The Politics of
Power

The Politics of Power

Joe Haines

JONATHAN CAPE
THIRTY BEDFORD SQUARE LONDON

FIRST PUBLISHED IN 1977
© 1977 BY JOE HAINES

JONATHAN CAPE LTD, 30 BEDFORD SQUARE
LONDON WC1

For The Survivors

British Library Cataloguing in Publication Data

Haines, Joe
The politics of power.
Index.
ISBN 0-224-01405-6
1. Title
354'.41'0009047   JN234
Great Britain – Politics and government – 1964-

PRINTED IN GREAT BRITAIN BY THE ANCHOR PRESS LTD
AND BOUND BY WM BRENDON & SON LTD
BOTH OF TIPTREE, ESSEX

Contents

Illustrations

Preface

This book is a very personal look at power and pressures in politics, but it is mainly about power, its use and its misuse. It is not so much about the theory and structure of power as about the way it operates in practice, which is a very different thing. In some chapters I have fallen for the temptation to offer some solutions to problems I have identified, but it was a favourite maxim of Harold Wilson's that any fool could give an answer; the real political skill lay in the ability to find the right questions. My purpose in writing this book is to stimulate the intelligent layman who is concerned about how his country is governed to ask the right questions. Its style is more heavily anecdotal than analytical, but I could never resist the opportunity to tell a good story. If in passing I have undermined some of the established legends about government and politics and some politicians I will be glad, but the achievement will be secondary.

I was never an advocate of the kind of 'open' government that would have us holding Cabinet meetings at the foot of Nelson's column. Sensible government ought to be sensibly discreet. But I am a passionate believer in truthful government and if I ever misled a journalist when I was Press Secretary at 10 Downing Street it was unintentional or because I had myself been misled. Truth finds it hard to survive among secrecy. The secret use of power, its aggregation by the unelected, becomes more dangerous as the tiers of government grow: from parish to district, to county, to region, to nation, to Europe.

In both local and national government the official is stronger today than he has ever been, not least because power has been thrust upon him. Perhaps this continued delegation of authority from the elected to the appointed is inevitable in a modern society. But it must never happen unseen. Unless society knows how, where and by how much and to whom power has been relinquished, it cannot make a judgment upon it and cannot decide whether to acquiesce.

It may be said that I criticise in this book the use of power by the unelected, yet I and my companions were among them. There was, however, a vital difference between those of us who were associated closely with Harold Wilson on a personal basis and the permanent civil servants: we were his choice as advisers. That choice is not a safeguard against abuse, but if abuse occurs it pins the responsibility upon the elected politician, who must answer for it.

The history of politics has fascinated me almost from childhood, but working at Westminster taught me how easily it can be falsified, which is why I have written this book while memory is fresh.

Politicians are diligent in recording—in diaries or in these days on tape, in speeches and memoranda—those events in which they played a part. Long before they have one foot in the grave they have one eye looking beyond it, surveying the niche they hope to occupy in their nation's history.

The trouble is that makers of history are not always the most objective recorders of it, for they see themselves as they would wish others to see them. Even a daily diary is not proof against adulteration if it is written for eventual publication; then it is no more than a book born prematurely and designed to conceal the private thought by the written word. Often what is written into the official record or preserved for the historian to discover in personal archives are not a statesman's true thoughts, but what he hopes will be thought to be his true thoughts.

The awareness of this trait in public figures first came to me some years ago when I was talking about Ernest Bevin, Labour's post-war Foreign Secretary, to one of his former Cabinet colleagues. I had just heard my companion express, in a radio interview, his warm admiration and friendship for 'Ernie'. 'He was a great Foreign Secretary and a good friend', he told the interviewer, 'and we were very close.'

To say the least I was surprised to hear it. He and Bevin did not appear to have much in common. I asked him if that was how he really felt about Bevin and his reply was abrupt. 'Joe,' he said, 'the only good thing I ever heard about Bevin was when they told me he was dead.'

I am not a candidate for posterity, so I hope this book will be accepted as a genuine impression of what life behind the scenes looked like to me.

It is not dispassionate and disinterested. I believe Khrushchev was right when he said there were no neutrals. I have dealt at some length with the Treasury and the Foreign Office, but I believe no more than they deserve. Almost every issue and incident recounted in this volume I was involved in personally. Very little is second-hand. Where I have criticised the civil service I have not named individuals because their names are irrelevant. They are part of the system; it is responsible for them and not they for it. In its upper reaches we have a magnificent civil service, but it needs constantly to be watched.

This book in no way represents the totality of my experiences during more than seven years as Harold Wilson's Press Secretary, a title which when he bestowed it upon me he said sounded impressive and did not explain what I did. However, I hope it brings together incidents, subjects, and people into an impression – a pattern – of power which taken together I found disturbing when it was not downright horrifying and which is the justification for writing it.

JOE HAINES

October 1976

I

The House of Fame

Such a position was never held by any Greek or
Roman; and if it only lasts three months, it will be
worthwhile to have been Prime Minister of England.

TOM YOUNG, *private secretary to Lord Melbourne*

No. 10 Downing Street has a more modest face than any of the
world's great buildings, but for 200 years the Prime Ministers
who walked through its unassuming portal were the navigators
of history. From the street outside it is a classic example of
British understatement, hiding the treasures of art and history
and experience that are within. Its façade is more deceptive
than any policy that was ever hatched inside its walls. Today
it harbours only Britain's crises, but it was once the eye of the
storms that shook the world. It is a magnificent building, easy
to love provided one does not get too attached to it.

Like so much of the British Empire over which its successive
occupants presided for so long, 10 Downing Street was the
creation of an enterprising but unscrupulous speculator, Sir
George Downing. Downing's father, a Parliament man, had
taken his family to New England in 1638, as did so many others
who sought their religious freedom outside the England of the
Stuarts. Young George returned to England, only the second
graduate from Harvard, following the outbreak of the civil war.
After serving as Scoutmaster-General – Chief of Intelligence –
in Cromwell's Scottish army and as a member of both the
Rump and the Barebones Parliaments he was appointed ambassador to The Hague in 1657.

Neither Downing nor his appointment was popular. Claren-
don said of it: 'he would add to any imperious command of
Cromwell's somewhat of the bitterness of his own spirit'.

B

Pepys called him a 'niggardly fellow' and a 'mighty talker' and later 'a most ungrateful villain'. Like a number of other Commonwealth men, Downing turned his coat when Charles II was restored to the throne and was strong in his allegiance to the Crown; he proved his loyalty by betraying some of his old comrades. They were executed and in New England a man who was not to be trusted became known as an 'arrant George Downing'.

He was granted in 1654 the Crown interest in the land which was to bear his name. Though his rights to it were jeopardised by the Restoration, his treachery to his former colleagues preserved them from forfeiture and he was created a baronet. Despite a short spell in the Tower of London after returning from Holland without orders to do so, he flourished, serving as Member of Parliament for Morpeth.

His plans for capitalising on the desirable site he owned so close to the Palace of Westminster, Whitehall and the River Thames were for long frustrated by an old lady, the mother of John Hampden and the aunt of Oliver Cromwell, who lived there in Hampden House until her death in 1662; and thereafter by her sons who retained the lease until 1682.

Downing's jerry-building—on, it is said, wooden piles sunk into swampy ground—of fifteen houses in the street was rapidly begun and completed around the middle of 1684, at which point he died, having done far less for posterity than posterity was to do for him. For Downing's houses then were no better than they look from the outside today. Some say he left part of his personality in the brickwork.

Much the larger part of No. 10, the real architectural inheritance that lies beyond the front door, consists of a house which originally fronted on Horse Guard's Parade and not built by Downing. It was a mansion erected on land granted by Charles II to one of his many bastard children, in this case the Countess of Lichfield, daughter of Barbara Palmer, Duchess of Cleveland.

The Countess did not live there for long. Her husband, the Earl of Lichfield, was made Master of the Horse to James II, an appointment without prospects; when he and the king fled, the building passed to Lord Overkirk, who held a similar post with William III.

From the death of Overkirk's widow in 1720 until his own

death in 1732, Lichfield's mansion was occupied by Count Bothmar, who came to England as the Hanoverian representative at the court of Queen Anne and was, consequently, a man of political importance when the Hanoverian George I succeeded her to the throne.

In 1732, George II offered Bothmar's house to his principal (or Prime) Minister, Sir Robert Walpole, who declined it as a personal gift but accepted it as the official residence of the First Lord of the Treasury, which it remains today (the Prime Minister being also the First Lord of the Treasury). Before Walpole moved in – in 1735 – there was an almost complete reconstruction, with many new rooms added, including three drawing rooms on the first floor and the Cabinet Room below. The whole was joined, under the supervision of William Kent, to George Downing's speculative building, the link being a long narrow room which today is the broad corridor which runs from the entrance hall to the vestibule of the Cabinet Room.

Downing's part of the unified property was substantially remodelled between 1766 and 1774, from when the present street front dates, but the house today is still basically the structure which existed after the reconstruction in Walpole's day, even with some of the same furnishings and fittings, though a State dining room was added in 1825.

A number of Prime Ministers during the eighteenth and nineteenth centuries preferred to live in their own London houses, which were no doubt even grander than No. 10, but between 1887, when Disraeli went to live there, and 1974, when Harold Wilson and Mary Wilson decided they would not, only Lord Salisbury declined to move in. Downing Street had become more of an office and less of a home, and Mary Wilson rightly resented the lack of privacy which living over the shop entailed. She may have started a trend.

My association with No. 10 began in the late 1950s – more than a decade before I went to work there – when, as a young political reporter, I first started to attend the off-the-record briefings for journalists held on most days by the Prime Minister's Press Secretary. (I continued these meetings in my first spell of office; Mr Heath's Press Secretary, Sir Donald Maitland, tried to end them, but compromised by transferring them to 12 Downing Street on three days a week; in June 1975, in what I believe were the best interests of journalists and Governments alike, I abolished them altogether, amid cries of anguish from those who did not object to being spoon-fed.)

The entrance hall, with its black and white marble tiled floor dating from the 1735 reconstruction, its Chippendale hooded hall chair, like a throne for the rainy season, and its gilt table, sun-ray clock and paintings, was therefore familiar to me when I took up my post. So was the Press Secretary's office which I was due to occupy after a few months' apprenticeship as his deputy.

But the rest was strange: the long corridor which was once the narrow room and its brooding bust of Disraeli (brought to the brink of disaster on one occasion when Harold Wilson's overweight Labrador, Paddy, almost hit it in pursuit of a ball thrown by a playful policeman); the Cabinet Room (which had heard of the loss of the American colonies, plotted the downfall of Napoleon and the end of Kaiser Wilhelm as well as Hitler, and in which the decision to grant India's independence was taken; how can the White House or the Kremlin compare with that?); the splendid staircase from basement to first floor displaying engravings and photographs of all the Prime Ministers who ever worked and lived in the building, with the mad eyes of Lord Liverpool at the bottom of the ground floor and the reassurance of Harold Wilson, photographed by Vivienne Entwistle, on the first floor, top.

The building was—and is—replete with minor treasures; busts of Wellington and Wilberforce, whose name was adopted in the 1970s for the office cat; portraits of Walpole, Churchill, Nelson, Wellington, Pitt the Younger, and a Charles James Fox whose face and figure are an uncomfortable and uncanny reminder of Lord George-Brown. There are pieces of Chippendale furniture outside the Cabinet Room and Georgian and Queen Anne silver candlesticks inside it. Gladstone covers a hole in the wall in the Prime Minister's study and L. S. Lowry's 'Lancashire Fair' reminds a Prime Minister, if he needs reminding, that there is a world beyond Watford. Next to the Study, overlooking both Horse Guards' and St James's Park, is the Boudoir, all gilt furniture by Adam, tables by Sheraton and paintings by Corot and Gainsborough. The Middle Drawing Room is Chippendale again, Van Dyck, George Morland and George Romney; *the* Drawing Room, often called the Pillared Room, is the most magnificent of all: settees by Kent and Adam, twelve gilt chairs by Kent; a pair of Kent side tables, and another, marble-topped. Its showpiece is a fine Persian carpet measuring 25 ft 6 in. by 17 ft 6 in. and the description of it in the official handbook says bleakly: 'It is probably 450 years old and took several generations to complete.' Its inscription in Arabic has been translated as:

I have no refuge in the world other than thy threshold. My head has no protection other than this porch-way. The work of a slave of the Holy Place, Maqsud of Kasham in the year 946. [i.e. in A.D. 1540]

All these rooms are at times working rooms, used for television interviews, receptions – where Philistines regularly grind their cigarette butts under their heels on the Persian carpet without any apparent lasting effect – and meetings with M.P.s and Ministers and visitors from overseas. The whole contributes to that atmosphere about No. 10 which makes impossible hours of work possible and frequent.

Only the housekeeper and his family lived there during the second Wilson era, but anyone could sleep there if duty prevented their leaving No. 10. Hours of duty at No. 10 under any Prime Minister are what happened to be required, and bear no relation whatsoever to any conditions of service agreed by any trade union negotiator since children and their mothers stopped working at the coal face. An annual allowance is paid in lieu of overtime.

Despite its occupation by officialdom, 10 Downing Street retains the atmosphere – relaxed, easy-going, pastoral – of a rural village, which is the principal charm of the house for those who work there. It is unhurried, and without tension, though the pressure is constant. Its population (100-plus) of messengers, telephonists, duty clerks, press officers, private secretaries, Honours staff – suitably proper – and ecclesiastical staff – suitably grave – mix like convinced egalitarians. Only the messengers insist on a proper regard for protocol. Everyone is nice to the Garden Room girls—secretary/typists so called for the obvious reason that their working room faces on to the garden – partly because they are pretty but largely because they can type.

At times of crisis, home for a private or press secretary might be no more than where a change of clothing is. During the General Election of October 1974, I did not travel the thirty miles to my home for nearly three weeks. But the atmosphere at Downing Street seems conducive to work without rest. (And work without food, too. Though Downing Street contains a splendid kitchen, it has never employed, except for a short period in 1974, any staff to use it. Anyone who wanted to eat on the premises either bought sandwiches or cooked for himself. During the October General Election I found that I could fry a better dinner than the Prime Minister's Senior Policy Adviser, but that he was more skilled in opening a bottle.)

On the whole, I was surprised to find myself working in Downing Street, even under a Labour Prime Minister. I was born and brought up in Rotherhithe, which when I was a child was one of the worst slums in south-east London. Today it is the prey of conservationists and others who are envious of not being working class and find Hampstead and Blackheath too conformistly middle class and expensive.

My father was a stevedore and died in 1930 when I was two, the youngest of three children. With a weekly income from the State of 18 shillings (90 pence in decimalised money) my mother ensured our reasonable comfort by scrubbing floors in the local hospital and carried on doing so even until she was sixty-five, because she refused to be dependent upon anyone, even her children.

Though Downing Street is only five miles by road from Rotherhithe, the conventional route to it is via Oxford or Cambridge. But between 1974 and 1976 we began to establish a colony of south-east Londoners in Downing Street. Bob Mellish, who is unmistakably not an Oxbridge graduate, and entered the Commons as M.P. for Rotherhithe in 1946, was as Chief Whip the occupant of 12 Downing Street. Albert Murray, from nearby Southwark, manager of Harold Wilson's Political Office, was there, too. The three of us shared the same sporting loyalty and the Prime Minister was heard to complain on occasions that he was surrounded by members of Millwall F.C.'s Supporters' Club.

I started work at No. 10 on January 1, 1969, having just been invited by Harold Wilson to be his deputy Press Secretary for a while until I took over as Press Secretary. I had been a political reporter—first for the *Bulletin*, Glasgow, then for the *Scottish Daily Mail*, and then for the *Sun*, the ill-fated successor to the ill-fated *Daily Herald*—for over fourteen years before then.

Once the newcomer has become accustomed to the splendour Downing Street emerges in its true role as the centre of power in the land. If at first the irrepressible impression of the building is that it compares with the police telephone box in the TV series, 'Dr Who'—which when you step inside it becomes a spacious time machine—the lasting memory is of the view out, a unique, panoramic view of Whitehall and its civil service machine, Westminster and its politicians, industry and the trade unions.

After a few days there, still feeling like a stranded minnow, I asked the Prime Minister why he had offered the job to me. He said: 'Because you got it right about 70 per cent of the time, which was more than anyone else.' I suspected that he meant that I agreed with him about 70 per cent of the time, which was not quite the same thing, but I was flattered by the compliment, back-handed though it sounded. When I realised just how little we know about how we are governed, I was even more flattered.

A little while later, when I found out how freely one could speak to him, I said that I did not know why I had taken the job; I did not agree with his industrial policy—it was the time of the 'In Place of Strife' battle with the unions—his immigration policy, or his incomes policy. 'That Joe,' said the Prime Minister, 'is loyalty.' He always placed great store by loyalty and so did I.

I worked for Harold Wilson for the next seven and a quarter years, after stipulating on appointment that I would serve no more than two years, largely because of the extraordinary quality he had of making people feel attached to him, even when he was not behaving very well.

When the Labour Government was defeated on June 18,

1970, I worked for him in Opposition, still looking after his press affairs but doing a dozen other things besides.

When he returned to Downing Street as Prime Minister, after the February 1974 General Election, I rode with him and Mary Wilson from Buckingham Palace to No. 10 and took up my old job there and then. It lasted for two more years until April 5, 1976, when for a variety of reasons Harold Wilson retired from office, three weeks after his sixtieth birthday, politically still a youngish Prime Minister, and I left his service altogether.

Though I had stayed for longer than the two years I originally contemplated, for excitement and stimulation it was not a moment too long. But privilege and power are dangerous drugs to work with; from that point of view, I parted from them not a moment too soon.

A British Prime Minister has virtually no executive functions, except in the field of patronage – making appointments and recommending honours. Though he is in Downing Street as First Lord of the Treasury, it is the man he appoints to be Chancellor of the Exchequer who manages or mismanages the nation's finances. Though he is Minister for the Civil Service Department, another Minister, usually a peer, is actually in charge. It is this absence of executive functions, however, which gives the Prime Minister his strength.

He is, in effect, as free as a bird to exercise the one real power he possesses – the power to intervene in the affairs of any department when he is not satisfied with their handling of Government policy or when he decides that the prestige of his office has become necessary to the policy's success. Every Minister of the Crown is appointed by the Prime Minister and he can unappoint them at will. If he wishes he can create a new department – as Harold Wilson did with the Department of Economic Affairs in 1964; and he can wind up existing Ministries – as Harold Wilson did with the Department of Economic Affairs in 1969.

Downing Street does not co-ordinate the work of Government departments, but if co-ordination is a failure then the Prime Minister will demand to know why. A successful Prime Minister will want to know everything that is going on, in the party in the country, in the party at Westminster, and in his Government. He must inquire and he must question. He is the leader of his party, but as Prime Minister he is the leader of the nation, and neither Whitehall nor Government can be allowed to forget it. He arbitrates when Ministers are dead-locked in dispute and he takes the sense of his Cabinet when a decision is needed. A Prime Minister of experience will always avoid a vote in Cabinet, not only because it emphasises the division, but because it circumscribes the power of his summing up. A Prime Minister must never be defeated on major issues in Cabinet, because if his authority is impaired then so is that of the Government as a whole. I have known occasions when the Cabinet has been narrowly, but clearly, against the opinion stated by the Prime Minister, but has accepted without a murmur his summing-up in favour of his point of view.

The Prime Minister is more than first among equals. He is unequal, and the staff and organisation of Downing Street has a first duty towards him; that duty includes the obligation to advise, to warn, to dissent and, in extreme cases, to resign. But except in that extremity, it is a duty at all times to support him in a post which is incredibly exacting, increasingly arduous and at times frighteningly lonely.

To work for a Prime Minister is a privilege only less than being Prime Minister himself. It compensates for the temporary destruction of one's private life; in return for total commitment if offers continuous excitement. To enjoy it to the full, it should never be out of one's mind that the job is, at best, temporary. The Prime Minister has no permanent senior staff, except for the Ecclesiastical Appointments Secretary. His other private secretaries are changed every two or three years; only his personal and political advisers stay longer, and they too ought not to stay too long, for their own good as well as his.

One of Harold Wilson's reasons for retiring from the premier-ship when he seemed to be secure in the post for many years ahead was that he wanted people to ask: 'Why did he go?' rather than: 'Why did he stay?' It is reason for long-serving travellers on his caravan to depart, too.

Politicians who acquire a Prime Minister's power will be under constant pressure to use it. Pressure is inseparable from power; unlike love and marriage, you cannot have one without the other. There is party pressure – greater upon a Labour than a Conservative administration – and the pressures of Parliament; there is the pressure of constituents who believe that if their M.P. is Prime Minister he can do anything for them and there is the pressure of every group with a grievance who want a Prime Minister's priority to be given to its remedying. Above all is the incessant pressure of decision-making and the distraction of being forever in the public eye. It all adds up to a terrifying physical and mental burden which is growing year by year.

The Pavlovian response to this situation is that those who cannot stand the heat should get out of the kitchen, but if the result of that advice is that the head chef is replaced by the kitchen porter then it might be better to install air conditioning. In other words, some of the load which has been increasingly placed upon the Prime Minister's back should be taken off. It was comforting to see Jim Callaghan in his early months as Prime Minister not trying to break into the *Guinness Book of Records* for the amount of work done in twenty-four hours.

Harold Wilson had remarkable physical stamina yet towards the end of his premiership the toll was being taken. Minor illnesses, stomach disorders, returning colds and susceptibility to 'flu all testified to the cumulative effects of physical exhaustion upon the strongest of bodies. Unless the pressure is eased upon his successors, Harold Wilson's peacetime record of being Prime Minister longer than anyone else in this century will be invulnerable to ambition.

He recognised the dangers facing him. He changed his style of premiership, deliberately withdrawing from the solo spot in the limelight, leading every charge, scoring every goal, composing every House of Commons motion, playing every instrument – to mix just a few of his favourite metaphors. But the rest of the army-team-orchestra-party were too often ready to bring their troubles to him; the Cabinet Office was always too ready to propose the establishment of a special Cabinet Committee – a Miscellaneous committee known only by a number – to deal with passing problems. In the last nine months or so of his premiership a more determined line was taken by him and his advisers. Ministers were told to try harder to settle their disputes. Fewer new committees were set up. Less successfully, an attempt was made to prevent the Foreign Office from insisting that he should see almost every ambassador or overseas Minister who wanted to call.

Some demands were too insistent to be ignored. Prince Fahd of Saudi Arabia would not come to Britain at all unless the Prime Minister agreed to receive him at London airport. The practice that British Prime Ministers never greet visitors, however celebrated, on arrival in this country was therefore breached; a tiresome addition to an overcrowded schedule and an unhappy precedent for future Prime Ministers who wish to husband their time. On the other hand, Britain is in trade and if we want the custom of countries like Saudi Arabia then we cannot jeopardise it by adhering to the conventions of the Empire of a previous age.

But during 1975 every American politician visiting Britain who had a pretence to his country's Presidency had to be seen by the Prime Minister, solely for consumption back home. None of those who came finished the course. Most of their hopes died in the paddock and the rest got strangled in the starting tapes. The most pitiful of the visitors was the deaf and paralysed Governor George Wallace, surrounded by strong-arm men and uncertain of the world's geography outside the Southern States of America, especially the difference between Holland and Belgium.

It is a cliché that Prime Ministers hate Question-time in Parliament, but it is true. After thirty years in the House Harold Wilson was still tense and nervous every time he waited to go on stage. He lavished great care on arming himself with every possible answer to every possible question. Off-the-cuff witticisms were invariably rehearsed at a gathering of his private secretaries, Dr Bernard Donoughue, the Head of his Policy Unit, Albert Murray, my deputy, and me. Indeed, all contributions from us were gratefully received.

But Parliament, or the cockpit of the House of Commons, is a place which only its members can possibly know. It was the one forum for which Harold Wilson always wrote his own speeches. Speechwriters cannot predict the moods of the House, only experience. That mood has to be sensed and exploited by the speech-maker. If necessary, the prepared speech must be

dispensed with, and that can only be done if it is his own
speech.

The other pressures crowd in, too: colleagues in dispute with
each other or with the party's philosophy or even the Government's policies. Cocooned within their departments, it is astonishing how politically maladroit some Ministers can be. One of
the most promising middle-ranking members of the Government
– later to join the Cabinet – was near to tears and resignation
in the summer of 1974, three months before the General Election, because the Prime Minister would not let him make a
speech attacking Tony Benn, then the Minister for Industry.

And always waiting to be seen and disposed of were the
famous red boxes, the strong metal cases covered in red leather
which are known the world over as the emblems of British
Ministerial office. The volume of paper deposited in them is
never-ending. As one box is filled by civil servants it is locked
and another is started on. They follow a Prime Minister everywhere – at home, on holiday or abroad – firmly clutched by a
private secretary whose job might not survive the loss of one of
them.

(When the Prime Minister and his delegation met Leonid
Brezhnev for drinks in the Kremlin in February 1975 the Soviet
leader gleefully snatched the Foreign and Commonwealth
Secretary's red box from the hand of Jim Callaghan's private
secretary and quickly disappeared through a door. The other
members of the Soviet Government present laughed and so did
we, though less cheerfully. The poor private secretary was
appalled. But Brezhnev reappeared within seconds, loudly proclaiming that he had 'all the British secrets'. After extracting
the maximum amusement out of his enterprise he handed the
box back.

Later two or three of us, almost simultaneously, had the
same idea: that a special red box should be made for presentation to Brezhnev on the next occasion that the Prime Minister
met him. That opportunity came a few months later in July at
the Conference on Security and Co-operation in Europe at
Helsinki. When Harold Wilson went to meet the Soviet leader
at the Finlandia Hall he was accompanied by his foreign affairs
private secretary, Patrick Wright, carrying a red box.

Brezhnev, unaware, played the part allotted to him to perfection. As soon as he saw Wright and the box he repeated his joke of February. He grabbed the box from Wright, who looked suitably dismayed. 'It's mine,' exclaimed Brezhnev. 'It's mine.' 'That's right,' said Wright. 'It's yours.' It took a while for the joke to sink in – until Brezhnev saw that the gold lettering on the box did not say 'Prime Minister' in English but 'General Secretary' in Russian. He was mightily pleased with the gift, which was promptly carried away by two burly Soviet security men, anxious to discover whether a 'bug' had been placed in the lining.)

The party pressures upon Harold Wilson were the pressures which arise from continuing tension. During 1974–6 he and the Parliamentary party were on friendly terms and the far left were largely paper tigresses. The party in the country remained as always the source of his strength, for no one knew them better or was more assiduous in nursing them. But relationships with party headquarters, Transport House, which he had always neglected and with the National Executive Committee were bad and forever worsening.

In the years of Opposition, especially from 1972 onwards, he had to fight against the party being committed to some breathlessly hare-brained schemes put forward during the preparation of the party's long-term programmes. It was more than a struggle between individuals; it was about the supremacy of the Parliamentary leadership and its freedom to resist domination by the party outside Parliament. A temporary reconciliation with the N.E.C. – which had moved decisively leftwards – came after the first election victory of 1974 but then the leader–N.E.C. relationship resumed its deteriorating course.

Labour leaders have never had an easy passage with the N.E.C. Clement Attlee dealt with a bumptious chairman of the party, Harold Laski, by writing to him: 'A period of silence on your part would be welcome.' Hugh Gaitskell fought the party conference but ensured that Transport House was packed with his followers. Harold Wilson gained the conference but lost Transport House through neglect. His tactic for dealing with the N.E.C. was simply not to turn up at its meetings and ignoring any decisions it took with which he disagreed. To be fair, he was sorely tried by it.

In recent years most of the trade unionists on the N.E.C. — with the exception of men like the Transport and Salaried Staffs' Association President, Tom Bradley, and the electricians' leader, Frank Chapple — have been second, third or fourth string in their unions, appointed to the N.E.C. as compensation for not getting a better post in their own organisation. The major trade union figures prefer to be members of the T.U.C. General Council, which meets at the same time as the N.E.C. each month, and to send an understrapper to Transport House. Several of the politicians on it are M.P.s whom no Labour Prime Minister would consider for the most junior post in his Government.

It has become unrepresentative of the Labour movement throughout the country; its majority represents a minority, never more amply illustrated than when it engineered the special conference of the party at the end of April 1975 into the position of outright opposition to Britain joining the E.E.C.

They then aggravated that idiocy — when every opinion poll was telling them that not only a majority of the country but a majority of Labour voters would follow the lead of Harold Wilson and Jim Callaghan — by a crude conspiracy to try to commit the party organisation to fight the policy of a majority of the Cabinet.

In the event — with Wilson and Callaghan out of the country but keeping hands on the steering wheel from Kingston, Jamaica — the N.E.C. was saved from further humiliation by the party's General Secretary, Ron Hayward; by the staff at Transport House who said they would not take part in such a campaign; and, so far as one member of the N.E.C. was concerned, by a warning from a friendly ambassador — friendly, that is, to the British Government — that a successful coup against the Prime Minister and Foreign Secretary would be damaging to Britain's wider interests.

The refusal of the N.E.C. to do anything to prevent Labour M.P.s being 'sacked' by their constituency parties raised again the spectre of a murderous struggle between the Parliamentary and outside party wings of the movement and soured relationships even more. By the end of Harold Wilson's premiership, the situation was little short of open hostility.

It was a pity that the relationship ever reached such a state.

There were faults on both sides, though the N.E.C. committed a clear majority of them. But Governments cannot continue to govern effectively in opposition to their own parties, any more than parties outside Parliament can govern. Party and Government are Siamese twins; war between them is impossible. A party anxious to help, eager to be constructive can assist the Government in a much more fundamental struggle: that against being suffocated by the civil service.

2

The Master Servants

'Tis mad idolatry
To make the service greater than the god.

SHAKESPEARE, *Troilus and Cressida*

The British political system embraces three 'Cabinets'—the
real one that meets at 10 Downing Street every Thursday when
Parliament is sitting, and sometimes on Tuesdays as well; the
'Shadow' one, which meets every Wednesday evening in the
Leader of the Opposition's rooms at the House of Commons and
hopefully understudies for the day when it will take the stage;
and the one that very few people outside Whitehall know anything about, that composed of the Permanent Secretaries of the
Civil Service. This committee of heads of departments, the
highest grade of civil servants, meets each week to discuss the
business which will come before Cabinet and whether—and if
so, how—Ministers will be advised on that business.

If the Whitehall machine has a collective 'line' on policy, and
it often does, it is at these meetings that it will emerge. A busy
Minister who requires to know the basic arguments on a particular question which might not fall within his responsibility—
the Secretary of State for Defence, say, may want to take part
in a discussion about invalid cars for the disabled—may well be
briefed by a Permanent Secretary who has already had a pre-
Cabinet discussion about it with *his* colleagues. In which case
the briefing will favour the conclusion which the responsible
Department—in the instance I have cited, Health and Social
Security—would like the Cabinet to reach.

The function of the Permanent Secretaries' meeting is similar
to that of the Pathfinder aircrews during the 1939–45 war: to

illuminate the target for the main force which is to follow. There have been occasions, however, when they have demonstrated an anxiety to camouflage the target rather than to expose it.

Together with the Steering Committee on Economic Policy and a group known as the 'DepSecs', the Permanent Secretaries' meeting is at the heart of the network of official committees which formulate the advice and guidance the Cabinet receives from the civil service.

The S.C.E.P. is composed largely of senior Treasury officials, a representative of the Bank of England and a few others. Their decisions – and they are more like decisions than recommendations – are crucial to the economic success of the country and therefore to the political success of the Government. Their secretiveness is of the 'Destroy before reading' variety and they keep very much to themselves.

Chairman of the 'DepSecs' – the Deputy Secretaries of the Cabinet Office, plus the Prime Minister's principal private secretary – is the Secretary of the Cabinet, a post held for most of Edward Heath's premiership, the whole of Harold Wilson's third and fourth administrations and into Jim Callaghan's first administration by Sir John Hunt. In terms of power, he made the Secretary of the Cabinet the most significant figure in the civil service; more than the Head of the Civil Service himself and certainly more so than the head of the Treasury, who lost ground.

The growing strength of the Cabinet Office under Sir John caused tension to develop between it and the Treasury, which is not accustomed to having its ascendancy questioned. But when the leaders of the six most important Western industrialised states met near Paris in November 1975, it had been Sir John Hunt who had attended the preparatory meetings on Britain's behalf and not a Treasury man. The Cabinet Office may yet fulfil the function which Harold Wilson conceived for the Department of Economic Affairs in 1964: to be an alternative source of power to the Treasury. The danger then would be that the Cabinet Office would become too powerful. There were signs of that in the 1974–6 period. The Office not only co-ordinated policy at the highest level, which is its function, but also showed strong desires to originate it.

c

A change of personalities in the post of Head of the Civil Service in April 1974, helped the rise of Sir John. Sir William (later Lord) Armstrong was much more assertive about his role in the Government's decision-making than his successor, Sir Douglas Allen. Armstrong—unlike Allen, not averse to publicity—was widely known during Heath's time at Downing Street as the 'Deputy Prime Minister'. His decision to become chairman of the Midland Bank—which greeted Harold Wilson when he became Prime Minister again—prevented a very awkward situation arising.

The importance of Sir John's weekly meeting with his Deputy Secretaries is that it plans ahead for the agenda of the Cabinet and its committees. That is a power function as well as a planning one. The timing of the presentation to Cabinet or committee of an issue can be decisive in its acceptance or not. Where it is placed on the agenda can be crucial, too. The Prime Minister may occasionally grumble at the timing of a committee—even, but rarely, veto a proposal because it was inconvenient—but he is far less likely to reject the proposed order of business put forward by the Cabinet Office.

This power of timing and placing could be of consequence. The civil service does not like delay which is not of its own making. There must always be the temptation, sternly though it would be resisted, to arrange committee meetings to take place when a Minister who might be awkward was due to be abroad.

In other words, meetings could be arranged to fit the inconvenience of Ministers. (Sometimes it can work the other way: I have known Cabinet Committee meetings to be timed so as to coincide with meetings of sub-committees of the National Executive of the Labour Party, but that requires a political decision. Ministers have a first duty, of course, to attend to their Governmental responsibilities and other meetings have to proceed without them. This is a defeatist practice, however; relationships between a Government and its party ought never to be so bad as to make this necessary.)

An outstanding example in my experience of the civil service attempting to influence the Cabinet came in the early winter of 1974 and the issue—unfortunately for the reputation of disinterestedness of the civil service—was the pay of senior civil servants. There is no doubt that the civil servants nurtured a grievance over their income – or the lack of it – due to the legal restraints introduced by the previous Government. At a time of rapidly increasing inflation they saw their comparative pay scales falling well behind those in private industry. (I do not accept the argument, but that is how they saw it.)

Some senior civil servants were determined to do all in their power to ensure that the Cabinet accepted the proposals made by the chairman of the Top Salaries Review Body, Lord Boyle, for substantial increases in their pay.

It was clear that the most prominent obstacle to be overcome was Michael Foot, then Secretary of State for Employment, who had publicly stated that no one anywhere needed an income of more than £6,000 a year. It was taken as certain that he would oppose implementation of the Boyle proposals.

There was no way of avoiding Foot's opposition, though some thought was given to the possibility of placing the T.S.R.B. report on the agenda of a committee of which he was not a member. But that was unrealistic. It would have been inconceivable for the Prime Minister to agree to any discussion which did not include the Employment Secretary. In the event, the issue went straight to Cabinet.

Dr Donoughue, who had been brought into No. 10 in March 1974 to head the Policy Unit, and I had the freedom to raise any matter with the Prime Minister. We were his principal 'political' civil servants. Although we both stood to gain over £3,000 a year if the Boyle proposals were accepted, we urged the Prime Minister not to implement them or at worst postpone and reduce them. Michael Foot was aware of our opposition to the increases.

But few other Ministers shared the Prime Minister's initial reservations or Foot's outright opposition, despite the fact that the T.S.R.B. increases averaged nearly 29 per cent – far more than could possibly be needed to offset the rising cost of living – and covered top service officers, judges and nationalised industry chiefs as well as civil servants.

Cabinet papers covering the pay and conditions of civil servants are given a more restricted circulation than almost any others – certainly more restricted than many documents which have a greater impact upon our national or economic security.

Rightly, it is thought that employees should not be privy to details of proposed salary increases which their employers are considering and which they might amend downwards. The trouble was on this occasion that all the civil servants in a position to advise Cabinet Ministers were themselves beneficiaries of the proposals. At No. 10, most of the private secretaries were kept in ignorance of the details of the T.S.R.B. report. Bernard Donoughue and I had to examine the Prime Minister's copy of the paper to be discussed by Cabinet in the room of the principal private secretary. There was no opportunity for a relaxed and considered study. Any reaction had to come from a quick reading of a document to which it was not possible to refer back. Our instinct rather than reasoning was that the increases should not go ahead in the way proposed, or anything like it. There were anomalies which ought to be straightened out flowing from the previous compulsory pay restraint. But without possession of the document – or time – the Policy Unit had no opportunity to prepare alternative proposals.

Time was vital. In breach of the normal Cabinet rule that papers for its consideration must be circulated at least forty-eight hours in advance, the proposals on top people's pay were distributed only twenty-four hours before the Cabinet met. Though it was, in its implications for the whole policy of wage bargaining in 1975, one of the most important decisions Ministers had to make, most of them came to Cabinet without adequate time to reflect upon where the wrong decision might lead them.

The item was not high on the agenda. Indeed, it did not look likely to be reached much before Ministerial thoughts were turning to the prospect of lunch; politicians get hungry, too.

Before the Cabinet meeting took place, Bernard Donoughue and I pressed the political objections to the increases upon the Prime Minister and one or two other Ministers. I had always felt strongly that the argument that a percentage rise in the cost of living had to be matched by a similar percentage increase in income was an illogical trap into which Ministers too easily fell. If the cost of living for an average family rises from £30 to £40 a week, that does not justify all-round pay increases of a third, which was the rise proposed for my own grade, under-secretary, and which would raise my salary from about £9,500 to nearly £13,000 a year.

A cash increase which is the same for everybody is certainly justified in times of economic stringency, even if it does distort cherished differentials, and that was the principle adopted for the £6 pay limit in the 1975-6 round of wage bargaining. Differentials ought to operate when the cost of living is fairly stable; their existence when prices are rising—because prices determine wage settlements—gives the higher income groups a vested interest in inflation. At such times the differential that really matters—the one between the well-off and the poor—continues automatically to widen, increasing the social strains and inequities which later result in a new surge in wage demands by the lower-paid.

When the T.S.R.B. report came before it, the Cabinet was uneasy enough to postpone taking a decision; at least, a few members of it were. Bernard Donoughue and I were held responsible by some senior civil servants. One stopped him in Whitehall shortly after the Cabinet meeting had ended and said: 'You think you've had a victory, but just you wait. You will not win this one.'

Nor did we. A fortnight later the Cabinet, after plenty of time to think about it, approved an amended scale of increases. Nationalised industry chiefs came off worse; the heavy increases proposed for them were rejected. Senior civil servants above the level of under-secretary had part of their increases deferred but they still received considerable sums (the Secretary to the Cabinet, for example, had his salary raised from £17,350 a year to £20,175, putting him £3 a week above the Prime Minister's basic salary. There were similar increases for other Permanent Secretaries. It was further proposed that the second half of the increases should be paid on New Year's Day, 1976, making the Secretary of the Cabinet's income £23,000 a year, but the £6 pay limit came into force before then and the further increase was postponed again.)

Under the amended proposals, only one grade of civil servants received the recommended increases in full: the under-secretaries. So Bernard Donoughue and I were among the favoured few. Well, we tried not to be. But the epitaph to this episode was not spoken until the following June when members of the Cabinet were gazing into the abyss of hyper-inflation and wondering if a compulsory incomes policy could possibly be avoided. 'I wish,' said one Minister, 'that we had not decided last year to increase top people's salaries. I think it was our biggest mistake.' 'Hear, hear,' said most of his colleagues. The civil servants present could literally afford to smile.

When I went to No. 10 in March 1974 the salary for a person in my grade, including London weighting (the justification for which has worn very thin) and the special allowance paid to No. 10 staff, was about £9,175. By the time I left two years later it had risen by about £3,800. I never asked for a penny of the increases and I actively tried to stop or delay the bulk of it. Whatever the genuineness of past grievances, during that period the top civil servants did themselves extremely well.

I have not the slightest doubt that expenditure on the civil service can be cut substantially, not by dismissing a few hundred counter-clerks in Social Security offices throughout the country, but by tackling over-staffing and over-expenditure at the other end.

The overburdened taxpayer is right to think he is paying too much to be governed. I remember my own outrage in March 1974 when I learned that a duty press officer at the Department of Environment who was required to answer press inquiries – from his home! – on a Sunday was receiving a payment of £50 for so doing. An agreement had been made between the staff there and the previous, Conservative, administration that Sunday duty would be reckoned as involving ten hours' work: two hours reading the newspapers – I used to queue up at Rotherhithe public library as a teenager for the *privilege* of reading newspapers – two hours watching current affairs programmes on television and listening to the radio, and six hours answering the telephone. All paid at double time, normal time being calculated at £2·50 an hour. This practice now, I am told, is widespread throughout Whitehall Ministries. Salary increases since 1974 have no doubt raised the rate of Sunday duty. But if that sort of unjustifiable payment was cut out, then perhaps it would not be necessary to reduce by so many the staffs who actually serve the public.

But the real spending excesses are at the Ministry of Defence, whose employees have brought to a fine art the practice of lying in the lap of luxury and telling the world how much it hurts.

The Ministry of Defence really is the fat cat of Whitehall. Despite continuing, and partly presentational, cuts in defence spending under Conservative and Labour Governments the knife has nowhere reached the bone. In concert with its accomplice, the aircraft industry, the Defence department greedily consumes, like a bureaucratic Billy Bunter, substantial slices of the national resources while whining that it is being starved.

It seems impossible for Government to obtain a dispassionate study of defence spending. Those most qualified to carry it out necessarily have a martial or military-technological background: the very people who are responsible for, and the beneficiaries of, the spending. The most vociferous opposition to defence spending comes from those who are strong on ideology but weak on facts. When Frank Allaun, the Labour M.P. for Salford East, demands a cut of £1,000 million in the 'arms bill' his argument is automatically devalued because everyone knows he is a pacifist. In any case, round figures make headlines, not policies.

In the public eye, the Labour Party is suspect on defence – despite taking a leading part in the formation of N.A.T.O. – and the Conservative Party is to be trusted. It is therefore easier for the Conservative Party to cut spending on defence. The public only remembers its promises to increase it. This public attitude explains why even after the defence cuts of February 1976 the Labour Government was proposing to spend more on defence than the Heath Government would have done if it had remained in office.

It also explains why the most effete of Conservative politicians can be appointed as one of the Ministers for Defence without public comment but in a Labour Cabinet the Secretary of State for Defence is usually the kind of man who could moonlight as a bouncer in a Northern working-men's drinking club, though Fred Mulley was an exception to the rule. And when it comes to examination of the defence budget, he can count on the support of the Foreign and Commonwealth Secretary (when Aneurin Bevan cried out in anguish against sending a Foreign Secretary 'naked into the conference chamber' he gave an inexhaustible weapon to lesser men) and the Prime Minister, who must be *primus inter patriots*.

That combination is irresistible, even against a Chancellor of the Exchequer like Denis Healey, who after spending nearly six years, October 1964 to June 1970, at the Ministry of Defence was better equipped than any previous Treasury Minister to know what he was talking about when he demanded cuts. He knew, in 1975 and 1976, that the Labour Government's great 'defence review' had left a vast area of spending – administrative 'tail' as opposed to front-line 'teeth' – almost untouched and unharmed. The waste in Whitehall – and if the people at headquarters are not thrifty, why should lesser beings down the line act any differently? – can be seen any day of the week.

At any time in recent years up to a dozen high-powered, expensive cars (usually Rover 3·5 litres) could be observed each morning outside Waterloo Station, London, waiting to whisk their military commuter-cargo to the Ministry of Defence H.Q. less than a mile away. In 1976 the senior staff at the Ministry shared between them some 200 cars, including more than sixty Rovers and over eighty Princesses (compared with tour Rovers and a small Wolseley at 10 Downing Street). Before he went out of office, Harold Wilson began to press the Ministry fo justify this excessive allocation of limousines. No adequate answer was forthcoming.

He also questioned the necessity for the department to employ 164 press officers (plus secretarial support staff – a tail for the tail) when the Home Office, whose range of responsibilities is greater than any other domestic Ministry, managed to get by on fewer than thirty; the Foreign and Commonwealth Office could speak for every British outpost in every corner of the globe with only eleven; and Downing Street itself, ever modest, provided a twenty-four hours a day, seven days a week, fifty-two weeks a year service to the press with only seven.

No doubt some of the 164 were engaged in devising convincing answers to journalists who wondered why the Ministry had spent over £100,000 on a flat for a Service chief who needed to live near the Ministry instead of spending a small part of that sum on converting some of the hundreds of rooms inside the Ministry itself into suitable living quarters.

When Dr Charles (later Lord) Hill was the Cabinet Minister in charge of the Conservative Government's press relations in 1961, he once grumbled to me that only one department of State needed to be preserved against its secrets being leaked;

that was the Ministry of Defence and it was the leakiest of the lot. Perhaps he never realised – as I did not then – that to the Defence Ministry the deliberate leak is what the offensive smell is to the skunk: part of its defences against attack. Whenever the Labour Government began to take a critical look at any aircraft project, or a missile development or some other jewel-encrusted armament then distorted leaks of what was being proposed would appear in the newspapers. The Government would get agitated and chase the leaker, who was never found. It is a successful policy for the department. More than one secret project has been reprieved by going public.

Parliament could do worse than to establish a Standing Committee on Defence Expenditure from which ex-officers and pacifists were barred.

I believe that the civil service today is at the peak of its power, a belief that is sustained by many of the episodes which are related in this book. The service contains many of the best, the most able and dedicated, men and women in British public or private life. Financially it is incorruptible, but as Lord Acton said and no one ever tires of repeating, power corrupts too. The danger we face today is that the civil service has achieved too much power. The base of that power, its enduring strength, is its permanence; in recent years it has been buttressed by an increasing lack of authority of British Governments, beset by economic failure and, consequentially, political catastrophe.

The civil servant is immune from the electoral caprice which can sweep the politician out of office overnight. In the fifteen years between October 15, 1959, and October 10, 1974, the political battle honours awarded by a distrustful electorate read: 1959, Conservative elected, handsomely; 1964, Labour (only just); 1966, Labour (handsomely); 1970, Conservatives (surprisingly); February 1974, Labour (biggest party, minority Government); October 1974, Labour (but only just again). The premiership changed hands six times in thirteen years between 1963 and 1976. The strength of government was thus sapped by the importation of too many Ministers with too little experience, men and women who had to spend more time learning their job than they ever did in doing it. Inevitably, in a world where decisions have to be taken many years ahead of implementation, this experience has lessened the respect of many civil servants for the democratic system.

Their impatience and frustration is understandable, even though I cannot share it. They labour to create a policy and then they labour to dismantle it, only to be told to start building again. Though they seek to stay above the party battle, this constant chopping and changing in the preparation of policy produces in a number of senior civil servants not only intellectual conflict but emotional strain. It cannot be easy for them, for example, to brief a Prime Minister one week on the virtues of a compulsory incomes policy and then a week or two later – as happened in February/March 1974 – be compelled to brief a different Prime Minister with facts and argument directly contrary to his predecessor's philosophy. Similar stories could be told of every Ministry in Whitehall. It demands an intellectual dishonesty which many civil servants find hard to swallow and to which the hallowed neutrality of the service is the only defence.

It is impossible not to feel sorry for those civil servants who have spent the best years of their working life obeying diverse instructions about how to tackle the problem of development land. First a betterment levy, and then its abolition; then nothing for more than ten years; then a Land Commission; then the scrapping of the Land Commission; then the Community Land Act which a Conservative administration is pledged to repeal when it gets the chance; and then ... ? If repeal should come, the civil servants who drafted the Act will have to arm a Conservative Minister both with the arguments against the measure and the legislation to end it.

Inefficiency is a necessary price we pay for democracy. But the repeated changes of gear have put a strain on the engine of the pantechnicon and it has developed a will of its own.

Rather than go left under one driver and then swerve right under another, it seeks increasingly to find its own road and stick to it. This tendency is not new, but it has grown stronger. It is an instinct for coalition, even though intelligent civil servants realise that coalition is a recipe for indecision and muddle rather than consensus and clarity.

The centre of the struggle for power between the elected politicians and the appointed officials is the management of the economy, and more than once in my experience the Cabinet has bent the knee to the Treasury, ultimately to its and the country's regret. In Chapter 4 I record an occasion when the officials were thwarted by the politicians, but it does not often happen. At times the determination of the Treasury to compel the Government of the day to accept the policies in which it honestly believes is ruthless, even to the point where it seeks to create the conditions which make it impossible for the Government to spurn its advice. That is exercising power.

The fall in the sterling exchange rate to below $2, which occurred in March 1976, was welcomed by the Treasury and the Bank of England though it came to the surprise and dismay of the politicians. The cuts in public expenditure of over £1,000 million announced by the Government in July of that year, following upon cuts of more than £3,000 million which had been decided upon only five months earlier, were a direct consequence of the collapse of sterling on the foreign exchange markets. Having failed in February to get all the cuts they were demanding – though they got most of them – the mandarins succeeded in July. Indeed, they tried to panic the Government into making the further cuts at the beginning of June. The pattern then, you can be certain, was exactly the same as it was on countless previous occasions. The Prime Minister, on his return from a Whitsun week-end in the country, would have been greeted by the Chancellor of the Exchequer with the news that large overseas holders of sterling were about to withdraw their deposits because of the falling exchange rate; that confidence had to be restored at once; and that the only way to regain that confidence would be further drastic cuts in public expenditure over and above those agreed by the Cabinet only a few months before.

The Prime Minister, initially, would have resisted the Chancellor, having spent three traumatic years at the Treasury himself. The Governor of the Bank of England, sitting in his car with engine running and bonnet pointed towards Downing Street, would be told to disembark. Instead, the Prime Minister would exclaim: 'Send for Harold Lever', the one Minister consistently able to outsmart and out-think the Treasury and therefore heartily distrusted by them. 'What are we to do, Harold?' the Prime Minister would ask. 'Negotiate a standby credit of $5,000 million,' Harold would reply. This advice being transmitted to the Treasury they would sternly reply that it was not possible; and then they would negotiate it because the Prime Minister insisted. Finally, when that had been obtained, the Prime Minister would stand alongside his Chancellor and demand cuts of £1,000 million in public expenditure for the following year.

That is how it happens. That is how it happened in 1975 and 1976. That is how it will continue to happen until the power of the Treasury is checked and diminished.

Not the least of these Treasury powers is the negative one which enables it to resist any change in its working methods which might decrease its authority with the Government and its command in Whitehall. It has prevented successive administrations, Labour and Conservative, from opening up the Budget at an earlier stage in its preparation for Ministerial scrutiny and examination, a point with which I deal in Chapter 3. Here I would only say this: in 1976 the annual Budget Day was April 6 – one day after the conclusion of the voting for a new Leader of the Labour Party and Prime Minister. The successful candidate, Jim Callaghan, did not know until the morning of the day on which he became Prime Minister what the contents of the Budget were. When the announcement about further cuts in public expenditure were made on Thursday, July 22, the Cabinet were only told on the previous day that it was also intended to add over £900 million to employers' National Insurance contributions, and no estimate of the employment or industrial effects of this measure was put before the Cabinet. The Secretary of State for Employment, Albert Booth, was forced to do his own calculations, on the back of an envelope while the Cabinet meeting progressed, about its likely effect upon jobs. Mr Booth, of course, was a new member of the Cabinet; older hands had become inured to this cavalier treatment.

It is by means such as this that the Treasury retains its exclusive rights to decide economic policy, subject only to the views of the Chancellor. The junior Treasury Ministers are usually of little account and, perhaps because they stand in greater awe of the officials, 'go native' more quickly than Ministers in other departments who are overcome by their civil servants.

From the moment of his appointment as Chancellor of the Duchy of Lancaster in March 1974, Treasury officials resented the 'interference' of Harold Lever and the fact that the Prime Minister repeatedly boasted that Lever was his own personal 'think tank'. Mr Lever—who has never had the sustained discipline of having to work for a living—is an ingenious and lovable man who believes it is more blessed to give advice than to receive it. The Treasury sought to undermine him from the start (though they suffered a temporary setback in the first week or two of that Government when on a technical financial matter officials presented the Chancellor of the Exchequer with four options and Harold Lever proposed a fifth which saved the Exchequer some £80 million).

The technique against Lever was to admit and admire his grasp of complex financial questions but to suggest that his judgment was sometimes affected by his desire to shock more staid colleagues with the unorthodoxy of his views. A bit of a card, is Harold, but he has got to be watched. And watch him they did: every speech, every interview he gave—and he was a compulsive interview-giver—was scrutinised to see if it could form the basis of a complaint. No Minister, not even Tony Benn, had more complaints laid against him to the Prime Minister than were laid by the Treasury against Lever.

This determination that the opinion of the machine should prevail—and it exists in other departments, too, notably the Foreign Office, but also in Defence and Environment—is anti-democratic. It is reflected in the contempt with which the manifestos on which a Government has been elected is held. (Whether that is a good thing or not is irrelevant; it is not a democratic thing.) From March 1974 Defence fought to spend more against a Labour commitment to spend less; Environment waged its war against the railway system when the Labour Party was pro-railway (and the re-establishment of Transport as a separate Ministry in September 1976 will not necessarily change that attitude); and the Treasury persuaded the Government in February 1976 to retreat far enough away from its commitment to a wealth tax to ensure that it did not operate during the life-time of the Parliament which began in October 1974. It was thought prudent at the time not to announce that decision, which at least gave a chance for second thoughts.

If at times the insistence of the Treasury upon its policies prevailing is disturbing, so is the inconsistency of those policies. While the Civil Service Department, in obedience to the Chancellor of the Exchequer, was seeking during the spring of 1976 ways of reducing civil service manpower, the Treasury was resisting a proposal favoured by the majority of the Cabinet, including the Prime Minister, to abolish the Vehicle Excise Duty – the car licence costing £40 a year – which would have reduced manpower levels by 2,000.

When the pressure on the Chancellor mounted, he stated flatly that he would not introduce the measure into his 1976 Budget. So much for Cabinet government. It was neither the first time nor the last that a Treasury Minister, failing to persuade his colleagues, insisted on his Budgetary rights. He wins because everyone is fearful of a Treasury resignation, however unlikely it may be.

Equally the decision to approve the submission of a tender to build half a dozen ships for Kuwait, the tender deliberately pitched at a level several million pounds below cost, will not help towards Britain's economic recovery. It is neither socialist nor sensible for a near-bankrupt economy to subsidise an oil-rich state whose quintupling of the price of oil caused the recession and the unemployment which the tender was designed to mitigate. Instead of subsidising an industry which has no future whether publicly or privately owned, the money could have been spent on establishing new industries which offered security and the prospect of prosperity to the workers, so that not only they but Britain itself might be stronger economically.

Some Government Departments are weak, responding only to the last pressure put upon them. Over the years Education has been a prime example. In the February 1976 round of public expenditure cuts it immediately agreed to give the Chancellor what he was asking for. The towel was thrown in before the fight started. The Department of Agriculture, Fisheries and Food, the most benign of Whitehall's Ministries, has come to represent the producers' rather than the consumers' interests. The Department of the Environment appears more often on the side of the local authorities than on that of the taxpayers. The Deparment of Employment is still the old Ministry of Labour at heart; it is not only the channel by which the voice of the unions is transmitted to the Cabinet, it mimics the voice. Defence represents the military establishment against the people, instead of the other way round, and the Foreign Office prepares new orchestrations of 'I surrender, dear' to every demand or démarche made to it.

The Treasury for its part reflects the power of capital: business, finance, industry, foreign exchange and commodity markets, economists, monetarists, shareholders, stockbrokers, the City of London and the Governor of the Bank of England. If there is an ignorance greater than that of politicians for the complexities of finance it is that of financiers and industrialists for the simplicities of politics.

Though their advice is often conflicting, the burden of the representations usually points in the same direction, which is that the Government – especially a Labour Government – should implement policies which contradict those on which they got elected. They are easily panicked, too, by the appearance of bogeymen. From the late summer of 1974 the insistent whisper distilled from all their advice and alarm was that 'something' had to be done about Tony Benn, the Minister for Industry. Undoubtedly, Mr Benn and his deputy, Eric Heffer – who should have been sacked that May for attacking the Foreign and Commonwealth Secretary's policy towards Chile – were scaring the wits out of some highly vocal sections of the City and of industry. The first draft of a White Paper Heffer prepared that summer was torn up by the Prime Minister on the grounds that it was hardly likely to achieve its purpose, which was the regeneration of British industry, but Harold Wilson got little thanks for his efforts at rewriting the White Paper; it was immediately and intemperately denounced by the Confederation of British Industries before they had had time to digest it.

The whispers from the Treasury's contacts grew stronger. Only if Tony Benn was sacked, it was said, would the confidence of British industry be restored. If confidence was restored then industrial investment would begin again. Investment meant prosperity and, although they did not add it, prosperity meant electoral success. It is astonishing that this sort of naivety is expressed by otherwise intelligent men. Tony Benn eventually was not so much removed from the chessboard as castled. His departure from Industry to the Department of Energy was welcomed in the City, but it made not the slightest difference to investment intentions, except that they continued to decline, along with the pound, profits, and the stock market.

While the Treasury's power is great – negatively, positively and by insinuation – it is not alone. The civil service is all-embracing, like convolvulus. When a new Government is elected it starts to operate even before the departing Prime Minister has said farewell to Downing Street and Buckingham Palace. It is his principal private secretary who courteously and efficiently makes the arrangements for the Leader of the Opposition to be received by the Queen so that she may give him her commission to form a Government. In March 1974 the principal private secretary, Robert Armstrong, who had travelled with Mr Heath to Buckingham Palace, stayed on to greet Harold Wilson. I had travelled in the car behind the new Prime Minister, together with Lady Falkender (Mrs Marcia Williams as she then was), Bernard Donoughue, and Albert Murray. It was as much a gesture of defiance as an assertion of our rights that we decided – at Marcia's suggestion – that when Harold Wilson came down to the Palace courtyard from seeing the Queen I would ride in the car taking him and Mrs Wilson to 10 Downing Street. That meant Robert Armstrong would have to make his own way back. There were few men wiser in anticipating trouble than he. He had a spare car waiting.

A wave to the crowd from the steps of No. 10, a promise into the television cameras to go inside and 'get on with the job' and the Prime Minister crossed the threshold into the embrace of the civil service which never afterwards voluntarily laid aside its grip. Though it was nearly 9 p.m., very few, if any, of the Downing Street staff had gone home. Beyond the hallway of No. 10, at the beginning of the long corridor which leads to the Cabinet Room, everyone – press officers, Garden Room girls, messengers, private secretaries and others – lined the passageway to applaud their new boss. So warm was their reception – so tired were we by the day's events – that for a moment the preposterous thought that they might actually have voted Labour trespassed on my sanity. But really it was like an Epsom crowd on Derby Day who cheer the winner while they tear up their betting slips.

By the time the Prime Minister had walked this short gauntlet of welcome he was deep in conversation with Robert Armstrong – who had arrived by the back door in time to greet Harold Wilson at the front – and other members of the No. 10 Private Office staff. We discovered afterwards that they were all expecting to be sacked from No. 10, but that was not Harold Wilson's way.

Introductions were unending as the parade made its way towards the Cabinet Room and the Private Office, which abuts it. Those of us who during the previous weeks had organised his campaign, staffed his office, written his speeches, shared his sandwiches, accompanied, encouraged, chided and praised him – and done it almost without pause – now fell back in the wake. The machine, after an interregnum of about two hours, had a Prime Minister again.

Bernard Donoughue and I became civil servants that night and Marcia Williams and Albert Murray remained members of the Political Office staff. The first division – only in name at that point, not then in fact – had taken place. After natural hesitations and suspicions, the civil servants at No. 10 made Bernard Donoughue and me welcome. The Prime Minister made it clear from the outset that we were to have complete access to information about domestic issues and to the European Economic Community's affairs and that he required our opinions, formal and informal, to be obtained.

Speeches prepared by the civil service, even of the 'I declare this community centre open' variety, had to be referred to us before they went to the Prime Minister. This system worked well. The principal speechwriter on the official side was Robin Butler, a young private secretary who brought astonishing energy and a rigid discipline to his work. He would provide the facts and the framework for the speech. My task was then to do for them what Van Meergeren did for Vermeer: forge them into a style that only an expert (Harold Wilson) might detect.

Albert Murray was made welcome too, but more for his own perky character and quick wit than for his position as manager of the Political Office or as the organiser of a highly unsuccessful betting syndicate. It was obvious from the start that the civil service had decided that they would not be able to work easily with Mrs Williams. They were unfailingly polite to her but little

D

more. Memories in the civil service are transferable, and those who had not known her in her previous spell at Downing Street had been well informed by those who had. Embroidery was not necessary, but all the private secretaries had bought or borrowed a copy of her book, *Inside No. 10*, the better part of which contained penetrating criticisms of the civil service.

The pressure of the civil service upon a Minister, especially the Prime Minister, is relentless, like a tide that is always coming in. If there is a gap in the Prime Minister's diary then the civil servants will try to fill it with another official engagement, but in the early days of the 1974 Government Bernard Donoughue and I spent a great deal of time with the Prime Minister.

In 1969 and 1970 there had been an excellent system at No. 10 whereby on most mornings of the week the five private secretaries and the Press Secretary would gather in the Prime Minister's study at 10 a.m. to raise whatever questions had to be decided by him. We each knew what the others were doing and we could each contribute solutions to any problems that had arisen. In 1974 it was clear that such a system had not operated in the intervening years under Edward Heath. It was some time before the private secretaries felt bold enough to speak freely in front of the Prime Minister; even when they did, there were no regular meetings, for the Prime Minister's timetable rarely gave him a free morning. Cabinets still met at 10.30 a.m., but meetings of Cabinet committees were more frequent, starting at any time from 9.30 a.m., shortly after the Prime Minister arrived from his home. Sir John Hunt and his Cabinet Office assistants were devotees of the dictum that work should expand to fill the time available.

The irregulars – those who entered Downing Street with the Prime Minister – would have been squeezed out, effectively if not intentionally, if the Prime Minister had not sought us out and called us to his study between official engagements or at the end of the day when they had petered out. Those evenings were a fertile period for ideas and debate.

To deviate for a moment: it was during one of these discussions that we developed a project which came to be known by an old song title I borrowed for the purpose: 'Little things mean a lot'. Bernard Donoughue and I believed that a great deal of public good could be effected – and political benefit obtained – by simple measures which called for the outlay of very little money or sometimes for no money at all, like the abolition of some unnecessary regulations of which there are always too many. During the summer months of 1974 we advanced a number of ideas which met this criterion.

They included proposals to improve the situation of, and career opportunities for, part-time workers, of which there are nearly 4 million in Britain; to standardise the size of food packaging, a help to the housewife; lifting restrictions on public access to areas of land, sites of reservoirs and canals where those restrictions could not be justified; the waiving of the television licence and a subsidy for telephone installation charges for the elderly who live alone (reasonably inexpensive – the TV licence proposal in 1974 would have cost about £7 million); a Caravans Act to protect those living on mobile home sites who were not protected by the Rent Acts and had no security of tenure; the preservation of the imperial pint measure; restrictions on the parking of lorries in residential areas; concessionary off-peak fares on the railways for pensioners; a death grant for the over-eighties who were outside the National Insurance scheme (it involved only £2 million a year and would decline); a short factual statement to be sent out by the Inland Revenue to every tax-payer explaining how his taxes were spent; a Gaelic radio station on the Isle of Lewis, where television reception was difficult if not impossible; and the making of May Day a public holiday.

Some of these ideas were adopted, others rejected on closer examination, either because they were unsound or because departmental bureaucracy resented our interference. Others had already been thought of. 'Little things mean a lot' was only a sideline operated by two or three busy people. But I think it would be worthwhile establishing a small unit of sceptics whose remit was to scrutinise our bureaucracy and request that regulations which serve no positive purpose should be scrapped; and to recommend projects requiring compara-tively little expenditure where the benefit to the public would be out of all proportion to the cost. There would be no shortage of ideas coming from the public themselves, and the electoral benefit of a continuing bonfire of controls might also be out of proportion to the effort involved.

It is important that Ministers, including Prime Ministers, should have access to opinions other than those of their permanent civil servants. However much they struggle against it — and some of them surrender straight away — Ministers do become cloistered within the privileges of office, nursed and comforted by a Department who want him to become of their flesh.

Richard Crossman noted in his diary, ten days after taking office for the first time in October 1964:

> At first I felt like someone in a padded cell, but I must now modify this. In fact, I feel like somebody floating on the most comfortable support. The whole Department is there to support the Minister. Into his in-tray come hour by hour notes with suggestions as to what he should do. Everything is done to sustain him in the line officials think he should take. But if one is very careful and conscious one is aware that this supporting soft framework of recommendations is the result of a great deal of secret discussion between the civil servants below. There is a constant debate as to how the Minister should be advised or, shall we say, directed and pushed and cajoled into the line required by the Ministry ... Each Ministry has its own departmental policy and this policy goes on while Ministers come and go. (R. Crossman: *The Diaries of a Cabinet Minister*, vol. 1, p. 31, Jonathan Cape, 1975.)

Crossman's perception was often clouded by his arrogance, but in that passage he identified within days of becoming a Minister a problem which is at the heart of our political failure to carry out the policies which were placed before the electorate for their endorsement.

What applied to Crossman as a departmental Minister applies even more to a Prime Minister. The support for the chief minister is luxurious rather than just comfortable. The intellects offering him advice are more formidable. He has the full resources of the Cabinet Office at his command, including the Central Policy Review Staff — the 'think-tank' established by Edward Heath when he took office in 1970.

Mr Heath's instincts were right when he sought to acquire

this source of independent advice. But the C.P.R.S. is not today the independent body it was when it was first set up under Lord Rothschild, and independence was its justification and its biggest virtue. It has now become a part of the permanent civil service machine. Many of its young men and women are still iconoclastic, but not so much. More than once it has compromised in order to do its work and in so doing compromised its independence. In November 1975, for instance, one of its younger members prepared a preliminary study of Britain's overseas representation – largely the Foreign and Commonwealth Office's efforts, but also including the work of the Trade and Defence Departments – in the hope that a more detailed investigation into its cost-effectiveness would be authorised.

The intention was that the study would be submitted to the then Foreign and Commonwealth Secretary, Jim Callaghan, for his approval of the substantive stage of the work. But the document he eventually saw, and approved, was modified – or doctored – on the way to his desk. The original proposals were not acceptable to senior F.C.O. officials, and the head of the C.P.R.S., Sir Kenneth Berrill, was asked to make deletions before it was put to the Secretary of State. That was agreed. The document placed before Jim Callaghan was not the original one.

The proof of the amendments was obvious to those in the know about the first prospectus: the story was leaked in part to the *Daily Mail*. Although the paper's story contained many inaccuracies, it did quote figures for the numbers of cars used by various British embassies overseas, an issue about which the F.C.O. is over-sensitive. Very few people saw the original document – it was never even sent to No. 10 – but I was assured by one who had seen *both* that the *Daily Mail* had quoted the reference to cars almost verbatim. It was deleted from the paper put before the Secretary of State.

The C.P.R.S. should not have given way. It would have been better to have risked a political decision to refuse the inquiry – which I do not think would have happened – rather than make the amendments. However radical its report the suspicion will remain that it might have gone farther. If the C.P.R.S. is to be just another unit of the civil service, another muscle of the Cabinet Office, there is little point in retaining it. Any future

investigations it carries out into civil service practices will be
open to the same objections which were always raised by police
inquiries into alleged misconduct by the police: that of the
interested party.

It is the *power* of the civil service — not least the power to
prevent things being done — which should be the constant concern of press and Parliament, and not its *size*. Its power grew
alarmingly during the years of the Heath Government, because
Heath was a civil servants' Prime Minister. It is especially a
problem for Labour Governments or any other Government
committed to radical policies.

There is no simple or complete answer that I know of, but the
system of 'special advisers' to Ministers, which first flowered
fully in the 1974 Labour Government but which began on a
restricted scale under Heath, is part of the answer.

The special advisers are politically committed, mostly young,
people who are experts in their own field and on party policy.
In the Ministries some of them, especially those recruited by
Barbara Castle when she became Secretary of State for Health
and Social Security, were of the highest class. The Prime
Minister's Policy Unit brought together under Bernard
Donoughue a team of real quality which made it the most constructive advance in the machinery of Government for many a
long year.

But most Ministers enlisted the help of only one or two special
advisers, which is not enough. The No. 10 Unit is the pattern
that other Ministries should follow. The criticism of 'jobs for the
boys and girls' should be rejected if the encroachment of civil
service power upon the executive and upon Parliament is to be
resisted and turned back.

The Wilson Government was too timid in defence of the
special advisers when they came under attack from some of the
empty-headed junior advertising executives who seem to com-
prise such a large part of the Conservative Party at Westminster (assisted, it must be said, by a handful of publicity-
seeking Labour M.P.s whose minds went down with the
Titanic). Harold Wilson had a success story to tell, not an un-
seemly failure to conceal. He should have boasted of it.

Of course, in departments like the Foreign and Commonwealth Office it would be difficult to recruit a team of special

advisers with a knowledge profound enough to challenge the aggregated expertise of men and women who have devoted their working lives to foreign affairs, but the effort ought to be made. It is essential to the future of democratic government, I believe, that Ministers should have access to more than one source of expert advice, particularly from those who are not civil servants. We may learn by our mistakes, but we survive by not making them.

3
All Brains, Little Sense

And when they're running short of cash,
They borrow from each other ...

From 'Nice People', popularised by Flanagan and Allen

The belief in their own infallibility is one of the Treasury's greatest mistakes. It is a belief, however, that dies hard in Whitehall and Westminster and especially among politicians who regard the Treasury knights with something of the reverence with which Red Indians approached their totem poles. If only the Treasury more readily admitted its mistakes – which on occasions would be a full-time job – a more balanced understanding of its limitations might prevail and as a nation we might be better placed to take corrective action before the next unexpected economic storm blew Britain off its course.

You do not have to be an economist, only a heretic, to recognise the Treasury for what it is: the custodian of the three-card trick. Not for nothing are the knights of Great George Street referred to as mandarins: like an Oriental tong, they have their agents everywhere. There is not a single Department in Whitehall that does not have within it senior civil servants who think of the Treasury as their real home.

With a certainty which successive Chancellors have invariably mistaken for wisdom, these financial Fu Manchus have presided over, nurtured, cosseted and brought to flower almost every kind of economic crisis which can afflict a declining economy: from overfull employment to overfull unemployment; from classic deflation to runaway inflation; from recession to excession; from cost of living explosions to standard of living implosions. From 1973 onwards they managed to achieve the worst unemployment since the war, deflation and inflation, recession, rising prices and falling living standards, and all at once, and yet their supremacy is rarely challenged.

Again and again in my experience – and never more so than in 1974–6 – they presented to the Cabinet estimates of future public expenditure, cost of living projections and the like which were not only not estimates – they were not even good enough to be classified as wild guesses. One calculation got the Public Sector Borrowing Requirement wrong by several *thousand* million pounds because a crucial element was left out of it. When the mistake was discovered, the immediate reaction was to try to cover it up.

Even those Ministers who are economically literate and numerate enough to contest the Treasury's argument have to do so on the basis of the Treasury's figures; if the premises are wrong, then so are all the conclusions. Other Ministers who do not understand what the hell everyone is talking about just feel uncomfortable at hearing the experts challenged and they tend to side with the Chancellor. And the Chancellor traditionally defends his advisers right up to the moment that he is sacked for their getting it wrong.

So the Treasury mandarins go on, their greatest achievement being that they have managed to repeal the law of averages which might otherwise have ensured that once in a while they got their stratagems right. It is time they were debunked.

They have neither the omniscience of the Orient nor the omnipotence of the Papacy. They have got butter fingers. Give them sterling and they will drop it against almost any other currency you can name, including the lira and the peseta. Give them a surplus of gold and, like a perverse alchemist, they will transform it into the lead of a deficit. Give them a problem and they will turn it into a crisis.

They are intellectuals, charming and formidable and classical scholars, but ask them what two and two make and they will answer that it is a straight line. They may be sovereign in Whitehall – they *are* sovereign in Whitehall – but they have no clothes on, and it is time that a child in the crowd stood up and said so. They may be technical wizards – though that is un-proved – but they are politically incompetent, and politics is the art of government.

Since the early 1960s, the Treasury has been in the grip of a fetish which has brought down at least two Governments – possibly three – and which, if they had had their way, would have brought down a fourth. This invisible raiment, this article of faith, crock of gold, Holy Grail and magic formula which has disaster built into it, like 'Blackpool' on a stick of rock, has been, and at the time of writing still is, a compulsory incomes policy. It is an affliction shared with their soul-mates at the Bank of England. Who infected whom I do not know, but it is virulent in both. If they cannot persuade a British Government to impose legal restraints on pay, then they press them for the alternative of public expenditure cuts. The best of all possible worlds for them is to have both.

With a compulsory incomes policy of sorts, the 'pay pause', they wrote *finis* to the career of Mr Selwyn Lloyd, dismissed as Chancellor of the Exchequer in 1962 almost a year to the day after he introduced it. With another, and tougher, version they helped Labour lose the 1970 General Election (indirectly, but the then Chancellor, Roy Jenkins, only abandoned the compulsory policy on the promise that he could have the 'In Place of Strife' industrial legislation instead. It was the most artless of exchanges since an American tourist parted with his money to an Arab in the streets of Cairo in return for one of the pyramids). And with the compulsory policy, the Treasury lost Edward Heath the General Election of February 1974 because they had induced him to forswear the pledge he had made in his 1970 General Election manifesto, 'A Better Tomorrow', which said: 'We utterly reject the philosophy of a compulsory incomes policy.' *And, finally, they brought the fourth Labour Government of Harold Wilson to the edge of disintegration and defeat in the summer of 1975.*

The consequences of Edward Heath's broken-backed incomes policy were responsible during 1974 for the wage explosion which took Britain to the brink of hyper-inflation during the first half of 1975. Mr Samuel Brittan, the *Financial Times* writer who probably knows more about the Treasury than any outsider alive, wrote on July 3, 1975: ' ... the recent [wage] settlements of 25–30 per cent can be classified as part of the explosion following the Heath controls'. But the Treasury answer to that situation was more legal wage controls!

The result of the General Election of February 1974 could be interpreted in many ways. But if it had not been for the compulsory pay policy there would not have been a General Election. In the months that followed, the minority Labour Government, inevitably facing another Polling Day within a matter of months, could not – even if it wanted to, and it did not – restore wage restraint upon an electorate which had just rejected it through the ballot box. It was totally excluded from its thinking.

In speeches, interviews, and statements, as well as in the party's two 1974 manifestos, Harold Wilson denounced a compulsory incomes policy as vigorously as Heath and with greater repetition. He did it so often that when I drafted speeches for him on incomes policy my typewriter almost knew the words off by heart.

In a television interview on September 27, 1974, at the end of the first week's campaign in the autumn General Election, he said: 'There is no alternative [to the social contract]. We are not a dictatorship ... Have I got an alternative policy in terms of going back to the legislation? – No.' Four days later he told a press conference at Transport House, the party headquarters in London: 'We believe any statutory interference ... would be bound to fail. We shall not do it.'

Again and again, before the second General Election, during the campaign, and afterwards, he argued that 'consent and consensus, not confrontation' with the trade unions was the only policy possible for a Labour Government. What is more, he frequently told me in private that it would be impossible for him to be the head of a Government which went back on those pledges and introduced laws to limit pay rises.

Furthermore, all his Cabinet colleagues agreed with him. Except, perhaps, for Reg Prentice, but he had always been a bit awkward on these issues. And the other Harold (Lever). And Malcolm Shepherd (but he was a peer, and a Lord's vote does not count for so much in a crisis). And Roy Jenkins, whose eye had that gleam reserved for an old love. There was a suspicion, too, that Jim Callaghan saw nothing wrong with the principle, except that it would not work. But the Chancellor was believed to be firm. I think. Anyway, Harold Wilson was.

Despite all this unity, the Treasury knights had sniffed the air during the summer and winter of 1974 and nostalgically reached for their files on incomes policy. As wage claims grew bigger and bigger, the hunt for a new incomes policy (i.e. the *old* incomes policy) was renewed in earnest.

Official committees, dominated by Treasury men, looked at — and discarded, on the grounds that the defects were so for-midable — every conceivable option placed before them; every option, that is, except an incomes policy backed by the com-pulsion of the law, because the Government was irrevocably committed — wasn't it? — against such a policy. But, of course, as they had not considered it, they had not discarded it. And then, at last, references to the possibility of a legal pay policy began to appear in their minutes.

The Treasury is alone among the major finance ministries of the world in placing first and foremost among its anti-inflation policies the compulsory restraint of incomes, or even the restraint of incomes; and by the New Year of 1975 they were suggesting to the Chancellor of the Exchequer that the Govern-ment should put a terminal date on the current phase of the Social Contract — under which some trade unions were justify-ing even the most extravagant pay claims — and the date they had in mind was Easter. At that point, they argued, the unions should be asked sharply by the Government what they were going to do about implementing their promises about not being too greedy.

One or two Ministers were more incisive. The Minister for Education, Reg Prentice, for example, told his colleagues that the choice facing them was not whether they would break their manifesto promise not to reintroduce pay controls, but whether they would break that one or the promise about maintaining full employment. He was wrong. Those were not alternatives; the pledge about unemployment was going to have to be broken whatever else was done to help the economy. All the manifesto policies, including that one, had been featured in 'Labour's Programme: 1973' which, in turn, had been drawn up before the quadrupling and quintupling of oil prices had made a world recession inevitable.

No one agreed with Reg, of course, except, much later, Malcolm, maybe? The other Harold, hesitantly? Roy, reluc-tantly? Shirley, shiveringly? Denis, delphically? The smell of a

bonfire of election promises was growing much stronger and the
high-bred nostrils at the Treasury were quivering in anticipa-
tion. Indeed, for months they had been drying the wood for the
blaze.

The timing of a new incomes policy to succeed the Social
Contract was economically difficult and politically simple. The
Treasury had no faith at all in the promises of the unions to do
anything; therefore the new policy had to be brought in as
quickly as possible.

The Prime Minister, at that point—early spring, 1975—was
equally determined that the policy must be a voluntary one and
that it could not be rushed. A decision could certainly not be
taken before Polling Day, June 5, in the referendum on entry
into Europe. Agreement on a voluntary policy when most of
the Government was in conflict with the trade unions, the
Labour Party Executive, half the Parliamentary Labour Party,
and nearly a third of the Cabinet over membership of the
European Economic Community was not to be hazarded.

The work went on within the official committees to draw up
the guidelines of the new policy, but week after week was
wasted because the Treasury could not and would not see
beyond the invocation of the law. If they understood that they
were asking the Government to court defeat in the House of
Commons and consequent resignation, they never allowed it to
deflect them.

After the referendum was over, the Ministerial consideration
of the new incomes policy was intensified. A meeting of Cabinet
Ministers at Chequers on June 20 looked back over the events
of the previous three years, and particularly Labour's sixteen
months of office; then it peered apocalyptically at the consequences of an unchanged economic policy in which wage and
inflation rates were climbing towards the moon. It could not
go on.

Inside 10 Downing Street work on shaping the guidelines for
the new policy had been going on for many months. It was
centred on the Policy Unit headed by Bernard Donoughue, but
anyone could contribute, which is the way of things in No. 10.
He and I frequently discussed with the Prime Minister what
might follow a successful referendum result. In the late spring
I suggested to him that for the coming year, when the country

would be expecting severe measures and would willingly, even cheerfully, accept rough justice, the best solution might be a flat-rate, all-round wage increase of £5 or £6.

The Prime Minister was attracted by the idea, but concluded wistfully and reluctantly that the 'unions would never wear it' because of its effects on wage differentials. The Unit was working on a policy which would be effective, but acceptable to the lower paid. It could not be a policy which merely asked the T.U.C. to propose a maximum level and was then left to the unions to police. It had also to be seen to be fair so that if an uncooperative union leader – nobody mentioned Clive Jenkins of A.S.T.M.S., but he was in everyone's mind – decided to try to breach it, the country would be mobilised behind the Government.

The search for the right policy was made more urgent by the threat of a railwaymen's strike. The National Union of Railwaymen, under a new General Secretary, Sid Weighell, had rejected an arbitration award which gave them a wage increase of 27 per cent (27 per cent!) and were demanding increases of up to 35 per cent, claiming all the while that such increases were within the Social Contract, of which the N.U.R. remained stout defenders, of course. The argument was humbug, and everyone knew it. But so inordinate had the claims become – not least because of vast increases for senior civil servants and others covered by the Top Salaries Review Body – that a new leader of a union could hardly seek less.

There was still a case for fighting the railwaymen. If the Government did decide to stand firm, however, the consequences for sterling would be grim (it had been noted before that overseas investors and speculators act to the detriment of the pound when the Government gives in to a strike threat; equally, they flee in panic from sterling at the consequences of the Government standing up to a strike).

The danger was that if the railwaymen won too easily then the chances of a new policy some time in July–August would be seriously damaged. It seemed to me, however, that there was a chance of using the railwaymen's claim to reduce substantially the level of future increases in other industries. The railwaymen were popularly supposed to be at the end of the 1974–5 wage round. Why not pay them something close to what they were demanding (the Government had already privately decided to go to 29·9 per cent anyway; the railwaymen's top claim was 35 per cent and we knew they would drop two or three percentage points without being difficult, so the extra distance to travel was not far), which would help their executive, on condition they helped us in return.

I suggested to the Prime Minister that we should, in effect, put the railwaymen at the head of the queue for the 1975–6 pay round by meeting their present claim (nearly), provided they would come to a watertight agreement to restrict the 1976–7 increase to 10–15 per cent, the figure then being discussed by Ministers, with the majority leaning towards 10 per cent. If the railwaymen would accept a two-year agreement, we would have established immediately the criterion by which other claims would be judged that autumn.

I minuted the Prime Minister on June 5, 1975:

> As a variation to this second stage, the industry could be offered X per cent *on the wage bill*. The advantage of this would be that if substantial manning reductions were made, X per cent could become Y per cent (a higher figure) for each man. The further advantage would be that if this led to a manning reduction, *the cash increase* in the wage bill the following year would be lower than if manning had remained static. This scheme need not be incompatible with flat rate increases in the higher wage and salary ranges.

The idea was not accepted. One Treasury official to whom I had presented the proposal informally was enthusiastic but his colleagues were not. Although the Treasury were pressing very hard for an upper limit of 10 per cent on wages during the coming year — which was not contradicted by my suggestion — they wanted a compulsory limit. The disadvantage of anything like I had described was that it was voluntary.

By now Jack Jones, the General Secretary of the Transport and General Workers' Union, was making great strides with his own flat-rate increase proposal. The T.U.C. were arguing for £10 a week all round up to salaries of £7,000 a year, above which there would be nothing. Those figures were absurd, but negotiable. Ten pounds a week was more than the country could afford (and more than many low-paid workers were dreaming of) and £7,000 a year cut-off would have excluded many power engineers, the men more capable than anyone else of stopping British industry overnight.

The Government were beginning to favour the flat-rate because of the appeal of the 'rough justice' label that could be pinned to it. But all the information that was coming to us at No. 10 – and it was substantial – pointed to a Treasury determination upon a compulsory policy. They were taking their fetish for a walk again.

Time and again, the No. 10 Policy Unit warned the Prime Minister of what was in the Treasury mind; time and again, the Prime Minister said he would not have it. The Treasury, in turn, were suspicious of the policy which was taking shape in No. 10. Since the murder of the Department of Economic Affairs in October 1969, the Treasury had not been accustomed to a rival economic team giving advice to the Prime Minister.

The question now was whether we could get the timing right for the new policy's introduction. Ideally, it had to be after the referendum but before the collapse of the economy which the pessimists of the Right and Centre foresaw and which at least one Minister of the Left (convinced of the benefits of a siege economy) looked forward to with optimism.

Not every economist at the Treasury agreed with the course of action which the machine there was preparing to force the Government to take. One senior official, whom I had privately warned about the Prime Minister's hostility to a compulsory incomes policy, asked me, almost despairingly, one day:

'Does the Prime Minister realise that the *same* men who advised Ted Heath to bring in a compulsory pay policy are *now* putting forward the *same* policies in the *same* words?'

By the time the Cabinet met at Chequers on June 20 the guidelines of the likely Government policy – which was largely the policy evolved inside No. 10 – had become clear and the Prime Minister adroitly led the Cabinet towards the policy he wanted. Some Ministers, with medium-to-heavy hearts, saw no hope for anything but a compulsory policy, but they were in a clear minority and not noted for their working-class roots, except one. The vast majority favoured a voluntary policy on incomes, with the hint of powerful sanctions on employers who breached the 'voluntary' limit, and statutory back-up on prices and dividends.

But despite the clearly expressed view of Ministers that day, nothing emerged very quickly from the Treasury machine over the next week. Perhaps they were made complacent by the public promise of the Chancellor that a statement of the Government's intent on incomes would be made 'within six weeks'. Perhaps not.

On June 24, the House of Commons was told by the Prime Minister that he hoped a statement could be made much more quickly than the six weeks Denis Healey envisaged. But he also said:

> 'What is important is to get the right answer and the right package ... on the basis of consent and consensus, which does take time. The Conservatives tried to do without it and they failed. We do not want a wrong answer on a basis which divides the country.'

On Friday, June 27, in yet another of its private submissions to the Prime Minister, the No. 10 Policy Unit warned that if another sterling crisis was to hit Britain – and July was the traditional time for it – it would be bound to wreck any incomes policy.

That same afternoon, an impatient Prime Minister decided to put some pressure on the Treasury to produce proposals for Cabinet examination, following upon the Chequers meeting a week earlier. He was concerned, as we all were, that the Treasury would make a further attempt to compel frightened Ministers to impose legal controls on pay in response to a sudden crisis.

Looking back on it now, and on other past crises, I find it incredible that we so readily accepted that the Treasury machine might try to upset the policy of an elected Government. It was as if we conceded the right of the permanent financial advisers to the Government to have a policy of their own in competition with the Cabinet's. It was—and is—a salutary example of how easily the intolerable can be tolerated because it is accepted as customary, in the way that Chinese women used to accept the binding of their feet. The Treasury were crippling the Labour Government's feet, or trying to.

It was, in part, a measure of just how dominant is the myth of Treasury infallibility among Ministers, who were wary of taking a strong line against officials in case they turned out to be right.

But Friday, June 27, was the vital day in the battle between the elected and the appointed. The Prime Minister told me that he intended to send a minute to the Chancellor of the Exchequer telling him not to let his officials waste their time on the two options which had been consistently rejected by the Government: a purely voluntary policy (which would be abdicating everything to the T.U.C.) and a statutory policy which would, in the end, raise the probability that action would have to be taken in the courts against trade unions or their members.

The imprisonment of five London dockers in July 1972 and their Dick Barton-like release after five days by the intervention of the Official Solicitor had given Harold Wilson and the whole Labour Party a great deal of electoral material at the time, and he had no intention of risking a repetition of that episode.

In his minute to Denis Healey, the Prime Minister told me, he intended to reaffirm what the policy should be. It was the one largely born of the work done by him and the Policy Unit and in principle was the one eventually announced on July 11. But Harold Wilson was in no doubt what the Treasury reaction would be. 'I expect', he said to me, 'that I'll have the Governor of the Bank of England round asking to see me at 3.30 p.m. on Monday.'

I said to a colleague at No. 10 (and jotted down my words immediately afterwards, which was a rare thing for me to do): 'I'm afraid that on Monday the Treasury will come knocking at the door saying the pound has collapsed, that we have got to take drastic measures—and here they are.'

The Monday we feared—June 30—was to be a busy one for the Prime Minister. He left Battersea Heliport early to speak at the opening of the Royal Agricultural Show at Stoneleigh, in Warwickshire, at 11.30 a.m. When the speech had been prepared a few days earlier it was intended that it should be fittingly sombre in tone, and so it was. But the accident of the events of that day, plus widely publicised photographs of Harold and Mary Wilson eating strawberries and cream (strawberries are fruit he does not enjoy, but they were all that were on offer that day) gave the speech itself an air of complacency.

In it, the Prime Minister described the world's economic crisis as 'the biggest recession since 1931'. It had had a devastating effect upon the British agricultural industry. The oil price increases alone had added £2,500 million to our balance of payments deficit in 1974, on top of an import bill for food and drink which itself had increased by £1,500 million a year since 1972. These figures were 'daunting', he said. They came at a time when we were already vulnerable, with the boom in industrial production petering out in 1973 and with industrial investment falling off; with a large and worrying Exchequer deficit; and with the inevitability that the rates of inflation and unemployment would rise 'inexorably'. Up to that point it was hardly a speech to justify denigration as 'strawberries and cream'. But he went on:

'Judged against that background, and without underrating the gravity and scale of the problems we still face, we can take some reassurance from what we have achieved.'

He then listed a few of the lights he saw at the end of the tunnel: we had not only eliminated the deficit on non-oil trade, we were even showing a small surplus. The monthly average deficit on the balance of payments was only a quarter of the deficit a year earlier. We had increased our share of world trade at a time when world trade overall was not increasing. And, finally, the fall in national output in Britain had been less than in other major western developed countries.

Politicians cannot only deal in misery, even when the public expects them — which is not always — to say that things are going badly. For the public will still want to be told that the unpleasantness is only temporary; the First World War was entered into with lighter heart in 1914 because of the widespread belief that it would be over by Christmas. Anyway, politicians are optimists. Winston Churchill, at the height of the Second World War's disasters, recognised that the ray of hope had to be kept alive: 'But look to the West, the land is bright.'

When Harold Wilson went off to deliver that speech, none of us thought that he was going to be accused the next day of being complacent, but he was.

In the light of later events, however, there were other words in that speech which were to be more significant. Like all speeches by the Prime Minister, this one at Stoneleigh had been circulated to the relevant departments in Whitehall for their comments – in this instance, the Ministry of Agriculture and the Treasury. As the speech was to be delivered on Monday morning, the two departments had received their copies in the middle of the previous week so that the facts in it could be checked and cleared by Friday evening. Therefore, when they went home for the week-end on June 27, senior officials at the Treasury were not only aware of the Prime Minister's minute to the Chancellor; they also knew what he intended to say publicly about the prospects for an anti-inflationary incomes policy. The speech read:

> We reject panic solutions, we reject the advice of those who want to see us thrashing about wildly, searching for some melodramatic solution which would make good headlines but would not work. The solutions we apply, and they will not lack courage and determination, must above all be workable. Effective, workable, relevant, speedy in effect, based on the recognition that the Government has the right – and the Government has the duty – to take every measure necessary to fortify and safeguard the defences against inflation.

'Panic solutions', 'some melodramatic solution', 'above all be workable' – these phrases meant only one thing to those who knew how to analyse the Prime Minister's speeches. He was publicly restating his determination to have a voluntary incomes policy which would be acceptable to the people, if not to the Treasury.

While he was at Stoneleigh, things began to happen. Sterling opened at $2·2250 to the £1 that morning and dropped rapidly to $2·1730, or more than 5 cents. The Governor of the Bank, Mr Gordon Richardson, rushed to see the Chancellor and then the forecast made by the Prime Minister the previous Friday – 'I expect that I'll have the Governor of the Bank of England round asking to see me at 3.30 p.m. on Monday' – began to come true. While Harold Wilson was still at Stoneleigh, the Treasury telephoned the private office at No. 10 saying that Richardson and the Chancellor had to see the Prime Minister as soon as he got back. The meeting was arranged to take place at 2.45 p.m. The Prime Minister had been forty-five minutes too optimistic in his forecast.

There is no need to speculate about what happened at that meeting. Harold Wilson had heard it all before, when the then Governor of the Bank, Lord Cromer, came to see him in November 1964. Selwyn Lloyd, James Callaghan, and Tony Barber had heard it, too, when they were at the Treasury as Chancellors. Sterling was collapsing; unless the drain on the exchanges was stopped there would be a catastrophe; foreign depositors – in this case, the Arabs – were taking out their money; drastic measures, painful but inevitable, had to be taken. The Government had to be seen to be in charge, etc. And what were the drastic measures?

Well, it so happened that the Treasury had them handy. So handy, in fact, that it would be possible for the Cabinet to discuss and endorse them at their meeting next morning. (In breach, incidentally, of the rule that Cabinet papers must be circulated forty-eight hours at least in advance of a Cabinet meeting. Exceptions can be made for a crisis, however, and this was a crisis. But it would mean – as crises always mean – that decisions vital to the life of the Government would have to be taken hurriedly and without proper thought and discussion.) And after Cabinet discussion, the Chancellor would be able to announce his measures to the House of Commons that very afternoon, Tuesday, July 1.

Once again, the Home Civil Service (Treasury Division) were throwing the Government a lifebelt when the ship and all its hands seemed lost. Well, a lifebelt is always useful if the ship is going down. But there were a number of us within No. 10, including one or two permanent civil servants as well as us 'temporaries', who were by no means sure that the ship was foundering.

For what was in the Treasury package to stop the sudden run on sterling? First and foremost, the compulsory incomes policy which for months they had been pressing upon the Government and which three days before they had been expressly instructed to disregard. Suspicions that the Treasury and the Bank of England act together to thwart the honest yeomen of a Labour Government are always dismissed as part of the paranoia of the Left. In this instance, they cannot be so easily dismissed.

The proposal was that the Chancellor should announce legislation forbidding employers, by law, to grant pay increases of more than 10 per cent. (This 10 per cent level in itself was interesting; it had been the Treasury's original proposal and they persisted in it, even though they knew by now that the T.U.C. and the majority of the Cabinet had come down decisively in favour of the flat-rate proposal of Jack Jones.)

A small group of Ministers, stunned by the suddenness of the crisis, gathered in the Cabinet Room under the Prime Minister's chairmanship. Besides the Chancellor, they included the Foreign and Commonwealth Secretary (Jim Callaghan), the Secretary of State for the Environment (Tony Crosland), the Secretary of State for Employment (Michael Foot), the Prices and Consumer Protection Minister (Shirley Williams) and the Trade Minister (Peter Shore).

They heard the Chancellor's report of the dramatic flight from sterling that had taken place that day and they agreed that a draft statement should be prepared for the Cabinet to consider the next morning before it was delivered at 3.30 p.m. by the Chancellor in the House of Commons.

Everything moved so fast that the meeting of these Ministers had begun before I was aware that it was being convened (after the Ministers, the No. 10 Press Office should always be the first to be told). Bernard Donoughue and I were suspicious about the sudden run on the pound so quickly after the Prime Minister's minute on the previous Friday and his speech at Stoneleigh, and we saw the Prime Minister immediately after his meeting had ended.

We talked in the spacious area outside the Cabinet Room. The Prime Minister had received the first tranche of bad news from the City of London while he was still at Stoneleigh. He was severely shaken by it. Substantial sterling deposits were, apparently, being taken out of London. Kuwait had long made it known that it considered the floor for sterling was $2·20 and that they would reduce their holdings if the pound dropped below that level against the dollar. Saudi Arabia, an even bigger holder of sterling, had set their floor at $2·17 and that level had almost been reached. (Sterling in fact improved a little during the afternoon and its closing rate was $2·1920, a fall of 3·30 cents on the day.)

If the drain of withdrawals continued at that day's rate then the Treasury had warned there would be disastrous effects for the economy. The published figures for the loss to the reserves of supporting the pound during June were to amount to over 550 million dollars. But so wild are the monthly fluctuations in money taken in or paid out that they are not truthfully published; sometimes the figure is complete fiction. If the Arab nations started to get out of sterling in a big way then either the rate would plunge or thousands of millions might be lost from the reserves in supporting sterling. That was the argument the Treasury used that day.

Though the circumstances of the crisis were familiar to him, the Prime Minister was facing up to what he had so fiercely, time and again, rejected: the necessity of a compulsory incomes policy. (When he announced his resignation from office the following March, Harold Wilson gave to his Cabinet one reason why he should not stay in office too long: that when old problems reappear there was a danger that a Prime Minister would resort to old solutions, to the exclusion of new ones. What he had in mind in particular when he drafted that statement were the events of June and July, 1975.)

Bernard Donoughue and I argued at length that the right way out of the crisis was the way that the Prime Minister and No. 10 had worked out in calmer days. One of the real joys of working for Harold Wilson – one could almost say 'with' – was his complete lack of self-importance. He would never extricate himself from an argument by asserting his primacy. He did not enforce deference to his views, nor did he, despite the legends to the contrary, want to be surrounded by sycophants.

On one occasion in his study I had said rather miserably that it depressed me that I always seemed to be opposed to what he was proposing to say or do. 'It's what I employ you for', he said. Bernard Donoughue's ways were more subtle with the Prime Minister, but at that time his influence with the Prime Minister was still growing.

On that afternoon outside the Cabinet Room, however, we pushed our licence to the limit. Donoughue, speaking as the financial expert, deployed the substantial economic arguments against a compulsory incomes policy, but naturally spilling over into the political arguments, too. I put the political arguments at length, with vehemence, and some impertinence.

I told him that I did not see how after all he had said that he could go back on his commitment not to bring in a compulsory pay policy and still stay in office. He retorted that he had *not* decided upon such a policy, but that the economy came before politics. I could not see how the two issues could be separated. I argued that a compulsory policy would not work, for the miners had demonstrated that Heath's policy would not; that the only result of bringing in legislation would be to split the Government, whereas the No. 10 policy had a great chance of success. What was more, I could not see that there was any hope of getting the legislation through the House of Commons.

The Conservatives would almost certainly trump up a reason to oppose it. The Scottish Nationalists, for their own parochial reasons, would oppose it; Enoch Powell – and thus most of the Ulster Unionists – would oppose it out of intellectual conviction. The only opposition party in the House to whom the Government could look for support would be the Liberals, who favoured a permanent incomes policy backed by the law. Their votes would not be enough to offset the substantial vote against the Government which we could expect from our own back-benches.

It was clear to Bernard Donoughue and me that the question of whether or not a compulsory policy was the right one for Britain in the summer of 1975 was academic, even though we thought it wrong. The truth of the matter was that there was no hope of getting it through the House of Commons, a fact stated very forcibly to his colleagues earlier in the month by Bob Mellish, the Government's Chief Whip.

I think Harold Wilson was very patient with us, particularly

me. He could be a baffling man to talk to. Sometimes he would
give the appearance of not listening, only suddenly later in the
day, or week even, to reply suddenly to what you had said. This
time, however, he was listening and beginning to get irritated
by our persistence. When the discussion finally broke up, the
impact of the day's events were uppermost in his mind but he
was not irrevocably bent upon a change of course and the adop-
tion of a compulsory pay policy. There was still a lot to play
for.

Treasury officials had been commissioned after the meeting
of Ministers to draft the statement which the Chancellor was to
present to the Cabinet before making it in the House of Commons the following day. The Treasury promised to send copies
to No. 10 by 7 p.m. that evening and a personal copy was to be
sent to me. Just before 7 we heard that the statement would not
be ready before 11.30 p.m. My copy, I was told, would be
waiting for me when I got into the office the next morning.

By happy chance, several of the No. 10 staff, including the
principal private secretary, Mr Ken Stowe, Dr Donoughue and
me, and my deputy, Mrs Janet Hewlett-Davies, were staying
on that evening for the reception and dinner which the Prime
Minister was giving for M. Leo Tindemans, the Belgian Prime
Minister. We knew we would be at No. 10 at least until 11.30
and probably later.

The statement had not arrived at 11.50 p.m. and Bernard
Donoughue, Mrs Hewlett-Davies, Ken Stowe and I left the
reception while Stowe inquired of the Treasury what had
happened to the statement. At last one copy – the Prime
Minister's – came across from the Treasury at ten minutes past
midnight. Bernard Donoughue, Janet Hewlett-Davies and I
gathered in my office to read it. We were appalled by its tone.

The Chancellor would be asking Cabinet to consider an
unabashed announcement of a statutory incomes policy, with
no mention of sanctions against employers – which, if any
statutory policy was embarked upon, Ministers insisted was
essential – and proposing nothing effective on prices.

It amounted to a straightforward attempt by the Treasury to
make the Government put its policies totally in reverse, abandon
its manifesto commitments and commit suicide. Though it
sounds melodramatic to say so, had they succeeded in the

attempt, it would have been a civilian coup against the Government.*

Bernard Donoughue and I did not want to approach the Prime Minister while he was surrounded by guests. It would have looked too suspicious for us to take him away from them on a matter which was clearly urgent at that time of night. But everyone was accustomed to the Prime Minister breaking off a conversation on these occasions to discuss a matter with his principal private secretary. So we asked Ken Stowe to tell the Prime Minister that we wished to see him urgently about the Treasury statement. The reply came back – for the one and only time in more than seven years as his Press Secretary – that he would not see me or Bernard Donoughue. Understandably, he was tired and must have been more than fed up with the fusillade we had fired at him on this subject earlier in the evening.

Bernard Donoughue, Janet Hewlett-Davies, and I returned to my room to discuss what to do next. It was nearly 12.30 a.m. Cabinet Ministers were due to arrive at 9.30 a.m. to receive a copy of the draft and to begin discussing it at 10 a.m. But once the draft announcement was in Ministers' hands the crisis – the political crisis – would be upon us. The Chancellor would have been over-committed by his officials – we had heard that twenty-five officials had contributed to the draft in one way or another, but we were uncertain whether the Chancellor had seen it or, if he had, whether he had had a chance to consider its implications for the survival of the Government. We decided that Bernard Donoughue and I would send – for only the second time, because such formality is strange to No. 10 – a joint minute to the Prime Minister, attaching it by tag to his copy of the draft so that he would be aware of our views. There was one further piece of evidence which had come to us during the evening which strengthened our suspicions about the behaviour of the Treasury. No attempt had been made by the Treasury

---

* An alarming allegation against Treasury officials by an unnamed but 'wholly authoritative' foreign source was reported by Peter Jenkins, columnist of the *Guardian*, on October 28, 1976. The source told him: 'One of the problems is the axis between your Treasury and our Treasury. They seem to be agreed that the Labour Manifesto is a manual for suicide . . . They are in constant touch with our people saying, "Don't bale these bastards out".'

and the Bank of England to keep the pound above the crucial $2·20 level. No money had been spent to bolster the rate. Knowing the effect it would have, sterling had been allowed to fall. We had a veritable cornucopia of coincidence and we were getting fed up with it. So I planted a typewriter on my desk and between us Bernard Donoughue and I, with Janet sitting near-by, composed the following minute to the Prime Minister:

PRIME MINISTER

We believe that the Cabinet are being faced with an attempt by the Treasury to stampede it into a statutory pay policy, against every pledge which we have given. We are reinforced in this belief by the knowledge that no money at all was spent in defence of the pound on Monday.

The proposed statement by the Chancellor is a straight-forward announcement of such a policy. It has no reference whatsoever about acting against employers; it is solely concerned with legal restraints against pay.

Paragraph 5, on dealing with prices, is so inadequate it will be laughed at in the House.

Paragraph 4 sets the alternative to a statutory policy as the T.U.C. policy. This was not the case. We have been formulating another alternative, part voluntary, part statutory, which stood a much better chance of success.

The phrase 'using the law in the pay bargaining process' will lead to a split in the party. It is not, as we understand it, what the [meeting of Ministers] decided today. It will lead to resignations from the Cabinet and the Government.

The commitment on public expenditure, which has serious implications, is being made in advance of any proper consultation or discussion with colleagues.

We believe the Treasury are trying to bounce the Government along the same old path they have trodden before, with incalculable consequences for the Government and the party.

JOE HAINES
BERNARD DONOUGHUE

The draft statement and our minute were then sent to the Prime Minister's study for him to see before he went to bed. It was then 12.45 a.m. There was nothing else we could do and so we went home.

When I arrived home – at 1.40 a.m. – my wife had left a message for me to telephone the Prime Minister. He was still working in his study and it was a joy to listen to him. Though he had refused to see us, he had read our minute. He told me that he agreed with every word in it and that he had given instructions that the Treasury draft statement was not to be given to Cabinet Ministers when they came to No. 10 at 9.30. It was to be withdrawn altogether; the Chancellor would bring a different draft to the meeting.

It was nearly 2 a.m. when we finished talking. I phoned Bernard Donoughue and told him what had happened. If I could not sleep there was no reason why he should.

The Cabinet when they met were told by the Chancellor what had happened the previous day and how urgent it now was to achieve an effective incomes policy. Their decision was what the Prime Minister wanted: a voluntary policy, but with statutory powers held in reserve if there was any widespread attempt to breach it. No one contemplated at that time that there would be no breaching of the policy at all. A small drafting committee, including the Prime Minister, the Chancellor of the Exchequer, and the Secretary of State for Employment, prepared the final wording of the statement shortly before Denis Healey made it.

It was a revealing feature of the Cabinet debate that the junior members of the Cabinet – people like Merlyn Rees, Roy Mason, John Silkin and John Morris – were foremost in supporting the Prime Minister against compulsory restraint. Their links with the back-benches were more recent than many of their senior colleagues' and they knew the damage a U-turn of the magnitude demanded by the Treasury would do.

On that Tuesday, hardly anything needed to be spent to stop the pound plunging further, and the withdrawals by Arab depositors ended, at least temporarily.

The statement which Denis Healey made to the Commons that afternoon announced the Government's target of reducing inflation by the end of 1976 to a rate below 10 per cent. That meant, he said, 'the increase in wages and salaries during the next pay round cannot exceed 10 per cent'. The Government had reached an advanced stage in preparing measures which were 'fair and just', measures that would 'ensure' that all sections of the community shared the burden equally. It was no good having an agreed pay limit, he said, unless we could be 'certain' it would not be exceeded. For this purpose the Government would use 'a battery of weapons', including cash limits in the public sector and action through the Price Code in the private sector. The Government would 'much prefer to proceed on the basis of a voluntary policy agreed with the C.B.I. and the T.U.C. But a voluntary policy will not be acceptable to the Government unless it satisfies the targets they have set for reducing inflation and includes convincing arrangements for ensuring compliance.'

The lightly disguised menace in the statement then became explicit, as the Old Adam of the Treasury had its final fling:

If, however, no agreement can be reached which meets these conditions, the Government will be obliged to legislate to impose a legal requirement on both public and private sector employers to comply with the 10 per cent limit.

That was the essence of the compromise reached by the Cabinet that morning: a voluntary policy or else, the 'or else' stated as a commitment. Everyone knew that if the compulsion clause in the statement was invoked then Michael Foot would resign from the Cabinet and two or three other Cabinet colleagues might join him. There would also be a number of resignations in the lower reaches of the administration. Indeed, one Minister, Stan Orme, then Minister of State at the Northern Ireland Office, was acutely unhappy with the agreement eventually reached and contemplated resignation.

There can be no doubt that Treasury officials, throughout their campaign for a compulsory policy, knew that success would involve Michael Foot's departure from the Government. But then he was not their kind of Minister, any more than Tony Benn was.

Nevertheless, when the Chancellor sat down that afternoon the situation compared with twenty-four hours earlier had been transformed. On the Monday the choice put before the Government had not been either a voluntary policy or a compulsory one; it had been a compulsory policy or the collapse of the economy. Of course, there were other possibilities: a compulsory policy *and* the collapse of the economy (which might follow if the trade unions decided to fight) ; or there might have been a compulsory policy and the collapse of the Government which might have then led to the collapse of the economy. It was even possible that, in a surge of fear about living standards, a compulsory policy would have been approved by the Commons and accepted by the country.

But the whole history of wage control by law in an economy where prices continued to rise was one of sullen acquiescence turning into active resentment followed by open defiance (even the very first prices and incomes policy in 1381 led to the Peasants' Revolt against the freezing of wages at a time when prices were doubling; that is why no portrait of Wat Tyler hangs in Great George Street).

The next ten days began disastrously. The Treasury were instructed as a matter of urgency to prepare a White Paper for publication at the end of the following week. But in line with their policy of never acknowledging defeat – if they had operated the *Titanic* they would still be taking bookings for it – they produced a draft of shattering dullness and insincerity. Their hearts were not in it.

On their own initiative, the Policy Unit at No. 10 worked through half the night and prepared an alternative designed, as much as a White Paper can do, to lift and inspire the people who had to make the policy work. Some of its ebullience was toned down, of course, but with the Prime Minister's title – 'The Attack on Inflation' – added, it formed the bulk of the document published on July 11.

There was one unpleasant incident, however, which might have left the Treasury completely in charge. The Chancellor of the Exchequer suddenly complained to the Prime Minister that the Policy Unit had leaked the Treasury's thinking to another body. Bernard Donoughue fiercely denied the charge (when a similar accusation came from the Treasury some time later I responded by telling the principal private secretary at No. 10 with which journalists a Treasury Minister had lunched the previous day; where the lunch had taken place; and what he had said. We heard no more accusations after that).

As a consequence of the Chancellor's complaint, the Prime Minister gave instructions that only the principal private secretary and his deputy should see the flow of papers for consideration by Ministers. When I asked for the documents I was told that I could not see them. I telephoned the Prime Minister, who was in Bradford that afternoon (July 4) and he confirmed that he had given the instruction but added that I could see his copy. It was clear that the directive was aimed against the Policy Unit, which had done more than any other body to prepare an acceptable policy.

I believed then and I believe now that the allegations against the Policy Unit were part of a campaign by Treasury officials to keep control over the development of the policy and the White Paper.

I told the Prime Minister that I could not do my job if papers so essential to the Government's policy were not mine of right and he rescinded the instruction relating to both of us. Bernard Donoughue asked the Prime Minister that he should be allowed to confront the Chancellor but his request was refused.

Meanwhile, we had moved a long way towards setting up a special publicity group – subsequently called the Counter-Inflation Policy Unit – which would work full-time on putting the new policy across. I was deputed to persuade Geoffrey Goodman, Industrial Editor of the *Daily Mirror*, to take on the post of Chief Executive. Goodman was only prepared to accept the post provided his office were in agreement, and provided that the policy was a voluntary one acceptable to the T.U.C. He knew it would be impossible to launch an effective campaign against T.U.C. opposition. It was another indication of the difficulties we faced if compulsion was finally decided upon. In the event, Goodman took the job and his unit was highly successful, helped by the fact that they had to bat on a wicket much easier than they could have hoped for.

On Monday, July 7, Harold Wilson went to Scarborough to speak to the annual conference of the National Union of Mineworkers. I had prepared a speech for him which I thought was tough, but he wanted it tougher. It warned the miners not to isolate themselves from the rest of the community, thinking

that whatever was the state of the economy they would be able
to look after themselves. Coal would have to pay its way, he
said. Subsidies meant higher taxation and everybody suffered.
He went on:

> When the music stops in this game, someone is without a
> chair. That is the man who goes to the wall. He is the one
> who becomes another figure in the queue of the unemployed
> ... Inflation is causing unemployment.

That message had got through already to the T.U.C. General
Council members who were negotiating with the Government.
It got through to the miners, too. The stage was now set for the
Prime Minister to make his statement to the House of Commons, on Friday, July 11, ten days after the critical Cabinet
meeting following the sterling crisis. He announced that the
Government had decided to accept 'an overriding limit of £6
per week for pay settlements during the next pay round, a
figure consistent with the aim of reducing inflation to 10 per
cent by the late summer of next year'. He went on:

> Our policy is based on consent and willing co-operation
> within our democracy. We reject, for the reasons I have
> so frequently stated, the idea of statutory policies based on
> criminal sanctions against workers.

The Treasury had fought to the last, through the Chancellor,
for a clear announcement that there would be reserve powers
which the Government would not hesitate to use if there was a
substantial breach of the new policy. On that, the Cabinet
largely agreed. If such powers had become necessary, and
Michael Foot had left the Government, there would have been
little sympathy for him in the party or the country.

There was to be one final flurry, however. The Cabinet had
decided that though the Prime Minister would announce the
decision on reserve powers when he made his Commons statement, the nature of those powers would not be spelled out
precisely; there would be no Bill published. The reasoning was
sound enough: if the Government printed the Bill it would
become the centre of a new argument, hypothetical though it

would be, and it would demonstrate, moreover, that the Government had little faith in its policy. In his statement, he said only:

> If our faith in the agreed policy is disappointed, if there are any who seek to abuse a system based on consensus and consent, or to cheat by any means, the Government will not hesitate to apply legal powers of compulsion against the employers concerned to ensure compliance. We must have these powers in reserve. Legislation has therefore already been prepared, for introduction if need be, which, when applied to particular cases, would make it illegal for the employer to exceed the pay limit. If the pay limit is endangered, the Government will ask Parliament to approve this legislation forthwith.

Though the House questioned the Prime Minister for an hour about his statement no M.P.—not the Conservative leader, Mrs Thatcher, not the Liberal leader, Mr Thorpe, not anyone from the Left of the Labour Party—asked the Prime Minister to publish the Reserve Powers Bill. No one thought of it as an issue. But at the subsequent press conference, he was asked:

> On those statutory powers, Mr Wilson, can we be told that the Bill will be published at least, so that we know what the powers are going to be, even if it is not to be taken through Parliament?

The Prime Minister was momentarily stumped. He had been out of the Cabinet Room when the final decision had been taken upon the question and he did not know the answer. He turned to the Chancellor, sitting on his left. 'Yes', said the Chancellor. Mr Wilson told the questioner: 'Yes, that will be published.'

Cabinet colleagues were upset when they heard of the Prime Minister's promise and the Downing Street Press Office had a hard task in explaining that when the Prime Minister said the Bill was to be published he meant that it was not to be published. The Treasury's officials, who had prepared the draft of the legislation, *did* want it published, primarily to help overseas confidence. But to have published would have meant that the argument would be over what might be; it would have soured the chances of the policy succeeding.

There can never be a final victory over the official machine because for them the game never ends, it is infinite. The civil service is occasionally defeated, but never banished from the field. When the next crisis occurs—or when a maverick union defies a voluntary policy—the plans for a compulsory incomes policy will once again be taken out of the files, the red tape teased loose and a minute prepared for the Chancellor to circulate to his colleagues. It will tell them in grave tones that because of a sudden loss of confidence in sterling, brought about by excessive wage settlements, the economy faces collapse; that we must demonstrate to the holders of sterling deposits that we are determined to put our own house in order—whatever election pledges were given—and that therefore he must ask his colleagues to approve, immediately, a legal freeze upon all incomes, accompanied, if possible, by cuts in Government spending. Whoever the Prime Minister or Chancellor is when that day comes, whatever he or they say, the truth will be that the machine has triumphed again. The voice may be that of the elected politician: the policy will be that of the appointed official. The Treasury are not so much the mandarins of Whitehall as the Bourbons.

I doubt if British Governments can wait until we reach a plateau of economic prosperity before they tackle the problem of the Treasury (indeed, I doubt if we will ever reach that plateau *until* we tackle the problem of the Treasury).

I find it astonishing that a Labour Cabinet can still tolerate a situation where the Chancellor of the Exchequer only acquaints them with the content of his Budget some twenty-eight hours before he presents it to Parliament. On that time scale, only a massive spontaneous revolt against the Budget can make a fundamental change in it. I have no strong opinions about whether the annual Budget ritual should continue, but the secrecy in which the Budget is drawn up is not only absurd and anti-democratic, it is a powerful buttress to the supremacy of the Treasury mind over that of the elected Government's.

The Chancellor's announcement in his 1976 Budget speech on April 6 that he would make concessions in direct taxation provided the trade unions would agree to wage increases for

1976–7 being in the area of 3 per cent was never discussed in detail with his colleagues.

First reactions to it from the trade unions and – to judge from the vox pop interviews on B.B.C. and I.T.N. – from the men in the street were hostile. It was unclear for several hours what it was Mr Healey *was* proposing. Had it been thrashed out in Cabinet in the weeks preceding the Budget it could have been launched with a powerful and co-ordinated publicity drive. But the Counter-Inflation Publicity Unit were told nothing about it in advance. The combined expertise of the professional information service in Whitehall was neglected. The Treasury kept it to themselves, bungled its launching and were lucky to get away with it by 'modifying' the 3 per cent to read 'four and a half'. With a massive publicity drive such as accompanied the £6 limit in 1975, they might have found 4 per cent acceptable.

The power which their obsessive secrecy maintains for them is at its most dangerous in the field of exchange rates. The greater the fall in the value of sterling against the dollar and other currencies, the greater the cost of imports, the greater the risk of further increases in the cost of living and in interest rates. It was recognised from the beginning of the 1974 Government that sterling would inevitably suffer a continual depreciation while inflation in Britain was greater than that of our trading partners overseas. But it had to be a *controlled* depreciation, not one consisting of sudden, violent and excessive movements downwards which would lead to panicky demands for changes in policy ranging from destructive public expenditure cuts to damaging import controls. It was, therefore, an integral part of the Cabinet's strategy during 1975–6 for reducing the rate of inflation not to let the pound sterling fall by more than was absolutely necessary. In particular, the Cabinet made it clear, on three occasions, that it would wish to be consulted before the pound sterling fell below $2 on the exchanges.

But on Friday, March 5, only six days before Harold Wilson was due to announce to the Cabinet his intention to resign the premiership, sterling suddenly dipped below that rate, closing at $1·9820. The 50 pence dollar had arrived. The Prime Minister, who had said all along that he would postpone his resignation if there was a sterling crisis, sent for the Chancellor. He was reassuring, clearly believing that the fall in the dollar rate was an aberration which would be quickly eliminated on the following Monday.

Bernard Donoughue and I had already heard unofficially on the Whitehall network that it was the Treasury officials' intention to get the rate down to $1·88. We believed that was the purpose of letting the pound go through the two-dollar psychological barrier. The fears of those who knew more about the exchanges than I — fears that were wholly confirmed — were that it was impossible to guarantee that once the pound fell to $1·88 there could be any way of holding it there. It would be known in the markets that sterling was being depressed with official encouragement.

At one point in the week that followed, with the pound showing no sign of climbing back above $2, I remarked to one of the best of the Treasury men that it seemed to me that the Chancellor did not appear to know everything that had gone on.

'That's right,' he said. 'All this is classified "Top Secret".'

'So?' I asked.

'Oh,' he said cheerfully, '"Top Secret" means you don't tell the Chancellor.'

4

Perfidious Foreigners

'If everyone minded their own business,' said the
Duchess in a hoarse growl, 'the world would go round
a deal faster than it does.'

Alice in Wonderland

General Elections in Britain today are fought almost entirely on
domestic rather than foreign or Commonwealth issues, except
perhaps in a handful of constituencies where the immigrant vote
is thought to be significant. In the realm of overseas affairs,
probably only the issue of Rhodesia—in the General Election
of March 1966—had even a marginal effect on the voters'
behaviour. In the two General Elections of 1974, the rest of the
world, the Common Market excepted, was ignored for the dura-
tion of the campaign; and even the Market was debated almost
exclusively in terms of prices in British shops. I know because
I wrote the Leader of the Labour Party's speeches on the subject.

Except in moments of sudden drama or unexpected crisis,
foreign policy is no longer the concern of the electorate, even
though it is an obligatory item on the Cabinet agenda each
week; and even though the Foreign and Commonwealth
Secretary, whoever he is, is one of the most important three or
four men in the Government by virtue of his post alone. That
importance is reflected in the quality of the staff at the Foreign
and Commonwealth Office, which, man for man, is more able
than that of any other department in Whitehall, including the
Treasury.

Unfortunately, a diplomat is, almost by definition, an expert
on countries other than his own. Most of his working life is
spent abroad; he is, in terms of personal experience, a stranger

to, and ignorant of, the pressure of home affairs which are the principal preoccupation of his Government.

Inevitably, the question of, say, educational policy is not seen by him as one between the establishment of a fully comprehensive system and the retention of the grammar schools; or the relative priority to be accorded to the development of polytechnics or the expansion of the universities. It is, rather, the level of grant from the F.C.O. to maintain his children at the public school of his choice in Britain. His concern is understandable. Education facilities in most countries are inferior to those of Britain. If a man is to serve his employer overseas he does not expect his children to suffer in consequence – therefore, they must attend boarding school in England. The practice does, however, narrow his view. On wider issues he is insulated both from the level of the cost of living in the country to which he is accredited – because of a generous expense allowance – and from that in his own country because he is not living in it. He also gets his drink and tobacco duty free and retires at sixty, unless he has served in posts regarded as particularly wearing on his physique, in which case he can put his feet up earlier. A year in the Gulf is worth two in Rome.

This absence of a 'home' outlook can have serious consequences for the F.C.O.'s political masters. Though particular issues of foreign affairs are rarely fought over in front of the electors, a Foreign and Commonwealth Secretary who relies too much on his official advisers and thus is insensitive to party opinion will quickly be in conflict with it and damage the overall impression given by the Government as a whole; and the Foreign and Commonwealth Secretary, too often, is the sum of his civil service parts.

Though the growth in civil service power during the years of the Heath Government (1970–4) was principally in the field of domestic policy, the Foreign and Commonwealth Office grew stronger, too. This should not be surprising. If the unelected élite are going to rule us, there are more of the élite in the Foreign and Commonwealth Office than of any other kind. What is more, the department has a tradition of action rather than recommendation, dating from the time when communications with London were so tortuous and uncertain that an Ambassador acted first and told his Secretary of State afterwards what he had done. The absence of the electric telegraph is no excuse today; but the complexity of the European Economic Community's bureaucracy, and the multiplicity of its organisations, has given the professional diplomats' influence new strength. If there is something a stubborn Foreign and Commonwealth Secretary wants to do, then his department will find an E.E.C. rule which prevents his doing it. If, on the other hand F.C.O. officialdom cherishes similar ambitions, it will find an escape clause to permit it to do what it likes.

Unlike other departments of state – to demonstrate that it is not size alone that counts – the number of officials in the combined Foreign and Commonwealth Offices fell steadily as the last patches of British red were bleached out of the world atlas by independence. They did not fight too much over numbers. Instead they supervised the breaking of the chains of Empire and the spinning of the frail threads of Commonwealth with an enthusiasm bordering at times on conviction; and then they fought for, and achieved, entry into Europe with an enthusiasm bordering on the fanatical. So strong, so determined, was that resolve to make Britain a member of the E.E.C. that no Government of any party could have indefinitely resisted it. Not even an adverse vote in the 1975 referendum would have stopped entry – only delayed it until the F.C.O. decided the time was propitious to raise it again.

In the event the movement towards Europe was so powerful, so insistent, not only in the F.C.O. but more widely throughout the Whitehall machine and among politicians, that it was unstoppable. Though the comparison is odious, it was not until I experienced its force that I fully understood how the policy of appeasement was so powerful in the 1930s. For many officials Europe was an issue which claimed their first loyalty. They were prepared to work hard in 1974–5 during the period of re-negotiation of the terms of entry into the E.E.C., because that was demanded of them by their political masters; but if the Labour Government had failed to recommend entry when the referendum was held, on June 5, 1975, then a number of them, inevitably, would have resigned from the service.

This determination to pursue particular policies, like that of the Treasury in pursuit of its fetish of a compulsory incomes policy and public expenditure cuts, raises issues of serious con-

cern to our political parties to which I return at the end of this
chapter. At times, the F.C.O. has acted like a state within a
state, semi-autonomous, a part disregarding the needs of the
whole. This situation is of particular consequence for the
Labour Party, even though its traditional involvement with
international affairs has now largely deteriorated into an occasional National Executive resolution about Chile, or Brazil, or
some other faraway country of whose people, in truth, the
majority of the N.E.C. know little.

For the Conservatives the attitudes of the F.C.O. are largely
their own and the department is the conventional stepping
stone to Downing Street itself. Every Conservative Prime
Minister since the war, with the exception of Churchill – who
reversed the order by taking charge of the Foreign Office after
he became Prime Minister, when Eden was ill – has served a
spell there. Eden, Macmillan and Douglas-Home were Secretaries of State; Heath was Lord Privy Seal, in charge of the
negotiations to enter Europe which collapsed in 1963. Lord
Butler did not make it to Downing Street, but that was nothing
to do with his being Foreign Secretary. Even Selwyn Lloyd,
arguably the worst Foreign Secretary since Sir Samuel Hoare,
though missing out on No. 10, became Leader of the House of
Commons and, subsequently, its Speaker, as though Suez had
never happened. In the Conservative Party, Ministerial office
is greater than the deed.

For a Socialist politician, however, while the F.C.O. is not
a positive block on the path to the premiership – at least, it did
not stop Jim Callaghan – it is just as likely to lead to a hyphen-
ated title and an ermine shroud, plus expenses. Though the
electorate does not bother its head about foreign policy, the
party activist, particularly the Member of Parliament, does. A
Foreign and Commonwealth Secretary who becomes the creature of his department will suffer for it if he aims for the very
top. If it were to happen to a Labour Minister of Agriculture,
on the other hand, no one would notice.

The F.C.O. is as strong on policies as it is weak on politics.
It is, in particular, fiercely pro-Arab and has been, despite
occasional aberrations, ever since primitive Eton man first set
foot in the Middle East. Large numbers of diplomats received
their early training there; they retain an affection, even love,

for the Arab people and a great many of them speak Arabic. Very few, however, speak Hebrew. This does not make for a balanced view. The pressure of sympathy for the Arab cause surfaced again and again during Harold Wilson's last administrations – and was particularly evident in votes in the U.N. – despite the fact that the Prime Minister himself, and his deputy, Edward Short, were overwhelmingly pro-Israeli in outlook.

Just as strongly, the F.C.O. is anti-Soviet, by past tradition and current inclination. If the Zinoviev Letter had not been invented, the pre-war Foreign Office would have found some other way of making sure it existed. Those pre-war attitudes were reasserted after the wartime alliance with the U.S.S.R. was ended and Stalin and Molotov were making the blood of the world run cold. The F.C.O. has remained anti-Russian ever since, except for those who have defected. Many of the diplomats who served in Moscow and other Eastern European capitals, who suffered grim winters and even grimmer societies, returned to the West and Whitehall with an implacable hatred of the Soviet Union and its satellites. It induced an attitude which is slow to see changes in the East and which led to an incident – trivial in itself but with serious implications – which is described later in this chapter.

If it were possible to compress the F.C.O.'s ideal world into a single concept, I suppose it would look something like a Common Market peopled entirely by crusading, anti-Communist Bedouin. If I lived in Gibraltar or the Falkland Islands I would not sleep at night for worrying about it, because, so far as *policy* is concerned, those territories are peripheral; if the British connection is to be preserved it will be up to the politicians to do it. The *officials* will never die in the ditch for either of them.

It was the Foreign and Commonwealth Office, as much as any Community government, which defeated its Secretary of State's attempt, at the European Council meeting in Rome on December 1 and 2, 1975, to achieve a separate seat for Britain at the world energy conference due to begin a few days later. In the run-up to that summit, the Foreign and Commonwealth Secretary, then Jim Callaghan, had advanced farther and farther along the limb of 'No seat for Britain – no energy conference', refusing to be represented by a spokesman (Luxembourg) for a Community in which Britain was far and away the major energy producer. He then embarked on a tour of the Middle East, still rumbling menacingly, in press conferences in Saudi Arabia and elsewhere, that it was a seat for Britain – or else. But while Mr Callaghan was declaring there would be no retreat, the evacuation of his position was being organised by his officials back in London.

When in Rome Horatius stood and fought, he not only had two companions; he also knew what the consul and the citizens of the city were doing behind his back. I doubt if Jim Callaghan realised what was happening until the timbers of his bridge collapsed and the Tiber closed over his head. No one else got wet. The fact is that he was provoking a crisis – and maintaining it during a desert safari when he was not in adequate touch with London – which threatened not only the energy conference but, much more serious, the unity of the Community. That was unacceptable. What Harold Wilson and Jim Callaghan eventually conceded, after a day of tension and bad feeling at the Council meeting, was a procedural device not much different from what had been worked out by his officials in London four days earlier.

When I joined Harold Wilson's Press Office in January 1969, his Government had a record deficit in the opinion polls, had lost to the Scottish Nationalists a by-election at Hamilton where previously it had an 18,000 majority, had embarked on a fateful and fatal battle with the unions over 'In Place of Strife', was having its morale and energy sapped by constant talk of, and fitful attempts at, conspiracies to topple the leader, and had had its attempt to join the Common Market frustrated by General de Gaulle. It was like becoming a public relations officer for the army after the evacuation of Dunkirk.

Of all the Government's misfortunes, the failure of the efforts to get negotiations going on entry into Europe – which from the narrow view of electoral popularity had had the least impact – rankled most of all in the official mind. The French President was seen as an old man harbouring the resentments of twenty-five years earlier, taking slow, deliberate and repeated revenge for the affronts dealt to him when he was a wartime irritant to Churchill and Roosevelt. If a spirit of revenge was within him, there was one, too, among some British officials, though with them the origins were of more recent date. Suddenly, in the first week of February 1969, the General gave them their chance, in an interview granted to the then British ambassador in Paris, Sir Christopher Soames.

That the General did not like the E.E.C., either as it had been created or as it had evolved, was well known, though perhaps the intensity of his dislike was not. In his meeting with Sir Christopher he had rehearsed, first, his familiar lecture about Britain being the principal satellite of the United States. British entry into the E.E.C. as it stood then would change the whole character of the Market. Every country in the Community — except France, of course, which had managed to break away — was an American satellite and Britain's membership would only make matters worse.

The trouble was, he said, that Britain and France in their long history had never been friends, only allies when necessity compelled it, or rivals; there had never been a genuine partnership between them. De Gaulle was willing to try to change all that, to make a new start. He had little faith in the E.E.C., he went on, and would willingly contemplate its breaking up. To that end, he wanted Britain to launch an initiative designed to promote a new form of Free Trade Association in Europe, which would include agricultural free trade. If we agreed to do that then he would issue a statement supporting us.

He was willing, in effect, to be an accessory after the fact of the murder of the Community, but he had no wish to be caught with the gun in his hand.

The first British reaction was to ask why de Gaulle did not launch the initiative himself; if he did that, we would certainly then indicate our willingness to discuss the whole issue with him, though without prior commitment.

To do it de Gaulle's way meant that if the initiative succeeded Britain's reputation would be that of a country which, denied partnership in Europe, took retribution by destroying the most promising adventure in uniting Europe ever undertaken; if the initiative failed, as it almost certainly would have done, then Britain would have the odium, plus certain exclusion from the E.E.C. for at least a generation.

The Prime Minister's reaction was precise on this point: 'We want to join the Common Market,' he said, 'not bury it.' But, on the whole, he refused to get excited about the development, taking the view that de Gaulle had said little to Soames that was different from what he had said when they had met at an earlier Summit. Few others shared that view, however; certainly not Dr Kiesinger, the Federal German Chancellor, with whom the Prime Minister had talks in Bonn on February 11, six days after the de Gaulle–Soames discussion. Harold Wilson faced a dilemma in Bonn: if he told Dr Kiesinger about the proposals put forward by the General then he was breaking the confidential seal which de Gaulle had placed upon them; if, however, he did not disclose them, the British Government would have been doubly suspect in German eyes, when news of the talks eventually leaked, for concealing them from the Federal Chancellor. Harold Wilson was pressed hard by the Foreign Office to 'tell all' to Kiesinger, but he refused, giving him only a sanitised outline of what the General had said.

In the event, it did not matter. When Harold Wilson returned home he discovered that the Foreign Office, against his clearly expressed wishes, had circulated an extensive, though far from complete, record of the Paris talks to our ambassadors to the other countries of the Community and to Washington, with instructions to disclose the contents to the Governments to which they were accredited, with the additional information that the British Government disagreed fundamentally with the General on almost every issue he raised. It was this behaviour which subsequently prompted Harold Wilson to write in *The Labour Government 1964–1970: A Personal Record*:

> I was getting concerned ... about the attitude which the Foreign Office, at least at official level, seemed to be taking against the French, and the joy that some purely procedural victories seemed to give them.

On this occasion, the F.C.O. were after a bigger prize than a 'purely procedural' victory. Having twice been thwarted by the General in our attempt to join the Common Market, they were determined to cast him in the role of the Community's Benedict Arnold. It was an opportunity to demonstrate our credentials for being a part of the new Europe and that it was the French who sought to betray it. That was the motive in informing

France's partners of the way the General's mind was working. It had the incidental merit, too, of ensuring that the world outside Washington and the Community would soon hear of it. Then as now, to tell our European partners anything in confidence was equivalent to handing copies to Reuters news agency, the Press Association, the Associated Press, United Press International and Agence France Presse. In my experience, only the National Executive Committee of the Labour Party can leak secret documents faster, more consistently and more accurately, and they are, of course, a much older institution. On this occasion, however, the secret *was* kept, incredibly, for about ten days, which only went to show how shaken the Community Governments were by the news. Then *Figaro* and *France Soir* received a version of it – garbled, but with enough truth in it to blow the whole story open. The 'Soames affair' had begun, and from that moment the Foreign Office were active in exploiting it to what they conceived to be de Gaulle's disadvantage.

The News Department at the Foreign Office is unlike any other information office in Whitehall. Its staff are diplomats, many with considerable service abroad. They are specialists in their subjects, but with a solid general knowledge of British policy in any area of the globe. On completion of his spell of duty there, the Head of the News Department can expect appointment as an ambassador or High Commissioner. The department is integral to the policy-making function of the F.C.O., because publicity is not only at times essential to the success of the policy but it can determine the course that the policy will take. It would be inelegant to describe them as aggressive in their propaganda, but they are firm to the point of dogmatism, especially about N.A.T.O. and Eastern Europe. They are suckled by a corps of highly-paid British diplomatic correspondents; in addition a substantial number of foreign correspondents stationed in London look to the Foreign and Commonwealth Office as a principal news source. But it is not only the News Department which has these contacts; the relationships between other F.C.O. diplomats and journalists are close and extensive; if the F.C.O. gives a luncheon or dinner for a visiting dignitary, or throws a cocktail party, journalists are represented. When the Foreign and Commonwealth

Secretary sets off for a tour abroad, the newspapermen assigned
to report the trip may well travel in his aircraft, paying the full
commercial fare but enjoying the luxury of V.I.P. travel. In so
doing they inevitably jeopardise the independence they never
stop talking about, but that is by the way.

When on Friday, February 21, 1969, the news about the
Soames affair began to break, sketchy and inaccurate though it
was, I was told by the News Department that they were proposing to leak to *Il Messagero* in Rome the version of the interview telegraphed to France's partners and to the U.S. State
Department. This ill-conceived manoeuvre was to be the
means by which we exposed the perfidy of the French and displayed the innate decency and desire to be good Europeans of
the British. It was true that General de Gaulle had placed an
embargo of confidentiality upon his talk with the ambassador
but, seeing that the story would be in an Italian newspaper, we
were hardly likely to be blamed for breaking it. Had this
clumsy exercise taken place – which was unthinkable – and had
it succeeded – which was unlikely – the Italian Government no
doubt would have been condemned for leaking it, an even-
tuality which, if it did weigh heavily on the official mind, no one
saw fit to mention. When I reported the plan to the Prime
Minister he instantly vetoed it.

That evening, Harold Wilson was due to speak at a party
rally in Felixstowe, some eighty-three miles from London but in
the Friday rush-hour three hours or more away by road. It
meant that once he left Downing Street he would be out of
touch for several hours (communications between Prime
Minister and Downing Street have since been improved).

Just before he left, at 4.20 p.m., he instructed me on the
course the No. 10 Press Office was to follow: not to leak the
story; not to deny the truth, but not to add to it. We were to
'keep our hands clean'. If the French decided to leak the story
then we could not stop them, but Harold Wilson did not want
Britain to be accused of being responsible.

There must have been a Black Santa operating that evening,
for a wish was never so speedily unfulfilled. As the Prime
Minister drove away I went to the general press office and
found a message asking me to go to the Foreign and Commonwealth Office's press briefing at 4.30. I arrived in time to hear

the official spokesman begin to read from a telegram in his hand. It was the same telegram which had been sent to The Hague, Bonn, Brussels, Luxembourg, Rome and Washington, and classified 'Secret'. The spokesman said:

General de Gaulle spoke to our Ambassador in Paris two weeks ago. He began by saying that it had been impossible to arrive at a European view because of the pro-American feelings of all the countries in Europe, and particularly ourselves, whereas France had succeeded in achieving a totally independent position. This was not so in the case of either Germany or Italy or the Netherlands, and certainly not of the United Kingdom. The whole essence of a European entity must be an independent position in world terms and he was not yet convinced that it was possible for us to accept this.

Once there was a truly independent Europe, there would be no need for N.A.T.O. with its American dominance and command structure. General de Gaulle went on to say that he had no part in the creation of the Common Market, neither did he have any particular faith in it. What was more, he was quite certain that if we and our friends joined it, it could no longer be the same. This would not necessarily be a bad thing. It might have been created differently and he by no means excluded that for the future.

But we seemed to have set our hearts on joining it, for better or for worse. He personally foresaw it changing and would like to see it change into a looser form of a free trade area with arrangements by each country to exchange agricultural produce. He would be quite prepared to discuss with us what should take the place of the Common Market as an enlarged European Economic Association. But he was also anxious first to have political discussions with us. His thought was that there should be a large European Economic Association but with a smaller Inner Council of a European Political Association consisting of France, Britain, Germany and Italy. But it was necessary first to see whether France and Britain saw things sufficiently in common, because this was the key to any such political association. General de Gaulle recalled a suggestion which M. Debré had made a few months earlier to our Ambassador, that Britain and France should have talks together on political matters, saying that he had understood we were not interested in this. Our Ambassador replied that we would wish to know what object the French had in view in these discussions. General de Gaulle replied that he would like to see talks between Britain and France on economic, monetary, political and defence matters to see whether we could resolve our differences. He would like to see a gesture by the British Government suggesting that such talks should take place, which he would then welcome.

That statement was given non-attributably to the reporters present; i.e., while they could use the substance of it, they could not quote directly from it, nor reveal its source. But sources nowadays are only secure on comparatively minor stories; in this case, the source was part of the story. By nightfall, every capital in Europe knew of it. By the following Monday, the French Government had bitterly protested about the briefing, the British press was ferocious in its condemnation of the Government and the Conservative Opposition was jubilant at the Cabinet's embarrassment.

At one stroke, the senior diplomats behind the move had destroyed any hope of Britain negotiating to enter Europe while General de Gaulle was still in power (in fact, he resigned two months later, having recklessly committed the continuation of his Presidency to the outcome of an unimportant referendum; but the F.C.O. could not have anticipated that happening); reduced relations with France to the depths they plumbed when the first de Gaulle veto was applied in 1963; made the rest of the Community wary about Britain (Europe without France was inconceivable; Europe without Britain was not only possible, it was the current position); provoked an embarrassed ambassador to the edge of apoplexy and resignation; upset the fervently pro-European members of the Cabinet; given the Opposition the time of their lives in the House of Commons; and enabled the British press to portray the Government as being as inept abroad as they said it was at home. All in all, short of staging a military coup, it was quite

1 At a Labour conference in Blackpool, not a gangsters' convention in Chicago. The *Observer* published this picture with the caption, 'Joe Haines and friend'.

2 No. 10 Downing Street. The Press Secretary occupies the bow-fronted room to the right.

3 The Pillared Room – and priceless Tabriz carpet – at No. 10.

an afternoon's work. As the Duke of Wellington said, 'The next greatest misfortune to losing a battle is to gain such a victory as this.'

I was not able to speak to the Prime Minister after the F.C.O. briefing until much later in the evening. Predictably, he was angry, and well aware that he would have to bear the brunt of the Opposition's attack in the Commons as well as the criticism from overseas. The F.C.O., however finely they may have calculated would be the effect in foreign capitals, had totally failed to appreciate the disarray their action would cause at home; or if they had appreciated it, they chose to ignore it. In diplomacy, whatever the public, purist protestations of prime ministers and presidents, the end is frequently held to justify the means, but at the conclusion of the Soames affair the Government could not even enjoy that consolation.

An incident three years later, when Harold Wilson was Leader of the Opposition, was to revive his distrust of the Foreign and Commonwealth Office and, as a consequence, a fundamental change took place at the News Department when Labour returned to power in 1974.

In late 1972 and early 1973 the Czechoslovak Government was pressing Harold Wilson to visit Prague as part of its campaign to rehabilitate itself in Western eyes after its collaboration with the invading Soviet armies in August 1968. Britain was a prime target for its attentions; the British Government was beginning to respond to the overtures of the Czechs and they wanted Labour's seal of respectability, too. Harold Wilson turned them down, or postponed a decision, more than once, because he needed a reciprocal gesture of some kind from them. Eventually, he agreed to go to Prague, subject to the Czechoslovakian Government agreeing to release the Rev. David Hathaway, a nonconformist minister from Yorkshire, who had been imprisoned by the Czechs for the bourgeois crime of smuggling bibles into the country.

The Czech authorities were at first reluctant, pointing out, solemnly, that the provisions of their legal code, to which they were bound to adhere, made the acceptance of such a precondition difficult. Nevertheless, they said, if Mr Wilson would agree to visit Czechoslovakia and *while he was there* make a formal request for clemency to be shown to Mr Hathaway, then the President, under the same legal code, would be able graciously to accede to Mr Wilson's plea. So he went, and graciously accede the President did—and with such celerity that Mr Hathaway was released from his prison about an hour before Harold Wilson actually got round to asking formally for his freedom.

The Foreign and Commonwealth Office, which had tried unsuccessfully over a period of months to secure Mr Hathaway's return to Britain were, perhaps understandably, piqued. But they recovered quickly and claimed a share of the credit by ingeniously pointing out that the fact that Mr Hathaway was freed before Harold Wilson formally intervened on his behalf was proof that it was the pressure of the Foreign and Commonwealth Secretary, Sir Alec Douglas-Home, which had succeeded. It was not a bad try but they would not have made much headway with it but for the unwitting assistance of Harold Wilson's companion on the visit, his then office manager, Tony Field, who sent me a telegram—through Foreign and Commonwealth Office channels—from Prague the day before Harold Wilson returned home.

Harold Wilson and I had already arranged that if Mr Hathaway was released in his charge, as the Czechs had promised, he would send me a one-word telegram, 'Shakespeare'— I still wince at the subtlety of it—and I would then know to arrange for a press conference at London Airport when he arrived back.

But the telegram that came read more like cloak-and-dagger melodrama, and third-rate at that. 'Shakespeare operation successfully accomplished', it announced. 'Leaves on our plane tomorrow ... Let the press all know to be there in force. Shakespeare will be spirited away and H.W. will take any press conference. Six British education correspondents on same plane.' This last sentence was a reference to a group of journalists to whom Harold Wilson had apparently suggested, in some off-the-cuff references to August 1968, that what had happened then should now be forgotten. The publicity for that was bad. The publicity for the telegram—when the Foreign and Commonwealth Office duly leaked it—was worse. It looked like a brazen attempt to grab, improperly at that, the credit for Mr Hathaway's release. That telegram, quite illogically, seemed to strengthen the F.C.O.'s claim that it was their success after all. It was widely circulated within the F.C.O. and a member of the News Department told a woman journalist about it over dinner.

That was going too far. Facilities for senior politicians of all parties when travelling abroad are readily available from our embassies and High Commissions. They are not dependent upon agreeing to save the face of the F.C.O.; in fact, the Government of the day gains considerable benefit from these visits, for any information of consequence which might be gleaned by the traveller is naturally passed on. In this instance, the leak was even more unforgivable, because before he left the F.C.O. had made a point of asking Harold Wilson to help the British ambassador improve his contacts with the Czech leadership. The release of Mr Hathaway was a small matter (except for him and his family). The result, however, of the F.C.O.'s action, whether it was careless – as they said – or deliberate – as we suspected – was to sour relations between the Secretary of State, Sir Alec Douglas-Home, and Mr Wilson. As Harold Wilson was to point out, during an acid correspondence with Sir Alec, his telegram would have been more secure had he sent it via the Czech embassy in London. Sir Alec, for his part, felt compelled to sign letters drafted by F.C.O. officials defending an action of the News Department – while grudgingly regretting it – which, had he known of it in advance, he would never have permitted or condoned.

That incident, like the only other episode which I want to recount at length in this chapter, was disturbing; the one for its sheer pettiness, the other because it showed the lengths to which the official machine is prepared to go to preserve the religion of the department from the revisionism of the politicians. Both had their consequences.

In early February 1975, the Prime Minister and the Foreign and Commonwealth Secretary were preparing to visit Moscow, in trade and political terms the most important overseas discussions they had undertaken since Labour returned to office eleven months earlier.

Almost everything about the visit was uncertain, including, for many months, the dates on which it was to take place. The agenda was largely unknown and so was the warmth of the reception we were to be accorded. (The degree of enthusiasm which the Muscovites manifest on these occasions is carefully ordained in advance, from the exact number of factory workers to be given time off to stand applauding in sub-zero temperatures at the airport to the size of the Union Jacks they will wave as the visitors pass.) We did not know how long the talks would last; and we did not know with whom they would be held.

In the months before the October 1974 General Election the Soviet Embassy in London had been pressing hard for the visit to be announced. Harold Wilson, remembering that the Russians had announced during the 1970 General Election campaign that he was going to visit Moscow after Polling Day, was not anxious to tempt Fate and refused. After October, the Russians became cool and then evasive about a date. This stalling exercise coincided with the disappearance from public view of Mr Brezhnev and the mounting reports that he was suffering from cancer of the lip or jaw. No one in the West knew for certain whether he was well or not; indeed, there was a moment when there was doubt whether he was alive or not. What was certain, however, was that during 1974 the Soviet leadership had been reviewing its foreign policy, particularly towards the Western democracies, among whom Britain is spasmodically accorded especial Russian attention and regard. Brezhnev had placed almost all his foreign policy eggs into the Nixon basket; now Nixon had gone. There had been other dramatic changes, too, during the year. Chancellor Willy Brandt had been destroyed by an East German spy in his private office; President Pompidou had died; Edward Heath had been defeated twice at the polls.

Perhaps old men do not like new faces; if so, the return to power of Harold Wilson must have been especially welcome to the geriatric leadership of the Kremlin, for no foreign statesman — no Ford, no Giscard d'Estaing, no Schmidt — had paid more visits to the U.S.S.R. or was better known to them. Suddenly the dates were fixed. In any case, the Russians, too, were eager to improve matters. Their foreign policy is not permanently decided by pique. In fact, they had made overtures for a visit by Mr Heath in 1973, though nothing had come of it.

For his part, the Prime Minister was determined to restore

good relations with the Russians, which had been soured more than three years earlier by the expulsion of over 100 Soviet 'spies' from Britain. If the Russians were willing to be friendly and to sign some useful trade agreements, Harold Wilson and Jim Callaghan were prepared to make a big effort to initiate a new start.

One major speech by the Prime Minister was due to be delivered at a Kremlin luncheon, which turned out to be an affair for Gargantuan gourmets, three hours long, a kind of 'Quo Vadis?' with food. He prepared his words with care before they were sent to the Foreign and Commonwealth Office for its Soviet experts to scrutinise and to propose amendments, improvements, deletions and additions. Discussion of it was one of the principal purposes of a briefing meeting held with the experts in the Cabinet Room two or three days before we left for Moscow. The other purpose, of course, the deeper one, was to examine the latest evidence – which was getting more hopeful – of our likely reception and to consider the range of our responses.

In the event, the second purpose was barely touched upon because the time available was wholly taken up with the speech and a textual deviation by the Prime Minister which led to a protracted struggle with the experts. In the beginning, the meeting followed a routine course, with the Prime Minister accepting factual corrections in toto, conforming to policy, but resisting changes proposed which were designed to remove any meaning to the speech whatsoever. Then the leading Kremlino-logist in the F.C.O. team asked the Prime Minister to remove from the speech a reference he had inserted to 'peaceful co-existence'. 'Why?' asked the Prime Minister.

The official said firmly that the Russians did not mean by 'peaceful co-existence' what we in the West meant by it. It was not *détente* – or, as Harold Wilson preferred to call it, 'live and let live' – but the continuation of the ideological struggle against capitalism and democracy by all means short of war – by espionage, subversion, intimidation and infiltration. The Prime Minister refused to make the change, and recalled that President Nixon had used those very words himself. The experts persisted: it was true that the President *had* used the phrase, but it was a mistake; once it had been realised he had never used it again.

Harold Wilson rarely used his Prime Ministerial position to cut short an antagonist in an argument, whether he was a Cabinet colleague or an official. For that reason, he allowed the discussion to run on as one expert after another raised objections. But eventually an irritated Prime Minister rose from the table and beckoned me to follow him outside. There he fulminated at the time that had been wasted. I said I thought the time had come to end the discussion.

When we returned to the Cabinet Room, he asked the experts' spokesman to state again his objections to the phrase. After he obliged, repeating what the Russians meant by it, the Prime Minister said: 'And in my speech I will say what *I* mean by it.' That ended the discussion and the meeting.

In fact, when the Prime Minister completed the final text, he dropped the 'peaceful' but used a definition of co-existence coined by Lord Attlee a generation before. He told his Kremlin audience:

> Clement Attlee, a great leader of our country, who was Prime Minister when I first came here as a young Trade Minister, said in the context of the threat to world peace created by the menace of thermo-nuclear warfare, 'The only alternative to co-existence is co-death.'

The next day, Mr Brezhnev—who had ended speculation about his health by bouncing energetically into the limelight for the first time in five months and taking charge of the talks— told Harold Wilson he had been thinking deeply about Lord Attlee's words, which were new to him and which he found impressive. Whatever the private Soviet view of what 'peaceful co-existence' means, Mr Brezhnev gave a very different public interpretation to the one we had heard from the F.C.O. The Soviet leadership, he said,

> are fully determined to do all in their power to impart an historically irreversible character not only to international *détente* as such, but also to a real turn towards the long-term, fruitful and mutually beneficial co-operation of states with different social systems on the basis of full equality and mutual respect. That is what we in the Soviet Union mean by peaceful co-existence.

It was almost as if he knew what our internal argument had been.

If that had been the end of it, the whole incident would rate as no more than an insight into the bureaucratic mind, irritating largely for the time it had wasted and illuminating for its meticulous devotion to detail. But it was not the end.

After several years of pressure and negotiation, the Soviet Union had succeeded in getting some thirty-five countries to agree on holding a Conference on Security and Co-operation in Europe in Helsinki on July 30 and 31, 1975. By the luck of the ballot, the Prime Minister was chosen to make the opening speech to the conference at its first full session. In preparing the speech, it seemed to him appropriate to refer again to 'co-existence', which was, after all, what the conference was about.

Once again, soon after noon, we met with F.C.O. officials in the Cabinet Room. The Kremlinologist of February had departed overseas, but though the team of officials was smaller, it was headed by a more senior diplomat. His approach was different. Casually, almost offhandedly, he asked the Prime Minister if he would not care to drop the reference to 'peaceful co-existence' from the speech. The Prime Minister said firmly that he would not and he did not intend to go through all that 'bloody nonsense' again. Another official said that the French had been upset by Mr Wilson's use of the word 'co-existence' during his Moscow visit. By chance, the Prime Minister had discussed the matter briefly with President Giscard d'Estaing, who had told him that he approved of what he had said. When the Prime Minister mentioned that conversation, the subject was dropped and the draft was agreed as a final text, subject to a few minor queries to which the F.C.O. promised to supply the answers by 4 p.m. that afternoon. It was then shortly before lunch and the Prime Minister asked that his private secretary seconded to No. 10 from the Foreign Office and I should meet at 4 o'clock in his room at the House of Commons to make the final changes. When we met the private secretary read to the Prime Minister a letter from the Secretary of State's senior private secretary, who had not accompanied Mr Callaghan on a visit he was making at that time to Hungary and Poland. Nor, significantly, had he been at the briefing meeting earlier in the day. The letter contained one startling sentence. It said in effect that the Foreign and Commonwealth Secretary was strongly of the view that the Prime Minister should not use the phrase 'peaceful co-existence' in his speech at Helsinki.

The Prime Minister refused to accept that that was Mr Callaghan's view. I pointed out that in the little more than three hours which had elapsed between the end of the morning meeting and receipt of the letter it would have been difficult to send a coded message to Budapest, have it decoded, considered by the Secretary of State, a coded reply sent and received, decoded, and put in a letter to 10 Downing Street.

The speech was not altered. There was going to be a heavy demand for it in Helsinki and my office prepared 200 copies for us to take with us the next day; another 1,000 were to be produced by the conference secretariat in Helsinki, and once that operation began, no change, however minute, could be made without its being known to the press.

The behaviour of the F.C.O. officials, their sheer persistence in the face of his clearly expressed wishes, had irritated the Prime Minister. Parliament was about to rise at the end of one of the most difficult summers politically known to any administration in peacetime. A needless annoyance in such circumstances can attain a disproportionate importance. Harold Wilson decided he would mention the matter to Jim Callaghan when they met in Helsinki (the Secretary of State was coming in from Poland and would be late; physically and mentally, he is a lark, not an owl. He is at his most sunny in the morning and at his grumpiest at night).

The latter-day partnership between Harold Wilson and Jim Callaghan was one for connoisseurs of political relationships. They had both entered the Commons as young men at the General Election of July 1945, when Wilson was twenty-nine and Callaghan thirty-three. They had been colleagues, but not friends; Wilson jumping to the top as the youngest Cabinet Minister for generations, Callaghan on the fringe of the Government as a junior Navy Minister. They each found a natural home in different camps within the party, Wilson to the left, Callaghan to the right of centre; but it was not until Hugh Gaitskell's death in 1963 and the subsequent leadership contest that they became active rivals (Callaghan departing the contest after the first ballot) and not until the late 1960s that they became sworn antagonists.

In 1968 and 1969 Callaghan badly wanted the premiership and badly went about getting it. Harold Wilson had no difficulty in preventing the Callaghan bandwagon from rolling in the Cabinet, not least because it had no wheels. But once Callaghan realised and recognised in mid-1969 that a change in the leadership could never be forced, the relationship between the two men, for the first time, began to grow closer. Callaghan gained Wilson's trust and respect with his handling of the Northern Ireland crisis in the summer and autumn of 1969. From that moment, having tried so hard and failed, he was destined to succeed without trying. Indeed, at the time of Helsinki, though Callaghan did not know it, Harold Wilson had already decided to retire from office within a matter of months (the choice, then, was varying between October and Christmas 1975) and his preferred successor was Callaghan.

But though, now, they were more than colleagues, more than allies if still less than friends, the memories of past antagonisms had never died and had even acquired a certain nostalgia. They still probed each other's guard, circling each other in conversation, feinting like ageless boxers destined forever not to land a blow, but making it clear that if they did … A Wilson barb would be gracefully deflected or, more subtly, deferentially accepted by Callaghan. A retaliatory Callaghan jab would be cheerfully ignored or misinterpreted by Wilson, thus indicating that so far as he was concerned it had never happened. Callaghan would acknowledge Wilson's command of all the political skills, but exaggerate his sincerity in expressing it; Wilson would praise Callaghan's ability—which is formidable —to get to the heart of a matter with a few simple, direct phrases, and regret that he did not possess an equal knowledge of the ways of the world, but the envy was always slightly mocking. It was a courtly game they both enjoyed, but it rested on a hard bed of commonsense. The bond which had developed between the two men held Government and party together during Wilson's last administration. But whenever they met, the tension that exists between top class competitors was always there.

The Foreign and Commonwealth Secretary and the small

team which had been with him in Eastern Europe arrived at
the British ambassador's residence in Helsinki some time after
the Prime Minister and his staff and a much larger F.C.O.
team had wined and dined. After a brief discussion between the
two men, Jim Callaghan crossed to an empty corner of the large
lounge and began to work his way through a red dispatch box.
I was talking to my deputy, Mrs Janet Hewlett-Davies, when
the Prime Minister, who was easily bored with diplomatic
small talk, joined us and suggested that we should descend upon
the Foreign and Commonwealth Secretary and 'pull his leg'
about 'peaceful co-existence'. We walked over and sat on either
side of Jim Callaghan. Unfortunately, when the magnet moves,
so do the iron filings. *Every* official in the room, including the
ambassador, joined us, too. What began as a half-tease by the
Prime Minister was taken seriously by the Foreign and Commonwealth Secretary. Harold Wilson began to take it seriously,
too, because at heart he was not in a mood to joke about it. Jim
Callaghan clearly did not know what the Prime Minister was
talking about, but he said sharply that he was not going to
discuss it 'in front of a mass meeting' and, calling to his senior
private secretary – who had travelled with us from London – he
left the room.

When he returned about twenty minutes later, we were
waiting to depart for the hotel. Jim Callaghan said abruptly
that he would like to travel in the Prime Minister's car. I felt
apprehensive. An F.C.O. official, quick to interpret his master's
mood, picked up a copy of the Prime Minister's speech and
began to alter it, there and then, to remove the offending words,
'peaceful co-existence'. I had that stopped.

Harold Wilson and Jim Callaghan left for the hotel, followed
by a troubled posse of officials who were fearing an almighty
row between the two men. I went straight to the Prime
Minister's suite. He was sitting alone. 'Jim looked upset', I said.
'Is it serious?' 'Yes', said the Prime Minister. 'He has just sacked
his private secretary.'

It appeared that the Foreign and Commonwealth Secretary
had known nothing of the letter, invoking his authority, the
previous day. He had no objection to the phrase 'peaceful co-
existence'. Like the Prime Minister, he thought the dispute
pointless and bureaucratic. What he did object to, however –

what *was* serious – was that his officials had used his name to try to change a decision by the Prime Minister. However unimportant that decision, it had been taken. What had given an essentially trivial matter substance was that officialdom had deliberately set out to deceive the Prime Minister in pursuit of departmental policy. In the end, the real sufferer was a young man, the private secretary, who had not been involved in the manoeuvre, not attended any of the meetings, not heard the Prime Ministerial arguments, but who had been responsible for signing the letter at the request of a more senior colleague. He took his dismissal – which, in effect, was a transfer to another part of the department – very well. The man I thought was the real culprit escaped unscathed. To this day, I do not know if Mr Callaghan was aware of the part he played, but I suppose he was.

If a civil servant blunders, he is still protected today by the doctrine of ministerial responsibility, which is as it should be. In any elective system, ultimate responsibility must reside in the Minister, because he is the person elected to decide. Civil servants are appointed to advise. The distinction is vital. If it is blurred, either by an official taking a decision which he is not authorised to take or by his so ordering a situation that his Minister is left without a real choice in the decision he has to make, then the entitlement to that protection – from ministerial or parliamentary wrath, or from public scrutiny – is removed.

My career as Harold Wilson's Press Secretary fell into three phases: in government in 1969–70; in Opposition from 1970 to 1974; and in government again from 1974 to 1976 and in this chapter I have chosen an instance from each phase where, in my opinion, F.C.O. civil servants went beyond what was permissible and the distinction between decision and advice was blurred. The first – the 'Soames affair' – concerned a matter of absolutely fundamental importance to the Government's foreign and domestic policies, the consequences of which might well have been much graver than they were. The second was gratuitously offensive to the Leader of the Opposition, who has a recognised, statutory role in our constitution and who is not to be sacrificed to departmental prestige. The third related to a relatively rarefied disagreement over words which, because they were against the received wisdom of the Foreign and Commonwealth Office, led to officials behaving recklessly in an attempt to preserve their theology, come what may. In one respect, however, this last incident had a beneficial consequence, because it demonstrated that, if pushed too far, elected Ministers are prepared to act decisively and surprisingly against a civil servant, even if it is the wrong civil servant.

Of course, three swallows do not make a summer. Defenders of the F.C.O. can point out that temporary civil servants with a political background – which described me – are notoriously obsessional about the power of the civil service and hyper-suspicious of its influence. Certainly many permanent civil servants have told me that is the case. For my part, I was alarmed by the complacency of senior civil servants when things went wrong, a complacency born of the fact that while governments may come and governments may go, the civil service will go on for ever, whatever the nature of the regime. I saw them as insulated from the outside world, the political world as well as the world of the working man, by the stockade of neutrality and impartiality which they have erected around themselves. Their resolution not to be involved politically – though the fact that their top tier, in the main, went to public schools where Conservatism is endemic, live in Conservative constituencies which are part of or adjacent to the stockbroking belt, and think conservatively, which makes them Conservative-inclined voters – has led them to be politically ignorant, which is neither the same thing nor a good thing. For the special reason that diplomats might spend two-thirds of their adult life working abroad – and when working in London are concerned only with overseas affairs – they are, despite their skills, likely to be more ignorant than most.

One example of this came in December 1975 when the F.C.O. drafted, for the Prime Minister's signature, a letter of congratulation to Mr Malcolm Fraser, leader of the Liberal (i.e. Conservative) party in Australia on his becoming Prime Minister; a potty suggestion which came within hours of the elected (Labour) Prime Minister, Gough Whitlam, being dismissed from office by the unelected Governor-General, Sir John Kerr, using powers everyone thought had fallen into disuse.

The 'Soames affair', the leaking of the Prague telegram and numerous other incidents convinced Harold Wilson when in

Opposition that changes in the structure of the F.C.O. News Department ought to be made if he returned to office. I proposed, and he agreed, that we should place a professional information officer, not a professional diplomat, at the head of the Department; not least for the benefit of the press themselves. Some months before the General Election of February 1974, Harold Wilson suggested the solution to Jim Callaghan and my nomination for the man to carry it out – Tom McCaffrey, a Scot who was then Director of Information at the Home Office – where he had worked with Jim Callaghan between 1967 and 1970 – and a former deputy press secretary at No. 10. At one point in the Douglas-Home–Wilson correspondence over the 'Shakespeare' telegram, Sir Alec had regretted that a slip had been made by a junior official (while still defending it). Under McCaffrey, who was politically sensitive, it seemed unlikely that such a mistake, deliberate or inadvertent, would occur again. It was the attitude which prevailed in the Department that counted.

Jim Callaghan was enthusiastic about appointing McCaffrey, and did so as soon as he became Secretary of State. By then I think, he had convinced himself it was his idea in the first place. With McCaffrey there, and with Tom McNally, head of the Labour Party's International Department, joining Callaghan as his special adviser, a new dimension was added to the advice given to the Secretary of State. But the service triumphed in the end. When Jim Callaghan became Prime Minister on April 5, 1976, he naturally took McCaffrey with him to Downing Street. The F.C.O. machine had already insisted that a diplomat should be appointed to replace him, and the monopoly was restored. McNally, too, went to Downing Street and the new Secretary of State, Tony Crosland, was accompanied to the F.C.O. by his special adviser at the Department of Environment, a young man whose principal expertise was in the field of housing and local government. Even though he later recruited a special adviser on Southern Africa, the clock had been put right back.

5

House and Home

Houses are built to live in, not to look on; therefore
let use be preferred before uniformity, except where
both may be had.

FRANCIS BACON

Since the 1950s, the housing policy of the Labour Party – its
councillors, its conferences and its Cabinets – has been based on
the need to build as many houses as possible. Numbers have
mattered ever since Harold Macmillan, the first post-war Conservative Minister of Housing, raised the total of annual com-
pletions to over 300,000 by lowering the standards.

Today, to build as many new houses as possible is no longer
an adequate policy and it is doubtful even if it is an effective
palliative. We have spent thousands of millions of pounds on
subsidising mortgages and erecting new council homes – spent
to the point where we have imperilled other social objectives –
yet the waiting lists for housing and rehousing get no shorter
and costs for the council tenant, which mean rents, become
more and more expensive. Not only does he have to put up
with his home becoming dearer each year, but he also has to
tolerate the abuse of ill-informed but better-off owner-occupiers
who think that they alone pay domestic rates and taxes.

It is about time that a measure of justice was brought to the
council tenant; I think it can be done, while helping also the
homeless, the owner-occupier, local authorities and central
Government. In fact, virtually everyone.

My sisters and I were raised in a gaslit terraced house in a slum
street so narrow that when an ambulance came to take my
grandfather away to hospital it could not get through the alley

entrance. He walked instead, and died on my ninth birthday in 1937.

No one who has ever lived among the scratching of mice and smelled the smell of bugs in the wallpaper – and at one time in Britain the slumdwellers were almost as numerous as the bugs – ought to feel less than passionate about decent housing. My family felt nothing but gratitude for Bermondsey Council which took us out of our home and moved us into a flat-cum-palace with electricity, a bath, hot water and an inside lavatory. But that was 1938. The commonplace slums of that era are rare today, except in pockets which still disfigure cities like Glasgow, and the passions of that time can no longer condition our policies.

So overwhelmingly important has it been to build new homes – and only local councils could have carried out the task – that a house too readily became a unit of accommodation on the credit side of the annual housing statistics. When it was built, local councillors, Conservative or Labour, Ratepayer or Independent, hemmed in the tenant with Bumble's restrictions, lengthily set out in the smallest possible type on the back of the rent book. No dogs. No noise. No arrears. No washing outside except on Monday. No painting the front door a different colour from the neighbours. Tenants could not be expected to possess the instincts of tidiness and good manners which came naturally to all owner-occupiers, but they could be instructed how to behave. Though they had been given a roof over their head, there was no security of tenure to go with it, and therefore the rules could be enforced. Fortunately, those attitudes have now largely disappeared, though many of the restrictions they engendered still remain.

Such were the needs of the homeless in past days, so wicked were the conditions in which people had to exist, that another restriction grew up in the minds of Labour councillors who cared about the homeless, which was most of them: no council house could ever be disposed of to the tenant or anyone else because to do so would reduce the total housing stock available for reletting. That was, and is, a substantial argument. It is irrelevant to ask whether it has the force today that it had many years ago because it is held with undimmed passion. I cannot see that in the near future Labour councillors, who administer the majority of Britain's six million council homes, will agree to a policy of freely selling council houses.

But a sizable proportion of the total number of council houses are in districts controlled by Conservative majorities and they contain thousands of tenants who are anxious to buy the homes they live in, not so much because it is a bargain—in strictly commercial terms council houses are less of a bargain than privately built ones—but because they want a home of their own. Many, many more thousands of tenants have the ambition to own their own home but regard it as forlorn because of the terrible inflation of house prices and values which more than doubled the cost of a house during the years 1971 to 1974.

The Conservative Party's concern for the council tenant contains a large measure of hypocrisy, but their policy, crude though it has been, has touched a chord. It helped, to say the least, to swell the number of seats which the party won in the district council elections of May 1976. What is more, since they lost office in February 1974 there have been signs that Conservative policy has been developing faster than the Labour Party's.

In September 1975, for example, Peter Walker, who was Secretary of State for the Environment in the Edward Heath Government and as such had responsibility for housing policy, advocated that council tenants of more than twenty years' standing should have the ownership of their houses transferred to them, free of charge.

I doubt whether that policy would work without leaving local authorities with an enormous burden of debt: most council houses have been built on loans spread over sixty years. But Walker is a man ahead of his time in the Conservative Party. He was demonstrating that the time had come, or is coming, when a radical new policy for housing must be adopted.

I was sufficiently impressed by the speech and the warning for Labour that I thought it contained to raise it during a discussion on housing with the Prime Minister. I told him (this was a day or two after Walker put forward his proposals) that I was worried that before the next General Election was due we would be outflanked on council housing policy by the Conservative Party; and if that happened our very substantial

4 February, 1974, General Election: Bernard Donoughue, Marcia
Williams and Harold Wilson walking to Transport House.

5 Harold Wilson with Dick (now Lord) Briginshaw and Albert (now Lord) Murray (right).

6 Sir John Hunt, who has made the Secretary to the Cabinet the most powerful man in Whitehall.

block vote among council tenants might be significantly eaten into.

With both justification and irritation, the Prime Minister replied that it was no use telling him that I was worried unless I had some proposals to do something about it; so what was I proposing? At that point, nothing. But that evening I tried to find a half-way house between the impracticability of the Walker proposals and the immovability of the Labour Party on the question of the reduction in the housing stock.

The next day, I submitted a brief outline of a scheme to the Prime Minister, who minuted that it could be 'historic'. He asked that it should be sent to the Treasury and to the Department of the Environment for their comments, which he wanted by the first week of November. He wanted to make a major move forward before he announced his resignation some time in the following March.

It was to be nearly six months after I first submitted the outline to the Prime Minister that Ministers collectively discussed it. In the meantime, the usual depressing, enervating, debilitating Whitehall stalling game was played. When eventually Ministerial discussion could not be held off any more because the Prime Minister *demanded* that it should be discussed, the proposals, much improved since I first told the Prime Minister of them, were deliberately changed – sabotaged – at the last moment.

The case I had put to the Prime Minister was this: there was an imperative political need for the Government to develop a distinctive new housing policy which would give a substantial measure of justice to the council tenants without enraging those who were not.

I started from the premise, which is not usually recognised, that the inflation of housing costs in recent years had hit the council tenant hardest of all. (To give a personal illustration: when I bought a new house in 1960, I committed myself to mortgage repayments amounting to some 15 per cent of my gross income at that time. In 1975, I was still making the same *cash* repayment, but by then it had fallen to less than 2 per cent of my gross income. Not only that: the appreciation of new domestic property over these years had been such that the value of my house on the open market and in cash terms had

H

risen, *each month*, by *five times* the monthly amount I was repaying to my Building Society. For the council tenant, on the other hand, inflation meant large rent increases to pay for higher loan interest charges, the costs of administration and the cost of maintenance; the latter, being principally labour costs, does not fall upon the mass of owner-occupiers, who do it themselves.)

I said that it would be an act of simple justice to say, as Peter Walker had said, to council tenants of long standing that they could have their home as a gift, but the debt problem made that impossible.

The official Conservative alternative was to sell council houses at a substantial discount, usually calculated on the number of years the purchaser had been a tenant. So far as the Government were concerned, it would not be possible to adopt such a scheme in face of the almost universal opposition of Labour councillors who would have to operate it. In any case, the tenant-purchaser would still be hit severely by inflation. A council house with a market value of, say, £5,000 in 1971 (discounted by 30 per cent, £3,500) might be valued at £10,000 (discounted to £7,000) in 1975. That would put it out of the reach of many tenants; those who obtained the maximum discount because they were long-time tenants were probably middle-aged and might find a substantial mortgage more difficult, too.

The first outline of my proposal read:

What I propose, briefly, is this:

That an entirely new scheme, which I've called 'Life-lease' for convenience, should be introduced.

It would work as follows:

A tenant would be offered the opportunity to buy his house at its *original cost*, minus the amount already paid off on the loan. In other words, he would take over the debt.

The conditions of purchase would be:

1 (Initially) That he had been a tenant of a local authority for at least 10 years.

2 That, like any owner-occupier, he would assume full responsibility for maintenance.

3 That on death (of himself, wife, or dependent relative, whichever is the last), *the house would revert to the local authority*.

This last condition is crucial: it would overcome the fundamental criticism of many Labour groups that to sell a council house is to reduce the number of homes in the council stock, and thus reduce the number available for reletting.

The advantages for the tenant would be:

1 That he would get all the advantages of owning his own home, except the right of disposal or bequest, at only a fraction, perhaps 20 per cent, of the current market cost.

2 It would insulate him from further rent increases.

3 When the loan has been repaid he will live rent-free, thus enjoying the benefit which owner-occupiers have in middle- and old-age.

The advantages for local government would be:

1 Reduction in subsidies.

2 Reduction in loan charges.

3 Reduction in maintenance and administration charges.

The advantages for central Government would be:

1 Reduction in subsidies.

2 Repayment of capital.

3 Eventually (though this may be minor) reduction in rent allowances and rebates paid to the elderly.

That basically was the scheme as an embryo policy, with a number of snags to be ironed out and assumptions questioned. It required a lot of work and the Prime Minister asked that I should send it immediately to Dr Bernard Donoughue for his Policy Unit to assess and comment upon. But Harold Wilson was enthusiastic. In my note to Bernard Donoughue, I added:

We have nearly six million council houses in Great Britain. A great many were built before the war for a few hundred pounds and I would therefore envisage a minimum price to be charged – say, £1,000.

If we managed to dispose of a million of the oldest houses, that would still reduce the loan debt by a thousand million pounds, or provide a sum approaching that order for the building of new houses for those in need.

It would, of course, be crucial to this scheme that the

finance should come from the private sector, principally the building societies, but I see no insuperable difficulty there.

I recognise the problems to be overcome – the particular difficulty of selling flats, for example, though that is a difficulty in the private sector today – but they can be worked out.

The advantages I see in this scheme, if it proved feasible, are so enormous for everyone concerned, however, that I hope a serious study can be made of it.

The Policy Unit began a 'serious study' there and then. In addition, I showed the idea to a number of other senior staff in Downing Street, all of whom shared the Prime Minister's enthusiasm. One of them, Robin Butler, the second senior private secretary on domestic affairs at No. 10 and an economist seconded from the Treasury, put his finger immediately on the problem that was worrying me: although the scheme might be tempting to single persons or childless couples it would have no appeal to parents who wanted, as most parents did, 'to leave something for the children when we have gone'. For those parents, the right to bequeath the house – or its value; children usually choose a house of their own – was an essential part of the desire for ownership. Butler took the scheme away to find a variation to it that would meet the need.

A day or two later he sent me a minute containing his solution, designed to complement my original proposal rather than supersede it. The scheme retained the 'life-lease' principle (at a later stage, the Prime Minister changed this description to 'life enfranchisement' because it sounded more encouraging) but gave the home a monetary value. (The right of children, as dependants, to continue to live in the house after the death of their parents was, of course, already in the original proposals.)

Butler said that he feared that my plan would have a 'locking-in' effect since an occupier, having purchased his life-lease, would have a strong disincentive to move house. (That is theoretically true, but the fact is that it is so difficult today for a council tenant to arrange an exchange with another tenant in a different part of the country should he want to move for employment reasons, that he is 'locked-in' anyway.)

He proposed therefore that a tenant should have the right to opt to acquire his house with the cost calculated on a different formula, one that would allow him to sell it back to the local authority and to receive part of the enhanced value that might have accrued during his ownership.

This new principle was a purely artificial and arbitrary one: that the cost of the 'life-lease' would be calculated on the 'capitalised value' of the current rent, less a factor for maintenance charges.

For example: if a tenant is paying a rent of £8 a week (excluding rates) and the maintenance element of that rent was estimated to be £2 a week, then the net value of the rent (excluding administration and debt servicing charges) to the local authority would be £6 a week. Assuming an interest rate of 10 per cent, the capital sum which a local authority would have to invest to receive an income of that order would be £3,000. That, therefore, would be the sum for which the local authority would sell the property's lease, always provided that the price was not below the sum outstanding on the debt.

If the owner of the lease or his heirs wished to dispose of the property they would have to offer it to the local authority, as in the original scheme. The rent which the property might bring would then be independently assessed. If house values, and consequently rent values, had risen between purchase and disposal which is almost inevitable, then the local authority would buy back the house at a higher price than they had originally sold it for. The lease owner's profit might be modest, but he would gain some of the cash benefits of the inflation in house values. The local authority would then be free to sell the 'life-lease' on similar terms to another of their tenants at no cost to itself. The new lease-owner would be purchasing the property at substantially less cost than its market value.

The figures above are only an illustration, but the principle is clear. The Butler variation had the merit of giving the life-leaseholder an asset which appreciated with inflation (though at a lesser rate, because he had bought at the lesser price) while retaining—which was vital—the ultimate possession of the property in the hands of the local authority. Butler, of course, was not concerned with the political issues involved,

only to try to improve a scheme in which the Prime Minister
was showing an active interest.

Nevertheless, we were hoping that we at least had demonstrated that it was possible to take a leap forward in housing
policy from which everyone—tenant, taxpayer, ratepayer, local
authority and Government—might benefit financially. If the
scheme was sound, the advantages would be considerable, not
only in human terms but politically.

As soon as a tenant entered into a contract with his local
authority he would be freezing his principal housing cost—the
weekly or monthly outgoing—in the same way as any other
mortgage owner.

Because we envisaged that the bulk of the money for purchase would come from private sources, principally building
societies, it would mean that local authorities would receive
capital sums for the houses they 'sold' which could be used to
repay outstanding debt; what is more, much of the money
outstanding on housing loans was borrowed at low rates of
interest and the capital receipts could be used to pay off debt
incurred at high rates of interest. Significant sales would hold
out the prospect of a reduction of the 'loan pool' rate, the
system which local authorities operate to average out interest
charges.

Further, every house disposed of would cease to qualify for
Government subsidy, though the interest charged on the new
mortgage would carry income tax relief. Every house sold
would also contribute towards reducing the Public Sector
Borrowing Requirement, which had become the Chancellor's,
the Treasury's, the Government's, and the Opposition's current
obsession.

For the former tenant, not only would the stabilisation of his
housing costs mean in real terms a continuing reduction in
them, but he would acquire the complete freedom to do whatever he liked with his home (except pull it down or do other
substantial damage—but a building society will not allow any
of its clients to do that, either). He could adapt it, extend it,
paint the door in stripes if he really wanted to or he could
remove the door altogether if his insurance company did not
object. If like most owner-occupiers he wanted to improve its
comfort and value he would gain the benefits in cash of those

improvements when he eventually disposed of the house. Under our schemes, improvements would be independently valued, too, and the *whole* of the value of those would be added to the price paid by the local authority on repurchase.

The interest burden, the cost of housing administration and maintenance charges added together far exceed for most local authorities the rent income from the tenants. Hence the need for housing subsidies which in 1976 were running at an annual rate of £1,400 million. With councils having to borrow at interest rates in the region of 14 per cent it could hardly be otherwise. Even a modest-cost house (say, £10,000) would need a weekly rent (in this case £28), far beyond most tenants' capacities, even to meet the interest charge. Add to that capital repayment and administration and maintenance and we are faced with a housing situation which is rapidly approaching crisis.

Government subsidies to local authorities are being swallowed up by the need to meet the interest charges on Government loans to local authorities, which to a non-economist like me seems the economics of a madhouse.

In an attempt to impart a special urgency to the schemes, they were submitted also to the Chancellor of the Duchy of Lancaster, Harold Lever, as well as Denis Healey, the Chancellor of the Exchequer, and Tony Crosland, who was then the Secretary of State for the Environment.

Lever, as a politician, was all in favour of helping council tenants to own their own homes; unfortunately his financial training and experience urged him towards straight sales at market prices – the Conservative scheme which we regarded as politically impossible. The Chancellor gave a guarded welcome, but his officials were uneasy about the implications for the Public Sector Borrowing Requirement, which were not as simple as I imagined them to be, though at a later stage they were to modify their reservations. The most important Minister, Tony Crosland, declined to react on the grounds that his Department were carrying out a major review of housing finance policy and he did not want to commit himself to a view in advance of that review being completed. It was a perfectly proper view to take, but it meant putting the scheme on the shelf at least until 1978, by which time it might be too late to introduce it.

The No. 10 Policy Unit was concerned that we should act quickly not only because of the Prime Minister's impending departure, which only Bernard Donoughue of the Unit knew about, but also because they estimated that by the beginning of 1977 the building societies and other sources of private finance might no longer be flush with funds for lending as the pace of the economy picked up.

On the human rather than the financial level, however, it would still have been the case that under our schemes many more families would be helped to buy their own home for the kind of sum advanced to a single purchaser in the private house market; five families at £3,000, for example, instead of one at £15,000.

Bernard Donoughue arranged a series of meetings with officials at the Department of the Environment to see if our schemes could be got moving.

One early argument advanced was more political than financial and it was one we had foreseen: the argument of equity; first, that it would give a life-lease owner an unfair advantage over the ordinary owner-occupier and, second, it would give him a similar advantage over the council tenant who had bought his house on the terms currently available under schemes operated by Conservative local authorities.

On the first point, while it was true that the tenant would be acquiring his home at a price far below its market value (but at or above its outstanding debt value) it was also true that that would be the basis on which he would have to resell it or return it. The advantage to the generality of owner-occupiers was that if the schemes were taken up in a big way there would be a reduction in their rate and tax burdens.

For the council tenant who had bought his house under a Conservative scheme, a real sense of grievance could clearly arise. But it would not be impossible to work out proposals under which he could, if he wished, switch into one of the new schemes. That might result in his receiving a lump sum repayment and would have the added advantage to the local authority of restoring a house lost to the housing stock. In any case, he was still free to dispose of his house at its full market value, though he had bought it for less, when any restrictive covenant had expired.

The savings in administration and maintenance appeared promising, too. They absorb two-thirds of the rent income of many local authorities. We discovered that in the Housing Department of one London borough it was calculated that the total cost of replacing a washer on a tap in one of their council houses was about £25, after all the administrative, labour, and transport charges had been taken into account. Coincidentally, I had just performed a similar task in my own home. Using my own labour, my own spanner and walking to a nearby iron-monger's to buy a washer, my total expenses amounted to three pence.

The opposition which we had expected to meet from Depart-ment of the Environment officials never materialised. From the beginning they were only too anxious to help. Such opposition as there was was coming from the politicians, the Secretary of State and his special advisers within the Department. They were terrified of any scheme to 'sell' council houses being denounced by Labour councillors in revolt. They feared, too, a similar revolt from the National Executive Committee of the Labour Party. We countered by arguing that we had met the main argument against the selling of council houses, which was that such policies reduced the housing stock.

I hope that *is* the main argument. Cabinet Ministers do not live in council houses, they own their own; so do most, if not all, members of the N.E.C.; so do most, if not all, Labour Members of Parliament—indeed, one member of the Tribune Group was buying the house he formerly rented from the council; most, if not all, special advisers to Ministers own their own houses and so do Bernard Donoughue and I. There is no reason at all— moral, legal, ethical or humanitarian—why we should not.

Perhaps one needs to have been reared in a slum house to recognise that the issue of ownership is irrelevant now that the day of the private landlord able to charge any rent he likes is over; and has been over since the first Rent Restriction Acts. Today, the biggest landlords in Britain are the local authorities and the New Town corporations and no egalitarian or socialist principle is served or furthered by insisting that ownership by a local corporation is better, for society or for the soul, than ownership by the person who occupies the house. If I am wrong, then we should start abolishing private ownership altogether, and I do not see that being put forward in any Labour manifesto.

Freedom is sensibly restrained when it impinges on the freedom of another. But if a man wants to own his house and to do what he likes with it, then let him do it. The cause of the homeless would not be retarded. Indeed, given the fact that privately-owned houses are better maintained than publicly-owned ones, especially in times of labour shortage, the number of houses falling into decay is likely to be fewer as home ownership spreads. If one man owns a number of houses then the homeless *are* threatened. The number of council tenants likely to be in that position is small and I do not think it would be difficult to prevent a former council tenant who already possesses a council house from adding to his stock.

The objections continued to come from the special advisers, however, some more absurd than others. Was it envisaged, it was solemnly asked, that the scheme put forward by No. 10 would be compulsory? In our wildest flights of enthusiasm the idea of compelling people to buy their own houses had never occurred to us. If our schemes provided money for the building of more council houses, it was said, that would be a strong point with Labour councils – but what if the councils then fell under Tory control? But what if they did? we replied. The schemes would continue to operate. In any case, councils were more likely to fall under Conservative control if we did not do anything about freeing council housing than if we did.

The idea of an owner-occupiers' 'backlash' against 'further featherbedding' of council tenants was raised again. If we had to move in the direction of selling council houses it should be on the basis of the 'half and half' scheme pioneered by Birmingham Corporation (that was acceptable to the Department presumably because it had been put forward by Labour Councillors). Once again, this argument overlooked the fact that we were not advocating the sale of the freehold, whereas the Birmingham scheme did. Under it, a tenant would buy half his house to begin with. He would pay a sum equivalent to half the value of the house and take out a mortage for it; the other half of the house would be rented, a sum that would increase as rents went up. We believed that the Birmingham scheme was right for houses most recently built where the cost was high. But five million of the six million houses owned by local authorities had been built before the explosion in house and land values.

Overwhelmingly, and patronisingly, the 'political' advice was for caution. We were being told how to suck eggs. Our schemes were described as 'full frontal attacks' by the Government on the issue of selling council houses in which, anyway, there were few votes to be won. If we went ahead there would be 'the most appalling demoralisation' among Labour party activists as we approached the local council elections of May, 1976. If we did decide to proceed, then we ought to conceal the fact from the electors before the votes were cast.

We found all this advice astonishing. Bernard Donoughue was one of the best-known lecturers on politics in the country. His connections with, and knowledge of, the Labour Party and its workers and members were widespread and of long standing. I had been a Labour Party 'activist' for a great many years. I had been a Labour councillor and member of my local authority's Housing Committee for nine years. At the very least we were able to calculate the likely effects of our proposals rather better than people with little practical experience in the field.

A further objection put forward was that council tenants would not understand our proposals. This concept of the council tenant as a species of sub-literate I found the most offensive and superficial of all.

But we persevered on the official side. Several meetings were held with officials from the Department. They assured us that there were no insuperable legal or technical problems which would prevent the schemes from operating if Ministers decided in favour of them, though of course there were problems which would be difficult. If the officials would have preferred a scheme along the Conservative lines they gave little sign of it; from the beginning they recognised its political impossibility.

Indeed, throughout our discussions they displayed a wider understanding of what was possible than the political side of the Department, which is not at all usual in my experience. In particular, they clearly understood that there was a distinction between party activists – who are a handful only in any constituency party – and the council tenants, who probably represent

10 million votes or more; votes which will not automatically continue to be cast unless the ever-increasing rents are
arrested.

Though progress appeared to be made, it was slow. By the
New Year it was apparent that we would not be able to achieve
anything before Harold Wilson went out of office; it was also
apparent that the reason was the prevarication of the Department flowing from the refusal at the top even to examine the
schemes with an open mind. The old objections were renewed
again by the political advisers: we were back again to the resentment which owner-occupiers would feel about council tenants
buying on favourable terms (but if the terms were favourable
why was it thought there were no votes in the proposals?); the
'selling' of council houses was gravely equated with the famous
Clause 4 of the Labour Party's constitution which aims at
securing 'for the workers by hand or by brain the full fruits of
their industry' upon the basis of 'the common ownership of the
means of production, distribution and exchange'.

We were entering the realm of the farcical, where the question of whether or not we gave greater freedom to the council
tenant was being incorporated into the theology of the movement. To compare our schemes with a breach of Clause 4 was
to liken a chihuahua to an elephant because they both have
four legs and a small tail.

One concession was made. It was accepted, at last, that the
No. 10 schemes had overcome 'one' objection to the selling of
council houses (we maintained it was *the* objection), and that
the housing stock would not be reduced by them. But still more
objections emerged. For example, we were told that it was
'never' right to sell off public assets at less than market cost.
'Never' is a word never to be used in politics. Public assets have
frequently been sold off cheaply where a social purpose was to
be met. The historic cost would certainly be covered, in any
event. What the Minister's advisers were now arguing was
that the advantage of the inflation in house prices since 1971
should accrue wholly to the local authorities. This was a fundamental difference between us, because our scheme was
designed to allow most tenants to escape from the penalty of
inflation.

As the time for any effective action began to run out, Bernard

Donoughue and I spoke to the Prime Minister again. He was still anxious, he said, to make progress. He convened a meeting of Ministers for March 24 which would consider our two main proposals plus two others included in a Policy Unit portfolio. But by March 24, the Prime Minister's intention to resign had already been announced. The Parliamentary Labour Party was proceeding, at stately pace, to choose his successor. There was little thought being given to anything else. Those around Tony Crosland, one of the candidates for the leadership, who favoured stalling had only to hang on for a little while longer and the Prime Ministerial pressure for a decision would be removed. Neither of the only candidates who stood a chance of becoming Prime Minister, Jim Callaghan and Michael Foot, knew anything about the schemes for these had never been circulated to their departments or come before any committees of which they were members.

The day before the Ministerial meeting took place, the Child Poverty Action Group published a pamphlet surprisingly strong in its support for council house sales. So did the Building Societies Association, which was encouraging in view of the warnings we had had from the Treasury that the societies would not provide finance for our schemes because their loans would lack security. Security could not, in fact, be stronger. If a tenant failed to meet his payments, the local authority would assume the obligation, repossess the house and decide whether or not to return to a tenancy or redispose of it.

But the death blow to our schemes came from an unexpected source: the civil service, who until then had been so helpful.

We had thought that our schemes, especially the first one, were simple, easily understood by Cabinet Minister and council tenant alike. But when the papers for the Ministerial meeting were circulated to Ministers, most of whom knew nothing about the particular item until then, the basis of what we called Scheme A—the Butler variation was called Scheme B—had been changed.

These schemes were 'novel', Ministers were warned. 'Novel' is the sort of word civil servants will use about proposals coming from Mr Tony Benn. It is what 'sin' means to a bishop. Care would have to be taken, they went on, to ensure that they did not contain surprising or unacceptable difficulties, ignoring the fact that we had spent a good many hours during the winter anticipating and ironing out unacceptable difficulties. Then all the sad old arguments were put forward: if a tenant was made responsible for maintenance then the condition of the property might deteriorate—a piece of monumental impertinence by civil servants who can afford to pay a builder and decorator to keep their own homes in repair. I would prefer working-class pride to civil service arrogance any day.

Ministers having been softened up, the civil service version of my scheme was laid before them; the basis for disposal of council houses which I had proposed—and which had never been challenged—was:

A tenant would be offered the opportunity to buy his house at its *original cost*, minus the amount already paid off on the loan. In other words, he would take over the debt.

This simple formula had been changed, without any consultation with me, without any consultation with the Policy Unit, without any consultation with anyone at No. 10, to read:

To pay to the local authority a premium based on the net rent (excluding maintenance and management) making assumptions about future rent increases and taking account of the life expectancy of the tenant and his named dependants and subject to a minimum charge.

I was not invited to the meeting. Ministers were never told that a fundamental change had been made in a scheme which had been under discussion for nearly six months; they were only told that the basis on which the scheme was put before them produced a 'much' higher figure for purchase than the original figure proposed by the No. 10 Policy Unit.

There was, I understand, a brief—very brief—discussion. The Prime Minister either did not recognise the scheme or was not prepared to fight for it. Indeed, after only a few minutes he suggested they move on to next business, abandoning a scheme which six months earlier he had said could be 'historic'.

I still think it might have been if the bugs had been taken out; not the bugs in the wallpaper, but the bugs in the minds of those more determined to frustrate the 'outsider' than satisfy a housing problem. With clinical efficiency it was killed off. If Labour loses council housing votes in future, they will know whom to blame.

6

John Bull's Other Island

Loyalty is a sentiment, not a law. It rests on love, not
on restraint. The government of Ireland by England
rests on restraint and not on law; and since it demands
no love it can evoke no loyalty.

SIR ROGER CASEMENT, speech from the dock, 1916

From the moment in August 1969 that British troops entered
Londonderry and Belfast in order to protect the Catholics from
Protestant bully-boys, British Governments, Westminster Par-
liaments, have lacked a policy for Northern Ireland. Since the
Ulster Workers' Council strike of May 1974, they have lacked
the power to enforce a policy, even if they acquired one.

Pacification, which by 1976 was all that was left to hope for
in Northern Ireland, is not policy enough. Even if it succeeded,
both sides of the divided province would be storing up ammuni-
tion and grievances until the violence could break out again.

The biggest – and therefore the falsest – hope of progress was
born of the Sunningdale Conference of early December 1973.
The month before, the leaders of the Northern Ireland political
parties had agreed on a power-sharing Executive, a Government of most of the talents available in Northern Ireland. At
Sunningdale, the Executive met with the British and Irish
Republic Governments and established the so-called 'Irish
dimension', the strictly advisory Council of Ireland, a joint body
of seven Ministers from the Republic and seven from the
Northern Ireland Executive. That agreement was the death
warrant of the Executive, because the Ulster workers and their
leaders were not prepared to have anything to do with any
creeping progress towards a united Ireland, which is how they
saw the All-Ireland Council.

So Sunningdale went the way of every other proposal ever

put forward by a British Government. As Harold Wilson frequently quoted from *1066 and All That*, 'Gladstone spent his declining years trying to guess the answer to the Irish question; unfortunately, whenever he was getting warm the Irish secretly changed the question.'

Indeed, Sunningdale, like every other proposal since the Civil Rights marches began in 1968 – direct rule, an Assembly, detention without trial and the end of detention without trial – was no more than another short-term expedient and the most disastrous one at that. The one lasting effect of Sunningdale and its final all-night session was that by exhausting the then Prime Minister, Edward Heath, both physically and mentally, it left him in no shape to turn and do battle with the miners over their pay rise, the struggle which led to his defeat the following February.

Edward Heath was not the first British statesman to be sacrificed to the bogs and fogs of Irish politics, but we ought to make sure he is the last.

The course followed by the Labour Government from the summer of 1969 onwards until their defeat in June 1970 was, primarily, to eliminate the violence and to establish the civil rights of the Catholics. These aims were understandable, but incompatible, for it was the burgeoning civil rights movement which provoked the Protestant violence.

Since February 1971, when the first British soldier was killed in the Province, violence, terror, murder, and sadistic maiming have filled graveyards and hospitals and emptied the minds of politicians on both sides of the St George's Channel.

In the process of righting the wrongs which fifty years of Protestant domination had institutionalised in Ulster, the Labour Government began to build up the grievances of the Protestants. Those grievances were in turn promoted and exploited by disreputable men who claimed to speak at Westminster and Stormont Castle for the majority population.

The reform programme initiated by Labour was carried on by Mr Heath's Government. It led, as was inevitable, to the eventual abolition of Stormont – which had become a monument to bigotry and one-party rule – and direct rule from Westminster. That inflamed the Protestant grievances even more.

The Heath Government tried almost every measure in the

I

civil service handbook of civilised administration. It tried to negotiate justice and commonsense and it tried to impose it. The Irish Republican Army, Officials and Provisionals, which had been thrown into confusion by the welcome which Catholic citizens had first given to the British troops in 1969, rejoiced in the renewal of Britain's traditional unpopularity. By gun and bomb they made impossible consideration of the one policy which, I believe, stands a chance of lasting success: the withdrawal of the Westminster Government from the affairs of Northern Ireland.

Violence paralyses thought. The I.R.A. assisted the traditionalists in Whitehall in preventing withdrawal from being effectively considered, because it would have taken a bold Labour Prime Minister—and an even bolder Conservative Prime Minister—to place such a proposal on his Cabinet's agenda.

There were times, however, especially in the Opposition years from 1970 to 1974, when I believed that the next Labour Government would take its courage to Parliament and announce that an orderly, but irrevocable, withdrawal was to take place. Courage it would certainly have needed, for withdrawal has been consistently denounced and categorised as cowardly by all who oppose it. It had become synonymous with retreat, collapse, surrender, appeasement, capitulation, and the lack of political nerve and will. It was as unmentionable in Whitehall and Westminster as devaluation had been until it eventually took place in November 1967 (even when we did mention it privately, in the irresponsibility of Opposition, we only did so under the code-name of 'Algeria').

Above all, it would need courage for a Westminster politician to renounce the efforts of Gladstone, Asquith, and Lloyd George and to admit, finally, that the English (I use the word deliberately in this context, even though it includes the Scots and the Welsh) cannot solve the Irish problem because the English are part of the Irish problem.

The Irish, North and South, are suffocated by their history. To some Dublin politicians, Drogheda and Wexford are as fresh today as Dachau and Buchenwald are to the Jewish people, though with infinitely less justice. The Battle of the Boyne has been refought for 285 years and the Easter Rising of 1916 is now celebrated almost as a religious festival, far removed from the Rising which Easter is supposed to commemorate.

For the Irish, the past is a refuge from the present, a reason for not coming to decisions about the future. Yesterday is their version of *mañana*. It enables them to talk, to speculate, to theorise and rhapsodise in the way that third and fourth generation New York Irish and Hollywood think is romantic and good for business. In reality it is the curse of an attractive people and a lovely island.

But so long as the history books remain a contemporary force, and Cromwell, and Wolf Tone, James II and William of Orange, Collins, Pearse, and de Valera and the host of others who are celebrated and execrated in song and toast remain as living ghosts, for so long must English statesmen recognise that England has only one more role to play in the future of Ireland, and that role is her withdrawal from it.

The arguments, of course, against this policy are formidable, but they are not overwhelming, and some of them are not even honest. It would be said that Britain had bowed the knee to the Irish Republican Army, a title with a not inglorious past which today is used to dignify fanatics, terrorists and gangsters. But there was an Irish problem before there was an Irish Republican Army, and it was insoluble then, too, while Britain remained the dominant power. The problem of what to do with Northern Ireland would only in little measure be diminished if the Special Air Service were given a free hand to wipe out every member of the I.R.A. overnight; or even if the I.R.A. decided to follow a political and parliamentary programme. If there were no injustices in Northern Ireland, or if there had been none in Ireland as a whole, there might never have been an I.R.A. But there would still have been an Irish problem, because in the final analysis the people are Irish before they are British.

It is said that if the British presence were withdrawn from the province there would be widespread bloodshed in the civil war which would inevitably follow, leading even to the massacre of a large part of the Catholic population. It is further said that this bloodshed would spread to the British mainland and that many innocent people, including Irish innocent people, would be killed on the streets of Glasgow, Birmingham and

London. It is further said – and these are all powerful arguments – that if such carnage resulted from the withdrawal of the British civil and military administration and it was seen – as it would be – on British television each night, a revulsion would grow up against the Government which had precipitated the massacre.

Nobody ought to contemplate increasing the risk to the lives of any of the world's peoples. But the British Labour Government withdrew from the Indian sub-continent in 1947 and the resultant fighting cost a million Hindu, Sikh and Moslem lives. Would anyone today say that Britain was wrong to withdraw? Or, that fewer lives would have been lost if that Government had decided to stay, come what may – which is our present position in Northern Ireland? I am not convinced that civil war, bloodshed and massacre on a scale greater *in the long run* than now exists would follow a British withdrawal. Indeed, I believe the opposite. Fighting and the Irish are synonymous in the public mind, but the image is misleading. They are a people with a great fund of human kindness and peaceable ways, too. I am, however, convinced that the killing will never stop until the constitutional link with Westminster is severed.

Between July 1970 and July 1976, more than 1,500 people died in Northern Ireland from acts of violence, over 300 of them regular soldiers or members of the Ulster Defence Regiment. The number of murders of Royal Ulster Constabulary members and its reserve was approaching 100. These were the men, and a few women, too, charged with defending the ordinary families of Ulster. At a Downing Street meeting during Harold Wilson's last administration, Dr Garret FitzGerald, the Republic's External Affairs Minister, was heard to say that 'soldiers were there to be shot at' when British Ministers were resisting his appeal for more troops to go on the streets of West Belfast to protect the Catholic population. But soldiers and policemen leave widows and orphans, too.

Already, Birmingham, Guildford, London, Coventry and other English towns and cities have had their citizens indiscriminately and senselessly mutilated and murdered. If the choice that faces a British Government is between a considerable number of people being killed in a short space of time and a considerable number – perhaps even more – being killed over a longer and indefinite period of time, then they ought to plump for the solution which makes possible an end to it all.

During my seven years with Harold Wilson I attended most of his 'restricted' meetings on Northern Ireland. I went with him on each of his visits, in Government and Opposition, to Belfast, Londonderry and Dublin. I stayed in the Governor's colonial-style mansion at Lisburn, where the cook wore khaki under his apron and there was an automatic rifle by the telephone in the kitchen; I slept at the Shelbourne Hotel (since bombed) in Dublin as the guest of the Irish Government, with an armed guard in the corridor outside our bedrooms all night. I was with Harold Wilson when he spoke to two soldiers in Londonderry at Christmas 1975, just before they went out on the patrol which cost them their lives; and I was with him when he met John Hume in Dublin, after Hume had fled there because of a serious threat to his life in the North.

I remember most vividly of all crossing the border late one wet night, en route from Belfast to Dublin, and being challenged at the army border by a youthful, whey-faced soldier, nervously clutching his automatic rifle and wearing a beret too large for him. The look of fear that passed from his face when he saw that the car's principal occupant was Harold Wilson and not a gunman told me more about the manliness of that boy than any army publicity hand-out could have done.

Each of these visits only reinforced my belief that the English/ Welsh/Scots political and military administration must leave Ulster because our very presence there is preventing a conclusion to its trial.

There would be, of course, a large number of problems in withdrawal which are not immediately obvious but would be very pressing upon a British Government. There would be serious concern in the North Atlantic Treaty Organisation if a gap was opened in N.A.T.O.'s defences. That position would have to be secured.

If the standard of living of the people in the North was to fall to that of the South, it would be a catastrophic fall. Dublin may be more romantic, but it is scruffy and seedy compared with Belfast, even bombed so severely as it has been. The removal of the British Exchequer and other subsidies would cause the standard of living in Ulster to fall by a third. But an orderly withdrawal would not take place overnight, nor would the withholding of subsidies happen immediately. Politically, financially, and militarily, a period of some five years of transition would be sensible.

In that time, there would be an opportunity to rebuild the province's industrial and business base, provided the politicians there at last shouldered the responsibility of behaving responsibly. Rebuilding the industrial and business base, incidentally, would require some harsh decisions; decisions which ought to have been taken by the British Government but which it dared not take because it feared they would provoke further violence. Such a decision would be to close down Harland and Wolff's shipyard unless its finances could be dramatically, even miraculously, transformed. In 1975, so the Policy Unit at Downing Street calculated, the weekly subsidy paid to H. & W.'s – a Protestant enclave, at that – averaged £74 for each employee. It would have been cheaper for the British taxpayer if we had doubled the dole and shut down the yard.

The closure of Harland and Wolff's, however, by a British administration would be the final straw for the Protestant majority and would almost certainly provoke another strike like that of May 1974. (There can be few administrations in history which would have shown a profit – or less of a loss – in its operations during a General Strike, but with the massive subventions to unprofitable industry in Ulster in recent years, we must have been getting close to it. Even the losses caused to the power supply industry during the 1974 strike were met by the British taxpayer rather than the Ulster consumers, most of whom were on strike, too.)

Northern Ireland has become a tumour in the United Kingdom and ultimately it is going to become the concern of the European Economic Community because it will damage them, too. However well disposed the Dublin Government is towards defeating the I.R.A. terrorists, its heart is still with the basic unity of the Irish people; it feels guilty at being seen to be co-operating with Britain against Irishmen, even if the Irishmen are terrorists.

For their part, the Protestants, the so-called Loyalists and the undeniable majority, want the British to remain, but only on their terms. Their loyalty is to the concept of a Protestant

Ulster; if the United Kingdom went Catholic overnight then they would declare independence for Ulster before the sun was up. While Ulster remains a part of the U.K. the Protestants represent a dilemma which the British Government and the Westminster Parliament evades by not thinking about it. Under almost any other democratic system – and certainly under any system where might is right – the Protestants would have the right to expect to be the government of their homeland; at the very least, to exert the governing influence.

But they are not. They have less influence, effectively, than do the Nationalist minority in Scotland. In order to mitigate their influence still further, we forced upon Ulster, in the Assembly elections of 1973, a system of proportional representation which we deny (rightly) to the Scots, the Welsh and the English – and the Northern Irish, too, when it comes to elections to the Westminster Parliament. But how in democratic logic can we refuse the right of the majority to govern Ulster? If forced to answer, the British politician will tell you that the Protestants cannot be trusted. But are they less trustworthy, say, than the Rhodesians were when they were given self-government?; less trustworthy than any of the other thirty-five or thirty-six Commonwealth nations who have been given full independence? The question has only to be posed to see how silly it is.

No doubt the inevitable consequence of British withdrawal would mean Protestant government of the territory. But I doubt even then that we would see a return to the blatant discrimination which the Stormont Government formerly practised against the Catholics. In the first place, the old links between the British Conservative Party and the Ulster Unionists have been broken; the Unionists would no longer be able to rely on their political friends across the water to protect them from the world's interest and inquiry. Secondly – and this at least ought to be a gain from the troubles that restarted in 1969 – the Unionists by now must recognise that it would not be in their interests to so misgovern their country that murder remained its main industry.

I believe that when the people of Ulster are faced with deciding their own destiny, instead of being able conveniently to shuffle it off to others and to blame Westminster for whatever results, then they will begin to find the formula for living together. Until then, they will continue to die together, along with the security forces employed to protect them. It would be reasonable to expect that the Catholic, republican and nationalist elements in the Province's population would keep alive their dream to be joined with their co-religionists in the South. It would be a proper ambition, if it was peaceably pursued and pursued no doubt at considerable leisure. (In the normal course of time, the Catholics should outnumber the Protestants anyway.) But there is no hope of union with the South so long as Ulster remains within the United Kingdom. That is the one option which seven years of violence has closed. *Enforced* union, enforced by Westminster, *would* cause bloodshed, *would* provoke a civil war, *would* ensure that bombing spread to the mainland. Voluntary union is the only way to a united Ireland, but only if the Westminster connection is first cut. Then, in the fullness of time, even the Protestants might look at it because it makes economic sense. Withdrawal offers something to both communities if only they will learn to live together. But if they will not, no British army is going to force them to.

Unfortunately, there is an allure about the Irish situation which enslaves, apparently, every British politician who attains responsibility for it. It is to rising young Ministers — as it is to declining old statesmen — what Mount Everest was to climbers before Hillary and Tensing conquered it. It offers everlasting fame to the man who succeeds where all other men failed. It becomes an obsession with them, as compulsive as blood was to Count Dracula.

His arduous duties as Secretary of State for Northern Ireland wore out Merlyn Rees. He ached, and looked as if he ached, with tiredness after his first fifteen months in office. In June 1975, Harold Wilson was concerned about Merlyn and offered him the less exacting post as Minister of Education, but still a member of the Cabinet. He refused. He had had a plan for an elected Convention to succeed the defunct Assembly and he hoped against hope — even though, realistically, he knew there was no hope — that at its meetings, which had begun in May, the Convention would be able to agree on a form of government for Northern Ireland.

The Convention, however, ended in November 1975, without producing a scheme acceptable to the British Government. Merlyn asked for, and was granted, the Prime Minister's agreement that he should stay on until the New Year when he intended to recall the Convention and ask them to try again to reach an agreed solution (as opposed to the majority Protestant solution, which the other parties rejected). They met again and dissolved in confusion at the beginning of March 1976, without a report of any kind.

When James Callaghan became Prime Minister on April 5, 1976, Merlyn Rees, whose great admirer Mr Callaghan is, could have accepted an honourable transfer to another Cabinet post. Again, he asked to stay on. A good, kind and able Minister had become trapped by his office and was too exhausted to realise he had little more to offer; that the solution lay not in his continuation in office but in the abolition of Britain's responsibility for it. Not until September 1976 did he finally relinquish office, fifteen months too late. His achievement was to end internment; he alleviated a symptom but not the cause.

Elsewhere in this book I have sought to describe where power lies in Britain today. It is just as important to demonstrate where it does not lie; in Northern Ireland, the Government cannot exercise its authority with the same confidence it will be respected as it can in the other component parts of the United Kingdom. In the Province we have responsibility without power, the prerogative of the eunuch throughout the ages.

Like many others who either attended after mid-summer 1969 the discussions about Northern Ireland's future or had some part in shaping policy for it, I had never visited any part of the island. Nor did I do so until Harold Wilson's visit in November 1971, which was his first visit as Leader of the Labour Party to which he had been elected eight years before. This lack of first-hand knowledge among British politicians and senior civil servants was over the years a crucial element in the failure to recognise that the discrimination practised in Northern Ireland would one day lead to an explosion. (The senior civil servant allocated by the Conservative Government to assist Harold Wilson during his visit had at one time been in charge of the Northern Ireland Department at the Home Office. He told me he had never been to Southern Ireland in his life. It had never been the practice, apparently, of the Home Office to encourage its civil servants concerned with Irish affairs to visit the Republic.)

During that November 1971 visit Harold Wilson, in a hectic three days, met every conceivable interest group: politicians, of varying shades of orange and green and pale pink; trade unionists, some courageous and a few racist; leaders of every religious denomination; businessmen; surgeons; and the General Officer Commanding. No one was turned away, except the I.R.A. – 'I would not meet any men who sought to change the existing order by violence', he told Parliament on November 25. It was an attitude he shared with Conservative Ministers. Less than four months later he had to modify it. We not only met the 'men of violence' but we went back to Dublin to do so.

The trouble with that particular stand – apart from the fact that throughout British colonial history we had not only treated with violent men but had usually installed them as leaders of their countries and invited them to Buckingham Palace – was that it rested upon a very narrow definition of violence.

The internment camp at Long Kesh – barbed wire and machine gun towers, like a German concentration camp and only fifty minutes' flying time from London – housed sullen and hard-bitten men for the main part, but there were a number of seemingly bewildered youths who protested their innocence to us. Harold Wilson asked the Irish civil servant accompanying us about the procedures for appeal against internment; what, he asked, is the response of the appeal tribunal to the claim by some of these men that they are innocent? 'Oh,' said the civil servant, 'they would be asked why, if they're innocent, they are in Long Kesh?' That is a kind of violence, too.

The rest of the journey was also depressing. The Social and Democratic Labour Party, under the titular leadership of Gerry Fitt, was a less cohesive force then than it is today. When we met them in Belfast they spoke with more voices than there were members of their delegation. The greatest progress made was in the emptying of the Irish whiskey bottle.

They spoke, and they spoke. They argued, disputed, debated, discussed, contested, and controverted, and they reminisced over and recounted recent – i.e., since 1690 – Irish history. And so did the next group, and the next. The clergymen drank less but talked as much. The women were earnest and the men were bigoted. One shop steward from the Rolls-Royce factory, arrogant and offensive, made it plain that he thought Harold Wilson ought to keep his nose out of Ulster's affairs. 'But you are not Irish?' Mr Wilson inquired mildly. 'No,' he said truculently, 'I'm from Southall. I left there seven years ago. I've seen it all before with these bloody Catholics; they're the same as the blacks ... ' Winston Churchill was reputed to have said about a fellow Member of Parliament that he 'brought sodomy into disrepute'. That shop steward did the same job for racialism.

Mr Ian Paisley, who bawls bigotry through his clerical collar with a violence more suited to the terraces at Old Trafford, announced to the press that he would see Mr Wilson in order to tell him a thing or two. What he was going to say was in the newspapers before we arrived at Stormont Castle for the meeting. Paisley was accompanied by another clergyman who appeared to be his political curate and Mr Desmond Boal, whose intellect is on a totally higher plane. An advocate of intense ferocity with a passion for meticulous detail, he did not let Harold Wilson or Paisley get a word in edgeways as he cross-examined the Leader of the Opposition. Harold Wilson listened patiently, but he had not gone to Stormont to be hectored by Mr Boal, whatever his intellectual qualities. Eventually he interrupted and put a question to Paisley about his views on detention. (He already knew Paisley's views on detention, having re-read them shortly before we left for Stormont, but it was the only way to stem Boal's eloquence.) Paisley repeated his views in a friendly, matter of fact way. The promised and publicised explosion by him did not come. But then ... 'Mr Wilson,' he said, 'there is one question I *must* ask before you leave.' 'Certainly', said Harold, bracing himself for the onslaught. Paisley stepped forward, towering above us. 'Would you mind autographing my copy of your book?' he asked, bringing a copy of *The Labour Government 1964–1970: A Personal Record* from behind his back. His companions stared. Paisley looked uncomfortable. 'I bought it wholesale', he excused himself.

From Belfast we drove to Dublin and meetings with the then Taoiseach, Jack Lynch; the leader of the Irish Labour Party, Brendan Corish, and a number of his colleagues; and with Mr Liam Cosgrave, leader of the then main opposition party, Fine Gael. At lunch with Mr Lynch, Harold Wilson aired some of the propositions he was later in the month to include in a fifteen-point plan for solving the problem of Northern Ireland: Ireland to rejoin the Commonwealth (a nonsense from which I was unable to budge him in an argument which the night before had gone on until nearly 3 a.m. in the hotel) and Irish unity, fifteen years after agreement upon it. The full fifteen points of the Wilson plan had much to commend them at the time and contained more positive and constructive suggestions in a coherent whole than had previously been advanced. But like every other plan for Ireland – like, indeed, one he had put forward himself only two months earlier – it was overtaken by the avalanche of events. The fascinating moment at the Taoiseach's lunch came when Harold Wilson put forward the plan for turning the dream of unity into reality. I had thought they would jump for joy. But their reaction was more akin to falling through the floor.

Like so many others we were to meet in Ireland, whatever their public pronouncements, in private they preferred to dream rather than do; I suspect they feared Harold Wilson was right when he added, rather insensitively, that he thought the out-come of a united Ireland would be that the South would be taken over by the North.

The speech Harold Wilson made in the debate in the House of Commons on November 25, 1971, after that Irish visit was the most thoughtful that he had delivered since the election defeat seventeen months earlier. It stilled for a moment a grow-ing disquiet in the party, especially on the right, about his leadership and reminded those who had forgotten, and in-formed those who had never witnessed it, why he was such a formidable force in public affairs.

Irish newspapers, north and south of the border, wanted to interview him, and so did the radio and TV reporters. So, more intriguingly, did the I.R.A. and in early March 1972, we received, through an intermediary – Dr John O'Connell, a Labour member of the Dail – a message that some leading 'friends' of the I.R.A. were anxious to discuss the problems of the North with Mr Wilson. After a meeting with Dr O'Connell in London and talks with Merlyn Rees, then the Shadow Cabinet spokesman on Northern Ireland, Harold Wilson decided to go, provided that secrecy could be preserved –

though he said he would privately inform the Prime Minister —
that it was understood that he was not in a position to negotiate
with them, and provided a suitable 'cover' story could be
arranged.

The last was not difficult. I telephoned Radio Telefis
Eireann, who had been asking for some weeks for a chance to
interview Mr Wilson, and told them that there was a gap in the
diary for March 13 if they still wanted him to come to Dublin.
They jumped at it and neither they nor anyone else inquired
why he should go to Dublin for an interview which could just
as easily have taken place in London and at less expense.

So to Dublin we went; Harold Wilson was warmly welcomed,
gave the TV interview, spoke to a puzzled press and bade
goodnight to everyone. Followed by a police car, Dr O'Connell
then drove us to his house, a gaunt and gloomy structure — or
so it seemed that evening, when fancy was likely to run wild —
on the edge of Phoenix Park, where Lord Frederick Cavendish,
newly appointed Chief Secretary for Ireland, and his private
secretary were stabbed to death on their first day in Dublin,
May 6, 1882. Five men were hanged and three sent to penal
servitude for life for that crime, and an assignation late at night
with their heirs, even ninety years later, put all kinds of silly
and sinister thoughts into the head.

We were uncertain who exactly were the 'friends' of the
I.R.A. who would be there; indeed, Harold Wilson had said
he did not wish to know whom he would be meeting. But two
of the three men there — they arrived early to avoid being seen
by the police — were easily recognisable by me as David
O'Connell, effective leader of the I.R.A., and Joe Cahill,
notorious north and south of the border, who had served a
lengthy prison sentence for the murder of a policeman. The
third man was John Kelly, from Belfast. There were no introductions, merely a polite 'Good evening'. The 'friends' of the
I.R.A. refused alcohol and drank soft drinks for the whole of
the meeting. Merlyn Rees, who had been in Dublin anyway,
was with us.

Harold Wilson began by declaring that violence would only
delay an eventual settlement of Ireland's problem; it had to be
ended before any move forward would be made.

David O'Connell, whose face had the pallor of a skin unused

to the sun, spoke quietly, and with some dignity, throughout. Though he and his colleagues were to us light years away from reality, especially when discussing what was politically possible, he demonstrated an intellectual quality greater than many politicians we had met in the North. It is necessary to say this, even if it gives offence to so many who have suffered at the hands of the I.R.A. He is not a man to be underestimated. O'Connell began by agreeing with Harold Wilson. He and his friends, for whom he was speaking, also deplored violence and they wanted to see peace restored in Ireland. But ... they had not started the violence, the Unionists had, and the British Government were continuing it. To stop violence before there was a satisfactory solution – i.e., a solution along the lines proposed by the I.R.A. – would only postpone bloodshed to a further evil day.

He seemed well informed about the military activities of the various Protestant movements in the North. The Vanguard organisation, he alleged, had been created with the connivance of Brian Faulkner (Prime Minister of Ulster until direct rule was imposed in 1972). It was growing and growing. The Protestants in the North had 121,000 guns, 400 of which were heavy calibre machine guns. Since June 1970 (that was, since the arrival of the Conservative Government) it had been the policy of the British Government to harass the Catholics. They were concentrating on 'ending the gunman' in order to avoid reaching a political solution. If the British Government made a declaration of intent (to leave Ireland) that was a genuine declaration, said O'Connell, then the Irish people, North and South, could work out a solution together.

That was not what we had heard from the Protestants in the North.

O'Connell went on:

The violence in the past will be nothing to the prospect and the actuality of the violence that is going to come in the future ... We are being driven into a situation of having to attack. If the British Government are not prepared to face up to the contrived sectarianism we are going to be forced into a bigger conflict to protect our own rights. Since 1969, we are capable of enlarging on the present

violence if violence is increased. There are signs of immi-
nent disaster unless there is someone prepared to take
responsibility again. We have given some leadership,
demonstrated that we are capable not only of stopping the
violence, stopping the war, but of going farther and talking, entering discussions.

Harold Wilson replied that children on both sides of the
divide in Ireland were being alienated and they would be the
ones to carry on the war in the 1980s. He feared that a civil war
was approaching in which the Protestants with their guns would
go on to the streets. (At that time, the Protestant 'back-lash'
had hardly begun. Though they had initiated the brutality in
1969, they were not in early 1972 anywhere near as well
organised and active as the Provisional I.R.A.) He recalled,
too, his November 25 speech and the possibility of a united
Ireland fifteen years after it had been agreed upon, and added:
'The way your friends are going on it will be a longer period.
If it could be cut down to eight or ten years I would be de-
lighted.'

Harold Wilson asked O'Connell if his friends would trust
anyone to speak for them in any talks that we held, given that
the Government could not negotiate with the I.R.A. 'What
would your friends feel about my friends in the S.D.L.P.?'
he asked.

Joe Cahill reacted sharply and abruptly: 'Our friends hold
very strong views. No one substituted for them in the fighting
and they do not want a substitute in the talking.'

Harold Wilson went on to say that some of the S.D.L.P.
leaders would like to talk about a solution to the problem of
Ulster (at that time internment without trial in Long Kesh had
brought Catholic hostility, including S.D.L.P. hostility, to the
British Government to a peak). Gerry Fitt, he said, would like
to talk 'but he had difficulties with your friends. He thinks that
one day one of your friends will shoot him in the back.'

'Hardly in the back,' said O'Connell softly. I remembered
that it was past midnight and we were still on the edge of
Phoenix Park. O'Connell went on:

'It is not a question of anyone not permitting Gerry Fitt to

talk. It is a question of his own survival. His own constituents won't allow him to talk. Gerry Fitt is subject to no
threat, no intimidation ... It is the feeling of those people
who have sons and fathers in Long Kesh. The S.D.L.P.
have completely lost touch with the situation.'

Wilson:

'What politicians have you confidence in in Northern
Ireland?'

O'Connell:

'None of them.'

Wilson:

'If there were talks could you promise that your friends
would not intervene? Not shoot them in the back?'

Kelly:

'That's absolute nonsense.'

O'Connell:

'In order to retain their own constituencies they cannot
afford to enter talks without release of all internees without
conditions.'

The talks went on until nearly 1.30 a.m. A meeting of minds
was clearly impossible. We were planets apart; words had
different meanings. 'Violence' to our side was what 'peace'
meant to the other; 'freedom' was 'oppression'. Harold Wilson
stressed that constitutional talks could only be between 'elected'
representatives. O'Connell insisted that they must be between
the British Government and 'our friends'. The I.R.A. leaders
wanted an amnesty for 'political prisoners'; Harold Wilson said
that if 'political prisoners' meant 'the men who committed
Aldershot ... I would not accept it, nor would any British

Government'. It had been, he said, an 'interesting and frank' meeting.

On the other hand, as far as I could see, it had got us nowhere, except that we had broken the taboo on talks with the I.R.A., and thus held a door ajar for the future.

We said goodnight and left. The I.R.A. men stayed behind to avoid the police escort which was waiting, hidden off the road, to take us to our hotel.

A few days later, just before a debate on Ireland in the House of Commons, the news of our meeting began to leak in Dublin. Harold Wilson decided that he would have to reveal that it had taken place and asked me to telephone 10 Downing Street and pass a message to the Prime Minister, Mr Heath, saying that in his speech he would add that he had informed him before going to Dublin that he would be meeting the I.R.A. A few minutes later one of Mr Heath's private secretaries phoned me back to say that Mr Heath said that Mr Wilson had not informed him of any such intention and that if he stated that he had then he, Mr Heath, would deny it. Harold Wilson had told me a week earlier that he had had a word with Mr Heath at a reception they had both attended. He was upset. It was an illuminating illustration of the distrust which for a long time soured the relationship between the two men.

In fact, the public reaction to news of the meeting was not too critical, and nor was that of the press. It had not been so evidently a failure that it could never be risked again; and three months later the Conservative Secretary of State for Northern Ireland, William Whitelaw, himself met a group of the Provisional leadership, secretly, in London. News of that meeting encouraged Harold Wilson to propose further talks with the I.R.A., this time at his home near Great Missenden in Buckinghamshire. Three I.R.A. representatives flew in a chartered plane to a nearby private airfield on July 18, 1972. We learned later that their Army Council had been divided on whether anyone should come at all. They compromised in the end by sending a lower-level delegation which meant that David O'Connell was not among them.

The three Provisionals were Joe Cahill, a man named Ford from Belfast, and Miles Shevlin, a hard-line lawyer from Dublin. The meeting was barren from the start.

K

Harold Wilson began by saying that the meeting was on his initiative; he was not representing William Whitelaw, or speaking for him, though he intended to report his impressions to him.

The Provisionals were taken aback. They clearly thought that the reason a former Prime Minister wanted to see them was that he *had* a message he wanted to convey; they did not, or could not, in their own councils, distinguish between British politicians, regarding them largely as interchangeable members of the same conspiracy. They would not accept the distinction on that day.

Harold Wilson was anxious to try to persuade the I.R.A. to resume the truce which had recently ended in the North, but the discussion sank deep into the details of why it had broken down: of harassment and intimidation of Catholics in Belfast; of complaints that the army had prevented Catholic families from occupying houses allocated to them on a Belfast estate — allocated it was added inconsequentially 'by civil servants who are Unionists and Protestants'. The army were 'taking orders' from the Ulster Defence Association and they had fired the shots which had broken the truce. Individual harassment that was instanced even included the case of a soldier who had 'raised two fingers to a Catholic' during the truce. All this may or may not have been true, may or may not have been cause for complaint, but set against a resumption of murder and arson and the need to secure the reinstatement of the truce it was not the kind of discussion we should have been having. When Harold Wilson raised the question of whether the troops should be taken off the streets in a resumed truce, Shevlin interjected — 'The I.R.A. want the British troops out of Ireland.' He went on:

> The British Government should give a commitment to withdraw British troops on or before January 1, 1975 and in the meantime withdraw from the sensitive areas. The timing of the announcement is negotiable, but the principle is not.

The discussion continued over a light lunch and was joined towards the end by Merlyn Rees, but it was completely meaningless. The Provisionals had only come to Great Missenden because they believed that Harold Wilson was empowered to negotiate on behalf of the British Government, or at least would put to them propositions on behalf of the Government, even if they were thinly disguised as his own; they had thought that he, like they, could speak on behalf of his 'friends'. They went back disappointed. On our side, the door left open on March 13 had been shut, bolted, barred and welded to its architrave. Harold Wilson never saw them again.

Despite strains within the Parliamentary party, the Labour Opposition stayed with the Government on Northern Ireland policy, supporting them generally and easing the party pressures by occasional criticism of the particular, especially internment. They stayed because there was nowhere else to go. But the search for a way out of the circle of violence and reaction to violence went on, and it was groping towards disentanglement from Irish affairs. But always the quest was confined and frustrated by the violence. Every move that might be made on the political front was judged by whether or not it would encourage the I.R.A. or help to defeat them. It was another chicken and egg argument: there could be no Progress without Peace, and no Peace without Progress. Anyway, what was Peace? Was it only an absence of violence or something more? What was Progress, if to the Ulster majority it meant Retreat?

There is no doubt that in Northern Ireland affairs a change of policy has to be preceded by a change of Secretary of State. The incoming Labour Government of March 1974, therefore, had an opportunity then, when all was new, to break out of the chains of the previous years, whether five or fifty. But it could not be taken.

The Government was a minority Government, destined and determined to fight another General Election within seven months – despite various false clues, October 10 was always the intended day – but facing the fact that if the opposition parties in the House of Commons were to combine on a vote of confidence to throw the Government out Polling Day could be within seven weeks.

The more immediate crisis, anyway, was the crisis of the economy, and everything was subordinate to that. Ending the three-day week was easy enough and it got the new Government off to a good start. The inflation projections from the Treasury, however, showed that price increases were about to raise their gait from a trot to a gallop. What was more, it was becoming clear that as soon as compulsory wage restraint lapsed, major unions would be seeking to get, generally, what had been conceded to the miners as a special case.

On top of all that, there was the problem of renegotiating the terms of entry into the European Economic Community, a prospect with the potential to destroy the Government from within. There was very little time for Ireland; more accurately, very little time for a substantial rethink of British policy. In the circumstances, the Government was willing to continue along the path which the Conservatives had trodden in the footsteps of the previous Labour Government. Bipartisanship is often not a policy but a disguise for the lack of one.

Of course, Merlyn Rees and his team of Ministers had some successes, on a personal and political level. There is no doubt that the Catholics in the North regard Labour as more sympathetic to them than any other party. The process of releasing detainees from H.M. Prison the Maze (as Long Kesh camp had been renamed) was welcomed, even by the Conservatives.

But that had its other side, too. If Labour was pleasing the Catholics more, then conversely it was bound to displease the Protestants. On May 14, the Ulster Workers' Strike began and continued until the power-sharing Executive lost its nerve, collapsed and resigned on May 28, after a life of less than five months.

The Prime Minister broadcast to Northern Ireland on May 25, when he summed up the purpose of the strike exactly:

> It is a deliberate and calculated attempt to use every un-democratic and unparliamentary means for the purpose of bringing down the whole constitution of Northern Ireland ... The law is being set aside. Those who are now challeng-ing constitutional authority ... have decided, without being elected by a single vote, who shall work in Northern Ireland and who shall not. They seek to allocate food, to decide who shall eat and who shall not ... The people of Northern Ireland and their democratically-elected Assem-bly have the joint duty of seeing this thing through ...

The democratically-elected Assembly followed the demo-cratically-elected Executive into hurried oblivion. Against No. 10's advice, Harold Wilson had also called the strikers 'spongers', which was good for winning votes from the electo-rate in England, Scotland and Wales, but which had a disas-trous impact in Ulster.

The strike had demonstrated that the Government's writ did not run in Ulster if the Protestant workers decided they were not going to man the power stations. It put a permanent, recognisable limit on the power of the British Government. From then on, we were not even refereeing the fight, only hold-ing the coats while the religious factions got on with it. We could only do such things in Ireland as the organised Protestant population were prepared to agree with, acquiesce in, or tole-rate with reluctance and grumbles.

It is often easier, much easier, to fight violence than it is to overcome the more passive resistance of a strike. If it were not for the proper restraints which a democratic and civilised administration must put upon its military forces, the British army could eliminate most of the I.R.A. gunmen very quickly (though in time another regiment of terrorists would step forward to fill their places). But the army cannot operate power stations, run railways, unload ships, distribute food *and* fight at the same time. Indeed, most of these things it could not do anyway, even if there was peace on the streets. Sympathy for the strike seeped into some army officers and senior civil servants, one of whom told me that because the only petrol available was from pumps operated by members of the Ulster Workers' Council he had authorised his secretary at Stormont Castle to go down to the garage and get an allocation for her car. When a member of the staff of the Chief Executive, Brian Faulkner, did that, then the U.W.C. could not be blamed if they thought that the local administration was on their side.

Nevertheless, they destroyed that administration as part of their larger bid to wipe off the agenda any possibility of the All-Ireland Council. An emergency social security scheme established during the strike cost some £5,000,000 to the British taxpayer, on top of the normal generous provision for Ulster. Since the troubles broke out in 1969, Ulster has received more money per head of the population than any other part of the

United Kingdom. One reliable estimate in 1975 placed the annual subsidy from the Exchequer at around £400 a year per person.

The U.W.C. strike had proved that though we were paying increasingly large sums of money to the piper we were not calling the tune. It had given us the second opportunity to start the process of consultation about eventual withdrawal and once again we had missed it.

In January 1975, Dr O'Connell approached us again, this time through Tony Field, who managed Harold Wilson's private office in Opposition until June 1973, and who had been responsible for making the administrative arrangements for our visit to Dublin and the visit of the I.R.A. team to Grange Farm. At that time, a temporary, uneasy truce was tottering towards its end. Field, who no longer had any connection with public affairs, passed the message to his sister, Lady Falkender, who telephoned the Prime Minister (I was with him in his study at the time) in a highly excited state, declaring that the truce was about to break down, that it was all the Government's fault, and that she was going to go to Dublin.

The Prime Minister replied that she would do no such thing. She was ignorant of the subject, he said, and did not know what she was talking about; and the situation was far too serious for her to interfere.

That ended her intervention but left the Prime Minister with the problem of what to do about the I.R.A. approach: whether to ignore it or find an unusual channel to see what it amounted to. The I.R.A. were claiming that they could not trust the British civil servants with whom they had been meeting; they said they had reason to believe that their messages and their attitudes were not being correctly conveyed to the British Government. The Prime Minister decided he could not ignore any chances, however remote, of saving the truce and making it permanent. The I.R.A. might be wanting to make progress; or they might only be wanting to make trouble. They might even be wanting to make both, but we had to find out.

The problem was Merlyn Rees, and his very powerful permanent secretary, Sir Frank Cooper, whose knowledge of, and influence in, Northern Ireland affairs surpassed that of any Minister or any other civil servant. If the Prime Minister told them of the approach their strong advice would undoubtedly be to reject it; after all, they were themselves, through officials, in touch with the I.R.A. at that time. But it was the I.R.A.'s distrust of those contacts, apparently, which made them want to speak directly to the Prime Minister. Harold Wilson decided that we should hear what Dr O'Connell had to say, and then tell Merlyn Rees afterwards. The question was how contact should be made.

I was in a different position from Lady Falkender. I knew O'Connell (John, that is); I knew the Government's current thinking and I had attended most of the meetings between the Prime Minister and Merlyn Rees. I was also a civil servant, with the advantages of travel and communication which that gave me. So I offered to go to Dublin to meet John O'Connell and anyone else he thought necessary, provided it was understood that I was a messenger, no more; able to receive but not to give.

The Prime Minister was attracted by the thought, but decided against it on the grounds that there were too many journalists, as well as some Irish civil servants and politicians of all three main parties, who might recognise me. Eventually, he decided to ask John O'Connell to come to London where I could meet him, unofficially and secretly, not as an official but as a friend.

The temporary truce was due to end at midnight on Thursday, January 16. John O'Connell could not reach London before the late afternoon of the following day. Although I was seeing him surreptitiously without the knowledge of Merlyn Rees and his office, we could not possibly have a situation where a member of the Prime Minister's office was meeting with a contact of the I.R.A.'s on the very day when violence was to be resumed.

I therefore asked Albert (now Lord) Murray, the manager of Harold Wilson's political office who was put in charge of making the arrangements for Dr O'Connell's visit, to tell him that if the bombing and shooting restarted after Thursday midnight, I would not see him and nor would anyone else. The point was made forcefully and effectively by Albert and the truce was briefly extended.

That Friday there was an all-day meeting at Chequers of members of the Cabinet, which I had to attend, but I left unnoticed by other civil servants during a break for tea and returned to Downing Street. From there Albert Murray drove me in his own car to the Old Vic Theatre in Waterloo Road where he had arranged for us to pick up Dr O'Connell at 6 p.m. Then we went on to the Southwark headquarters of Albert Murray's union, Natsopa, where Dick (now Lord) Briginshaw, the union's general secretary, had provided a private room and asked no questions about it.

John O'Connell is a gentle man who genuinely believed he had a role to play as a bridge between the I.R.A. and the British Government; he was not seeking personal publicity, indeed, he had been severely criticised by his Labour colleagues in the Dail for his earlier mediation activities in 1972. He always seemed to me very sincere, but he grossly over-estimated his chances of success.

He told us that he had been with David O'Connell (no relation) until 5.30 a.m. that morning. He had requested that the truce be extended and the deadline had been put back until Saturday midnight. He feared that when violence was resumed it would be against selected targets in Britain rather than in Northern Ireland.

The conditions for a permanent truce, he said, were:

1 The appointment of a Commission of Three – a small team of mediators who would investigate what common ground might exist between all the various elements in the Irish problem and make recommendations for a solution. The Commission was an idea of Dr O'Connell's and he believed the I.R.A. had come round to accepting it and would agree to Mr Sean MacBride, former Minister for External Affairs in the Republic, Chairman of Amnesty International and the United Nations Commissioner for Namibia, representing the 'republican' side. The acceptance by the I.R.A. of the principle of the Commission was a step forward, Dr O'Connell thought. He also thought that Desmond Boal, the lawyer colleague of Ian Paisley, would be suitable to represent the Northern Protestants, while Jo Grimond, the former Liberal Party leader, might represent the 'British' side, though that would be for the Government to decide.

2 The steady release of detainees.

3 Some kind of private commitment on a political amnesty when peace was permanent.

4 Movement 'on the conditions privately submitted', on which a reply had been promised but which had not been forthcoming. (These included freedom of movement for all members of 'the Republic Movement'; the ending of harassment of the civilian population; cessation of all raids on lands, homes and other buildings; the ending of arrests of members of the Republican Movement; no more screening, photographing, and identity checks; the right of members of the Republican Movement to carry concealed short arms for self-defence; no provocative displays of force by either side; no reintroduction of the Royal Ulster Constabulary or the Ulster Defence Regiment into designated areas; agreement on an effective liaison system between British and Republican forces; a progressive withdrawal of troops to barracks to begin with the implementation of the bilateral truce; and confirmation that discussions between the Republican Movement and the Government would continue towards securing a permanent ceasefire. In the event of any of these terms being violated the Republican Movement reserved the right of freedom of action.)

5 Two representatives to be sent to talk to the I.R.A., principally David O'Connell.

John O'Connell said that both Jack Lynch and Liam Cosgrave (who had succeeded Lynch as Prime Minister in March 1973) were interested in the idea of the Commission of Three. It was accepted by the I.R.A. that violence would have to cease while the Commission deliberated, but that position he later modified, for it became clear that the appointment of the Commission would not in itself be sufficient to guarantee a ceasefire. The other conditions would have to be met, too.

For the rest, it was a familiar story; the sincerity of the British Government about the continuation of the ceasefire was doubted; during the current truce harassment had continued by the British army and photographs were being taken of Catholics for identification purposes. The army 'fortresses' in the Catholic areas had to be dismantled, the troops with-drawn to their barracks and internment ended. The I.R.A. complained that there had not been any 'meaningful response' to their initiatives, which made them think that the military were in control rather than Harold Wilson.

I told John O'Connell that I could only receive messages, not give any and I had none to give. I could not in any sense negotiate. I would ensure that his words were passed on in full, but in my opinion forty-eight hours – which was the time by which the truce had been extended – was impossibly short in which to prepare a considered reply. I then returned to Down-ing Street and dispatched a transcript of the meeting to the Prime Minister who had remained at Chequers after the Cabinet meeting ended.

Dr O'Connell was to come over to London again a week later and amplify his proposals to Albert Murray. But the suspicions of British motives and actions was paramount once more. Dr O'Connell was passed a message from the Prime Minister making it clear that all the points he had raised were matters for consideration by the Secretary of State for Northern Ireland. But the object of the I.R.A. was to bypass him and, especially, his civil servants. Dr O'Connell then discovered that his second visit to London had become known to civil servants in Northern Ireland within hours of his making it and the initiative, if it ever was one, followed all the others into the sand.

Later the truce was resumed, which meant after a while that people went on being killed but not in such large numbers as before. Eventually it expired altogether. There were some shocking acts of violence, especially in Co. Armagh. Merlyn Rees denounced them all, but he and everyone else knew it did not make the slightest difference.

After the resuscitation of the Convention early in 1976, followed quickly by its final collapse, we started to look again for a solution and we were no nearer to it than we had been in August 1969. The search for a policy for peace was as fanciful as trying to trap a leprechaun.

The ruthless men on both sides of the sectarian barrier con-tinued to commit crimes which were as idealistic in their com-mission as were Capone's, Dillinger's and Jack the Ripper's. Eighty per cent of violent crimes in Ulster were listed by the security authorities as the work of gangsters, criminals in any country or in any language.

Many of those elected to represent the people of Ulster – or claiming to represent them – continued to betray them with bigotry. Not the least advantage of a British withdrawal might be that those who are leaders in Ulster would have to start working for the Province's recovery rather than prolong its agony, or give way to decent, able, and responsible citizens who today play no part, out of fear or distaste, in community life.

Left to themselves, the people of Northern Ireland will one day find a solution to the disease that is killing them. The English never will. It is a lesson we will have to learn.

7

Doing the Honours

... Let none presume
To wear an undeserved dignity.
O! that estates, degrees, and offices
Were not deriv'd corruptly, and that clear honour
Were purchased by the merit of the wearer!

The Merchant of Venice

The occasional unaccountable award of public paid appointment to a party war-horse owes more to gratitude than to graft. Governmental, Ministerial, and Prime Ministerial patronage in Britain is not, as it is in America, a system for providing 'jobs for the boys', despite the regularity with which the accusation is made. Though nearly 5,000 paid public appointments are within the gift of Ministers, only about 1,200 carry salaries of more than £1,000 a year. Almost all these – and the more than 5,000 who fill unpaid appointments – are the fruits of a careful sifting and sorting by the civil service machine, which, whatever else it may be, is not corrupt. In most instances, Ministers merely stamp their approval upon the recommendations which have been put before them.

Those names are unlikely to be the best possible choices from the best possible list of candidates, but there have usually been discreet inquiries – including, where necessary, inquiries of the police – about their suitability. They would probably have been drawn from the register of 'The Great and the Good' which is kept in Whitehall, compiled over the years somewhat haphazardly by civil servants. A great many of the names, of course, are the personal selection of senior civil servants, which tends to give it an upper-to-middle-class, South of England bias. Permanent secretaries know more directors than they do dustmen. In any case, directors usually have more time to spare for part-time appointments.

Nevertheless, paid public appointments usually go to people who will do a tolerably good job and sometimes to those who will do an exceptionally good one. Even those whose recognition owes more to who they know than to what they know might not do a bad job. However, as the number of paid appointments to public bodies grows, then so do the dangers; these were recognised during Harold Wilson's last administration by the establishment of a Public Appointments Unit, whose responsibilities include broadening the geographical, industrial and social base of those from whom public office holders are chosen.

Of course, the top few per cent of the paid posts will still be heavily influenced by Ministerial choice, but if that choice is too capricious, particularly in a party or personal sense, public reaction – and Prime Ministerial frowns – act as a restraint. In fact, this does not happen very often because the two main political parties in Britain are as one on public appointments: they both usually select a majority of Conservatives.

Some appointments over the years have been indefensible. In particular, part-time membership of the boards of nationalised industries has been offered to – and eagerly accepted by – men whose qualifications for, and knowledge of, the industry concerned had not previously been the sole topic of conversation in Wigan or anywhere else. Such appointments have done more to supplement the basic State pension for those who have grown old in the service of their party than further the efficiency of public corporations.

It is also the case that too many Members of Parliament are rewarded with public posts, often as compensation for the loss of Ministerial office, even though in some past administrations a man would have to be very incompetent indeed to be dismissed from his post. It would not be a bad idea if M.P.s were ineligible for public appointments until two years have elapsed from the time they voluntarily retired from active politics (involuntary retirement – defeat at the polls – would be a different matter). A rule similar to this used to exist in local government for councillors who wished to apply for senior posts with their local authority. It would not be a bad idea, either, if the rule about civil servants not joining outside industry with which they had dealings during their civil service career until two years have passed was enforced more rigidly than it has been of late. The board established to run the nationalised aircraft industry could surely have survived without Lord Beswick just as the Department of Industry survived with him; the British National Oil Corporation could have waited for two years for Lord Balogh, and the Midland Bank could have done the same for Lord Armstrong, the former head of the Civil Service.

Where the real problem about patronage lies is in the field of honours – especially honours with titles – and it is a problem not because of the patron but because of the desperate lengths – humiliatingly sycophantic lengths sometimes – to which those desiring to be patronised will go. (Curiously, it is nearly always men, not women, who seek titles, though they frequently excuse themselves by saying, 'Of course, I don't really care, one way or the other, but it's the wife who really wants it...') A peerage is most fervently desired, but a knighthood is more than acceptable and so, even, is appointment to the office of Commander of an Order commemorating a long-liquidated British Empire.

Even some of those who are quick in their opposition to any form of privilege within our society and who condemn the House of Lords as an undemocratic anachronism have been known to be even quicker in seizing the opportunity of becoming a peer when it has been offered to them explaining, in the self-sacrificing tones of Sydney Carton, that it gives them one last chance to serve the party. Nor are they slow to recommend minor honours for their friends and constituency workers. But that is not a left-wing phenomenon: Conservative M.P.s deliver their recommendations in a cascade and will cherish an invitation to a Buckingham Palace Garden Party or to the Prime Minister's stand for the Trooping the Colour on the Queen's official birthday.

The obsession about titles, especially, can descend to unpleasant and degrading levels. During the 1969 Labour Party conference at Brighton, a few months after I had become the Prime Minister's Press Secretary, the political correspondent of a Conservative Sunday newspaper put the most bare-faced proposition to me on behalf of a Conservative M.P., Captain Henry Kerby.

Kerby represented the safest Conservative seat in the country,

Arundel and Shoreham, in Sussex, but he wanted to surrender it for a seat in the House of Lords. The proposal as it was outlined to me was crude and blatant: in return for a peerage Kerby would betray his party by 'passing over all the Conservative election secrets' when the time for a General Election eventually came.

If this were a novel, I would have risen to my feet at that point, declaiming, 'Sir, you dishonour me', or some other cliché from Victorian melodrama, but I never moved. I found the conversation irresistibly fascinating. It is not every day, even in the world of politics, that one hears anything so outrageously treacherous.

I told the intermediary that I would think about it. I then told Michael Halls, the Prime Minister's principal private secretary at that time, who was not surprised. He said that Captain Kerby had made approaches about a peerage before. I thought then, and still think now, that the M.P. was more to be pitied than anything else. I suppose I ought to have felt indignant or offended, but I did not, largely because it seemed so unreal. I did no more about it and I heard no more from the intermediary until the following May, when the Prime Minister announced that there was to be a General Election on June 18. At that point, he approached me again.

Captain Kerby, he said, was still anxious for a title, even though he had modified his ambitions. His offer still stood: in return for the promise of an honour in a (near) future list, he would ensure that the Prime Minister was informed of 'what the Tories are up to' during the General Election campaign. The honour sought was now a knighthood.

I listened, as I had before, but this time did not even report the approach. Michael Halls had just died and his successor was newly in post. The proposition was an obvious absurdity. At the basest level of consideration, to convey agreement would have put the Prime Minister in pawn to a Conservative M.P. who, to say the least, had raised question marks about his loyalty to his undertakings.

But a few days later, proof of Captain Kerby's seriousness began to come through my letter box. On almost every day during the 1970 General Election campaign letters posted from within the Arundel and Shoreham constituency, were delivered to my home addressed to my wife in her maiden name. There was no accompanying letter and no clue to the sender, other than the postmarks on the envelopes. The contents were unimportant, usually Conservative Central Office advice to candidates on how they should reply to awkward questions asked on the doorstep or at public meetings. (By definition, not 'secrets', because if the questions were asked the circulars were designed to provide the answers.) But on a couple of occasions there *were* confidential documents enclosed, including reports from Conservative agents in the south-east; one for example, detailed the impressive success which the party machine had achieved in securing 1,500 postal votes in the Dover constituency, a traditionally marginal seat which was held by Labour. All the other information was like that: interesting but valueless. Knowledge that it is going to rain does not stop it raining. Knowledge of the Conservative Party's ability to organise a substantial postal vote would not have helped the Labour Party in Dover, which lost the seat.

The only lesson to be learned from the episode, perhaps, was never to recommend anyone for an honour who asks for it, which followed my natural inclination, anyway. Kerby was an eccentric in politics. Though a Conservative, and a right-wing one, he detested the top-drawer Tories and the upper-class attitudes of some members of his party. He was a man of the right who spoke fluent Russian, a Tory with a great admiration for Harold Wilson, largely, I suspect, because he had no time for those inscribed on the social register either.

Nor was it the first time that he had been willing to dish his Parliamentary colleagues and help the Labour Government. On September 2, 1965, the then Speaker of the House of Commons, Sir Harry Hylton-Foster, had collapsed and died in the street. His obvious replacement was his deputy, Dr Horace King, a Labour M.P. for Southampton. But that meant that a replacement had to be found for Dr King; if the Conservatives in the Commons refused to co-operate (and that is what they were threatening) the Government would be under an obligation – or so it seemed – to find a replacement from its own ranks, thus halving its already minuscule majority of two.

In the event, a Liberal M.P., Mr Roderic Bowen, Q.C., took the post and preserved the overall majority. But the Prime

7 Marcia Williams and Harold Wilson relaxing during a Labour
   Party conference at Blackpool.

8 Victory night, February 28, 1974. Harold and Mary Wilson at
   Huyton.

9 An election campaign meeting at the Wilsons' Lord North Street home. *Seated, left to right*: Peter Davis (now Lord Lovell-Davis), Dennis Lyons (now Lord Lyons of Brighton), Dr Bernard Donoughue, Mary Wilson, and Marcia Williams (now Lady Falkender). *Standing in the doorway*, Bill Housden, B.E.M., M.B.E., Harold Wilson's driver.

10 Economic crisis press conference, July 11, 1975. Harold Wilson and Denis Healey, with Joe Haines on the left.

Minister was never worried, despite dire newspaper predictions of loss of his majority leading to a General Election and catastrophic defeat. Captain Kerby had already approached him and volunteered to fill the post. The irony was that if that offer had been accepted Kerby would automatically have qualified at a later date for the knighthood he coveted so much. Perhaps even in 1965 that was part of his motive. In the event, he did not long survive the Conservative victory at the polls and died with only his army rank to distinguish him from all the other misters.

When Labour emerged from the General Election of February 1974, as the largest party and the certain Government —delayed though that was by Edward Heath's reluctance to relinquish the premiership—the telegrams of congratulation began to flood in. One of the first, and certainly the most enterprising, came from a defeated Labour candidate: 'Congratulations,' he proclaimed, 'on a magnificent victory. I stand ready to serve you in another place.' 'Another place' is the euphemism by which members of the House of Commons describe the House of Lords, which is where the sender of the telegram is today.

Of course, there is good reason for sending ex-M.P.s to the House of Lords; not least the fact that they already have a knowledge of the legislative process which it can take a newcomer years to learn. But Westminster is an irresistible magnet to those who have known it; Lords or Commons does not seem to matter. One of my most regular correspondents during Opposition between June 1970 and February 1974 was a member of the 1945 Parliament who lost his seat in the 1950 election and was still hoping, more than twenty years later, to return. In all those years away from Westminster he had defended the Labour Party and its leadership on public platforms and in the correspondence columns of the newspapers. He was unswerving in his loyalty. Perhaps that was his mistake. He never received the ennoblement he craved. His last letter to me was a plea for a peerage, but wanting is not enough. If it was, all the bank vaults in London would not be large enough to accommodate the coronets that would be deposited within them.

For a socialist party, we certainly pay too much attention to

L

preserving the honours system broadly as it is and too little to considering a sensible modification of it. Between the extremes of the argument – those who wish to abolish any form of honours whatsoever, even an Order of Lenin, and those who want their trunks sashed, their legs gartered and their breasts bemedalled – there are very few who advocate a middle course: a system of honours awarded either for really exceptional service within the recipients' chosen field or for some other distinctive contribution to the community.

If we are to continue with an unelected second legislative chamber – and hope of a really radical change is non-existent – then we should separate the creation of life peerages from the honours system. There can be no excuse today for sending anyone to the House of Lords who is not prepared to work at the legislative task and only wants to gratify a desire to be addressed as 'My Lord' or 'Milady'.

Tinkering with the powers and composition of the Lords is unthinkable after the 1969 failure to get quite minor changes through the House of Commons. But one useful and uncontroversial amendment could be made to the Life Peerages Act: namely, that a life peer should be stripped of his (or her) title if there is a persistent failure to take part in the work of the Upper House. Then if there was any truth in the suspicions that some people elevated to the peerage were more concerned with the title than the obligations, we would be able to identify them.

Though during his first term of office Harold Wilson greatly reduced the number of honours automatically allocated to civil servants, there are still far too many of them. Every permanent secretary has a knighthood in his knapsack to cap the other honours he has collected on the way to the top. (The progression up the scale of honours for permanent secretaries, C.M.G. – 'Call Me God', K.C.M.G. – 'Kindly Call Me God', and G.C.M.G. – 'God Calls Me God', is Whitehall's oldest statutory joke.) But there is no reason why a man who is paid at the rate of over £20,000 a year (1976 levels), has a job whose security even dynamite could not dent, has an inflation-proofed pension waiting for him on retirement at sixty and the prospect of a further few years' profitable employment in industry after that, should also, as the Scots say, be dunted by the Queen. If that is what he wants he should climb Everest.

There is a serious case for removing the compilation of the Honours List out of the hands of the civil service and the Prime Minister. At present, 10 Downing Street houses an Honours section, staffed by permanent civil servants and under the direct control of the principal private secretary to the Prime Minister. The section keeps an index of everyone ever suggested for honours, those awarded them (and those who have refused), prepares the lists for submission to the Queen and dispatches the formal letters which go to intended recipients. The advice and recommendations to the Prime Minister stem from a network of official sub-committees and a main committee which are under the direction of the Head of the Home Civil Service. (This system ensures that senior civil servants who are candidates for honours are recommended by senior civil servants who have been, or are likely to be, candidates for honours. There is inevitably a tendency to regard this as a 'You scratch my back and I'll scratch yours' system.)

Anyone can recommend anyone else for an honour in one of the twice-yearly lists: that published on the Queen's official birthday on the second Saturday in June or that issued on New Year's Day. A letter to the principal private secretary at 10 Downing Street, giving some supporting reason why your nominee should be honoured, is enough. Then the civil service machine will begin the process of sorting and sifting which eventually benefits the chosen six or seven hundred every six months. While there is no reason why an individual should not recommend himself, the prospects of success are not bright. (If you are minded to try to secure an honour for someone you admire, bear in mind that the wheels of the system turn exceedingly slowly and thoroughly. To ensure inclusion in the June list, for example, recommendations have to be submitted by the beginning of February, and by mid-September for the New Year Honours.)

At least 90 per cent of the honours awarded each year, perhaps more, come through the machine in this way; inevitably, they often reflect the opinions, enthusiasms, and cultural inclinations of civil servants rather than the Prime Minister himself. The incidence of organists and architects in recent years has always seemed high in relation to their contribution to our music or to our public buildings.

I cannot see any fundamental constitutional principle which makes it inescapable that the Prime Minister – in effect, though not in theory – should be the fount of virtually all honours. An Honours Committee composed of disinterested and distinguished men and women – to belong to which might itself be regarded as an honour – could be made responsible for drawing up recommendations to the Queen. If the numbers of awards were strictly limited, say, to about 250 a year, civil servants could then take their chances along with the sportsmen, the musicians, the district nurses, the exporters and the rest, and their worth would be enhanced. The Prime Minister would retain his right to nominate life peers because of their legislative functions.

We might also, then, remove some of the ridiculous inequalities and attitudes which led, until recent years, to Rugby Union players being more favourably regarded than Rugby League players, or amateur cricketers having an edge over professional cricketers and footballers. Hockey, fencing, show jumping, real tennis and other such minority sports have always been a more acceptable source for quarrying honours candidates rather than the sports of the masses.

I remember one occasion when Harold Wilson, in preparing the 'stardust' to complete the Honours List called a small meeting of civil servants and one Minister to discuss possible names. I had suggested including the name of a popular woman athlete who had brought great distinction to her chosen event. But we were told that the advice of the responsible department was that she should not be included in the list. When the Prime Minister insisted on knowing what the objection was to her he was told that she had been having an affair with another (male) athlete and that all the British team knew about it. The Prime Minister raised his eyebrows above an otherwise straight face and asked me what I thought about that. I said that the department's objection appeared to me a valid one and that the girl should be left out – but only on the understanding that everyone else in the list under discussion, as well as future lists, who was thought to have slept with someone not their spouse should also be omitted.

'That,' said the Prime Minister, 'settles that. If we started taking that line we could end up with a very thin list.' I am prepared to bet that similar objections were never raised on behalf of any Rugby Union internationalist.

That honours are often gained by influence is certain. If an M.P. recommends you, then you have a better chance than if the local postman does, because the Prime Minister will be made aware of it. A Minister's recommendation matters even more, and someone who has access to the ear of the Prime Minister matters most of all.

In the latter days of Harold Wilson's premiership there was a widespread, not to say universal, belief among the staff at 10 Downing Street that many of those who had been honoured were friends of Lady Falkender, herself created a baroness suddenly and surprisingly in June 1974. That decision had contravened the criterion for ennoblement that the Prime Minister had himself laid down, that only those who were prepared to work in the Upper House should be given life peerages, and subsequent creations were to infringe the rule, too. Lady Falkender explained that it would be invidious for her to speak in the House of Lords while she was still political secretary to the Prime Minister. So she toiled not in the Upper House, neither did she vote, though there was no good reason why she should not join the small band of Labour peers who regularly supported the Government in the Division Lobbies. If she did not intend to use voice or vote while Harold Wilson was Prime Minister then there was no reason why she should not have waited until his retirement for her ennoblement. After all, she was one of the select handful who always knew that Harold Wilson did not intend to spend more than two years in office in his second term.

In the event, his Resignation Honours List caused enough controversy as it was. Several of the more inexplicable names were leaked in advance to various newspapers, but principally the *Sunday Times* and the *Daily Mail*. When they were eventually confirmed – only one person, Mr Jarvis Astaire, the impresario, among those tipped was not included in the published list – there was an outcry in the press, in the Parliamentary Labour Party, and in the party more widely.

By tradition, the Resignation Honours List rewards those people who have been of personal service to the Prime Minister during his term of office, but on this occasion they were accommodated in the steerage section of the list: Chequers staff, a senior telephonist, the policeman who guards the door at No. 10, the Prime Minister's driver and so on. Transport House staff and other Labour Party workers were modestly recognised, too. Two former M.P.s, Terry Boston, who had assisted on the press side during the two 1974 election campaigns, and Albert Murray, sorely-pressed manager of Harold Wilson's political office since the autumn of 1973, were also included.

So also were two knights, the brothers Lew Grade and Bernard Delfont; Sir Joseph Kagan, an old friend and manufacturer of the Gannex raincoats which the Prime Minister habitually wore, even when it was not raining; Professor John Vaizey, who reportedly had left the Labour Party and was a trenchant critic of Harold Wilson's (but had been helping Lady Falkender in her search for a suitable public school for her two children); Sir Max Rayne, a property millionaire; and Sir George Weidenfeld, Harold Wilson's and Lady Falkender's publisher. All joined Murray and Boston in the Lords.

Of the eight new knights, James Goldsmith was the most controversial. He, like most of the peers and knights, was a Lady Falkender nomination.

When that list was still in its earliest stages – that is, when Harold Wilson was still Prime Minister – I had warned him strongly, through his principal private secretary, Ken Stowe, that the public reaction to it would do considerable damage to his reputation. He had given to me and Stowe, in the previous October, the task of drawing up the plans for an orderly, dignified, and sensible transfer of power when the time came for his resignation to be announced. That we had done. Throughout our deliberations we had been anxious to bring about a constitutional innovation that would stand any government in good stead as a precedent. To obscure the valuable by the indefensible – for the original intention had been to publish the list on the day the Prime Minister ceased to hold office – seemed to us a dismal prospect, out of keeping with all that had gone immediately before.

The warning was not heeded, but the reaction, when it came, proved its validity up to the hilt. When the list was published on May 27, 1976, the *Guardian* commented:

Sir Harold can do — and has done — what he likes. But that does not mean that anyone else has to like it much. Today's list is frankly distressing for two prime reasons — both of them, in essence, a matter of honour. There is the point at which personal patronage has to stop. And there is the point at which straightforward commonsense dictates a certain seemly restraint. On both counts, Harold Wilson has strayed into grey territory.

The *Daily Telegraph*, a newspaper which succours the Conservative Party, like a Fleet Street St Bernard, when no one else has a good word for it, naturally relished the list, even though its proprietor had reached the Lords by way of an earlier Harold Wilson recommendation and its proprietor's wife occasionally lunched or dined with Lady Falkender. After exulting over the retiring Prime Minister's 'choice of cronies', the *Telegraph* went on: 'It is a fitting legacy from an in many ways absurd Prime Minister.'

George Hutchinson in *The Times*, sensing that a near-mortal blow had been struck at an institution which he venerates (and whose proprietor, too, was a hereditary peer though of Sir Alec Douglas-Home's creation) wrote fiercely:

Sir Harold Wilson's retirement from office, to all appearances well managed at first and dignified by his own appointment as a Knight of the Garter, has been irretrievably damaged. No honours list, resignation or otherwise, has ever been attended by such farce ... no individual recipient, however deserving, can feel altogether happy. Who could wish for inclusion in a roll call giving rise to universal astonishment and derision?

The answer to that question, of course, was the very people whose names had given rise to the derision. Hutchinson thought that Harold Wilson had 'demeaned' the office of Prime Minister, 'embarrassed' the Crown, 'injured' the Labour Party, and discredited the honours system. He went on:

While it is right that principals should accept the blame when things go wrong, Sir Harold's amanuensis and adviser (one might almost say accomplice) can hardly be exonerated. Lady Falkender has claimed too much influence and responsibility in the past to escape comment and attention now.

Hutchinson advised Lady Falkender 'to lie low for a while', but Lady Falkender pays a lot of attention to what appears in *The Times* and she exploded into print, despite the fact that it was a Bank Holiday week-end, and wrote furiously to *The Times*. She had, she said, 'read with disgust' George Hutchinson's article. It was not the first time 'wounding and highly inaccurate' stories about her had appeared in *The Times*. Two years earlier two articles about her were written more in the manner of *Private Eye* than in that of 'what was once our leading newspaper'; indeed, *Private Eye* had been quoted to her (by a *Times* representative) as a precedent justifying the newspaper's behaviour. The inaccuracies in those articles were 'so legion' that she had refrained from comment. But she had always respected George Hutchinson (although she did not know him personally, she added later) so she could not allow what he had said to pass without reply. She stated, flatly and firmly: 'The Resignation List was Sir Harold Wilson's list and his alone.'

Lady Falkender said that the 'leaks and comment', which preceded the publication of the list and emanated from the *Sunday Times*, must be a matter for concern. It was unprecedented and represented leaks within the Government machine on a subject which she understood was kept as tightly secure in No. 10 as matters affecting state security. It was clear that someone in the public service had broken their trust by leaking 'a secret and confidential document'. She plainly thought that these indiscretions should be placed on the same level as the most sensitive intelligence matters, for she said that 'those who uphold our liberties and security' should be concerned about them. The secret nature of the Honours List, however, has more to do with not offending the Queen than anything else. It is a matter of courtesy, not security.

Lady Falkender said that she found the comment on the list 'sickening', not just that by George Hutchinson but by others too. It was a 'sanctimonious protest by the unimaginative half of the Establishment on their own behalf'; 'unadulterated snobbery'; and, 'much more serious, it has often been covert anti-semitism'.

The letter continued in that vein for another 1,500 words or so, full of the hints of conspiracy, malice, and dark motives which anyone who knows Lady Falkender well could write blindfolded – 'Perhaps behind this whole affair lies some other story, some other motive for it, where frustration, malice and envy are being expressed in a final attack upon a man who has contributed so much to our national life ... '

She rejected Hutchinson's suggestions that she had too much influence over Sir Harold, saying: 'The press have continually claimed I had it, or claimed that I claimed that I had it. But that does not mean I did. Nor is it true.'

Lady Falkender then quoted from a letter she had sent to the *Sunday Times*, in which she had written:

> ... it is the case that the Prime Minister would consult certain members of the staff about names for inclusion in the Arts and Sports sections, and together with Bernard Donoughue and Joe Haines and others, I have been consulted specifically on those parts of the Honours Lists.

The casual reader of *The Times* that day – if there is such a creature – might have thought that Lady Falkender was saying that Bernard Donoughue and I had been consulted on the Honours List which all the fuss was about, but of course she was not.

Her flat declaration that, 'The Resignation Honours List was Sir Harold Wilson's list and his alone' was true, but only in a narrow, technical sense: that he and he alone had the right to submit a list to the Queen (after all, he was the Prime Minister who was resigning) and that no one else could bear the responsibility for making recommendations.

But the list from which Sir Harold Wilson prepared his own list was Lady Falkender's written out in her own hand on the lavender-coloured notepaper she often used. It was that list, with a few deletions and a few additions in the Prime Minister's handwriting, which the principal private secretary used when he set in motion the inquiries and procedures which are always followed before a submission is made to the Queen.

In the event, some of the names did not survive until the

published list. Prudence removed a couple. One or two declined. The names added by Sir Harold improved the quality of the list, but the substantial majority of the knights and peers who were in the published list were those originally proposed by Lady Falkender.

I was shown her proposals for the list by the principal private secretary, who acted quite properly because he knew it was the Prime Minister's custom to consult me about honours which might provoke public comment; because of my reaction to them he specifically asked the Prime Minister to speak to me before he went any farther. But, exceptionally, on this occasion neither I nor Bernard Donoughue was asked to comment.

I had, however, discussed some of the Resignation Honours List's obvious candidates with the Prime Minister over a long period before his resignation was announced. I was anxious to ensure that two people who had served him with devotion – Albert Murray, the manager of his Political Office, and Bill Housden, his driver from his Board of Trade days under Clement Attlee's Government – should not be overlooked. After I had seen Lady Falkender's preliminary list I asked that two further names should be added at the M.B.E. level – which were accepted – and another at C.B.E. level, which the intended recipient later declined.

It is true, as Lady Falkender had written, that a tight security net was drawn round the Honours List operations at No. 10. It is also true, however, that she, together with Bernard Donoughue and I, were inside the net. We were all regularly consulted on the Arts and Sports sections, but also more widely. There was no Sports section in the Resignation List, unless the description is applied satirically, and the Arts section, by my interpretation of its meaning, was confined to knighthoods for the actors Stanley Baker, who died a few weeks later, and John Mills, two awards I heartily applauded.

But as so often and depressingly happened where Lady Falkender was concerned, the shadow became the substance. It was the leak, by malicious persons unknown, that became the primary issue. It was evidence of 'anti-semitism'; and of the hostility of the Establishment. That there might have been some justification for criticism of the list was never admitted. That members of Harold Wilson's staff who had worked with and for him for years shared that criticism and expressed it, for his reputation's sake while there was still time to change it, was ignored.

The fact is that almost every person on the upper slopes of the list was as well known to Lady Falkender as to the Prime Minister himself. Some of them were undoubtedly better known to her than to him.

For example, until only a few months before his resignation, Harold Wilson had never met James Goldsmith, the City of London financier and chairman of Cavenham Foods, Ltd. In 1974, the then Mr Goldsmith, according to David Butler in his book on the October 1974 General Election – one of his standard works on British General Elections – was still a contributor to the funds of the Conservative Party. George Hutchinson, in his article in *The Times* on May 29 which provoked Lady Falkender's 2,000-word response, stated: 'James Goldsmith is a declared contributor to Tory funds. As such he is much esteemed by the party treasurers.'

Mr Hutchinson is a former senior official at the Conservative Central Office, and few know better what would earn a Tory treasurer's esteem. It would not be peanuts.

A dinner engagement at the home of Mr David Frost, the television interviewer, which was arranged through Lady Falkender in the autumn of 1975 was cancelled when Harold Wilson discovered that the other guests were to be Goldsmith and Jim Slater, of Slater, Walker Securities. The Prime Minister made it plain to me that he could not, as head of a Labour Government, be known to be dining privately with City of London financiers. He had, after all, made it a consistent theme of his speeches over the years to condemn 'those who *make* money rather than *earn* money'.

A few weeks later, Harold Wilson did meet Goldsmith when David Frost brought him to No. 10 for a discussion on French economic planning techniques, of which Goldsmith knew a great deal. The Prime Minister was impressed with Goldsmith's exposition and by his ability in and mastery of financial matters. That meeting merited a letter of thanks, but not inclusion in the honours list.

Marcia's admiration for Goldsmith's abilities was reciprocated. Shortly before Harold Wilson left office, but after the announcement of his intention to resign, Goldsmith was a luncheon guest at No. 10. The only other person there, apart from the mandatory private secretary, was Lord Ryder, chairman of the National Enterprise Board, and the discussion centred on what lessons the French industrial planning experience might have for Britain.

After the lunch was over, the Prime Minister told a small group of us at his room in the House of Commons that Goldsmith intended to offer a directorship of Cavenham Foods, Ltd, to Lady Falkender. Though he recognised that if it came about it would mean her leaving his employment, he was facing the prospect with cheerful fortitude.

The publication of the list temporarily overshadowed the remarkable career and contribution to public life of Harold Wilson. But the most depressing feature of its aftermath was the refusal by him or by Lady Falkender to acknowledge that there was justification in the press, public and parliamentary anger that was aroused. Instead, the allegations of 'anti-semitism' were renewed and the former Prime Minister demanded of the new Prime Minister that a thorough inquiry should be carried out to discover the culprit, the person guilty of leaking the controversial names he had recommended—or, in the Jarvis Astaire case, not recommended—to the Queen. (A subsequent inquiry into who leaked the news of *that* inquiry to the *Observer* would, if successful, produce a highly amusing result!)

Sir Philip Allen, a former permanent secretary at the Home Office and thus an expert in intelligence matters, who was about to become a peer in Mr Callaghan's first list, was nominated by Harold Wilson to take charge of the investigation. A number of civil servants were interrogated, and so was I. But on Harold Wilson's instructions, neither Lady Falkender nor any other members of his Political Office staff were interviewed by Sir Philip. In other words, there was a presupposition that the disclosures must have been made by a civil servant or by more than one. But I know for a fact that a small group of people outside the civil service knew if not the whole list at least parts of it.

At the end of my interview with Sir Philip, a charming if reluctant detective, I expressed the hope that if he discovered the leaker he or she would qualify for inclusion in a future list. In the event, Sir Philip drew a blank and, I suspect, was heartily relieved to have failed.

8

Mirror, Mirror...

'Now, I give you fair warning,' shouted the Queen, stamping on the ground as she spoke; 'either you or your head must be off, and that in about half no time!'

Alice in Wonderland

That Lady Falkender's influence with Harold Wilson was powerful – indeed, all-pervasive – is undeniable, however much it may be denied. No one who worked in his office, in Downing Street or in Opposition, for more than a few minutes could be unaware of it. Every typist and every civil servant knew of it and could testify to it. Many of them went in dread of her; the fact of her power was like a baleful cloud hung permanently over their heads. By the time Harold Wilson went out of Downing Street in April 1976, there were only two views about her held by the staff, and they were both unprintable. But those outside or who only knew her from the showbiz/social round were always strikingly impressed by her charm and intelligence, and her admirers included some of the most honoured people in the land, often the most recently honoured.

Any future historian's appraisal of Harold Wilson's role as Prime Minister and Leader of the Opposition will be incomplete unless he comprehends the full extent of her sway. When Harold Wilson left office his reputation as a leader stood more secure than at any time since 1964. He had not got out when the going was good, but when it seemed to be getting better. A large part of the nation was sorry to see him go and grateful for what he had done for it. It had not always been like that. The years between 1970 and 1974 had dealt some terrible blows both to his standing and to his morale. The apparent changes of front over the Common Market and the referendum, the appearance of weakness over policy in relation to the National Executive of the Labour Party—every Labour leader appears weak in Opposition—all contributed to the image the Conservatives sought to promote: of a man who would do anything in order to stay in office. That was not true—at the party conference in October 1972 he was ready to resign if the N.E.C. and conference pressed a proposal that the party should commit itself in principle against entry into the E.E.C.—but it was widely believed.

The years 1974 to 1976 marked a long climb back from the cynicism that accumulated about him in the years that went before. But it was achieved during his last premiership. For months he accepted that his appearances on television, which had been too frequent in the past, should be sparing almost to the point of non-existence. Television exhausts a politician's appeal and encourages cynicism. When a Prime Minister is speaking on the small screen it should be an event, not an incentive to the viewer to switch off. Between the end of the February election campaign and the opening of the October one he got on with his job and largely stayed off television and radio except for one major interview with Granada.

All this, the more relaxed style of his premiership, his willingness to let his colleagues get on with their work, the creation not only of the public image of an experienced team of Ministers but also a real team spirit in Government, regained the credit that had been lost.

Yet in the end he was ready, as I showed in Chapter 7, to put it at risk—a risk of which he was well aware—by deferring to the views of Lady Falkender. That is the measure of the power she exerted.

A close friend and confidant of Harold Wilson's, one of the very few who knew of his intention to give up office, said to me in December 1975: 'Mr Haines, he will not go down in history as one of the great Prime Ministers, but if it had not been for that woman, he would have gone down as the greatest.'

That is a harsh judgment, but I have some sympathy with it. By her unpredictable tempers she demoralised not only those who had to work with her, but Harold Wilson also, yet she wielded power with the Prime Minister to a degree unequalled by any person in my experience. If, in the latter years,

that power had no effect on central issues of policy, that was a
tribute to the democratic structure of the Labour Party and
the Government, which limits what even a leader or a Prime
Minister can do.

There were many times when the smallest imagined slight by
a colleague might be transformed into a major scene into
which an unwilling Prime Minister was dragged to act as
peacemaker. Particularly after the trauma of the land deals
affair in April 1974 and the subsequent conferment of a peerage
upon her – with both of which I deal later – an eruption of
suspicion and accusation could spring from the most trivial
of causes. At this time her dislike of Bernard Donoughue
became obsessive. I was in his office on one occasion in 1974
when he asked the telephone operator to get Marcia for him.
That alone – going through an operator, not making the call
himself – was enough to provoke an explosion of bad temper.

A telephone call from her one day to Albert Murray could
not be put through because he was speaking to me at the time.
When the operator told her that Albert was engaged, Lady
Falkender instructed that our call be disconnected so that she
might speak to him. The operator – to my fury – did so and then
told me what had happened. That demonstrates power.
Rightly – as I believe – or wrongly – as she would maintain –
the staff at No. 10 were afraid of her wrath and afraid that the
unintended or imagined slight would lead to a complaint to
the Prime Minister.

Why was so destructive a force so influential? Why was she
not in turn destroyed by the simple act of dismissal? After more
than seven years with Harold Wilson, with him almost every
working day – spending more time with him, indeed, than any
member of his staff, including Lady Falkender – I do not know
the answer, except, perhaps, that it lies deep in his own
insecurity.

Because of the insidious gossip which persisted over the
years, it needs to be said from the outset that I never saw the
slightest sign of any affection between them. But she met for a
great many years a deep craving within him: for someone else
to whom politics was meat and drink and the very air that was
breathed; someone who, at her best, had a political mind
capable of testing and matching his; someone who, again at

her best, possessed a deadly ability to slash her way through the woolliness and verbiage of political argument to get to the heart of an issue. Someone who was prepared to devote all her time to Harold Wilson's service; and someone who, at the very worst moments, was always there.

Lady Falkender was not always a just target for attack.

In 1956, when she was only twenty-four, Mrs Marcia Williams (née Field) had a flash of political insight which amounted to a stroke of genius. She recognised, as few others did, that Harold Wilson was the natural future leader of the Labour Party, to succeed Hugh Gaitskell, the anti-Wilson leader of the party, when in the fullness of time he retired. Most political animals in those days would have chosen someone else: Alfred (later Lord) Robens (who would have been Alf Robens's choice); George Brown; Jim Callaghan; even Patrick Gordon Walker or the up-and-coming Roy Jenkins or Denis Healey. But towering above all others was Aneurin Bevan, and Harold Wilson was regarded, at best, as Bevan's junior silk. Both Bevan and Gaitskell, however, were significantly older than Wilson and none of the others – all standard bearers of the right – had any solid experience in Government as a senior Minister.

Though it is easy today to look back and see that Wilson was almost the inevitable successor, it was a remarkable choice in 1956 by a girl of twenty-four, a shorthand typist in the office of the General Secretary of the Labour Party, Mr Morgan Phillips, a renowned Gaitskellite. But, then, Marcia was remarkable. Whether consciously or not, she not only recognised Wilson's leadership potential but she detected his principal weakness as well: his readiness to believe that someone, somewhere, was engaged in a conspiracy against him (of course, sometimes there *were* plots against him, but never as many as he supposed), symptom of a chronic insecurity.

Lady Falkender has herself recounted in her book, *Inside No. 10*, how while in Morgan Phillips's office she wrote anonymous letters to Harold Wilson warning him, as Chairman of the important Organisation sub-committee of the N.E.C., of a 'putsch' that was being prepared against him. I can believe it was so. Wilson was Bevan's man; Transport House at the highest level belonged to Gaitskell. Bevan never could stand Gaitskell, whatever the surface reconciliations. It would have been im-

11 Harold Wilson and Joe Haines at Chequers, March, 1976.

12 Marcia Williams leaving her Belgravia home with Joe Haines during the 'land deals affair' in April, 1974.

13 As Jensen of the *Sunday Telegraph* saw the decision by Joe Haines in June 1975 to end the twice-daily 'non-attributable' briefings of political correspondents.

14 The perfect cartoon. John Kent in the *Daily Mail* after the publication of Harold Wilson's Resignation Honours List.

portant, in the never-ending battle against Bevan, to get Wilson out of such a key position. And for a party of principle, Labour does tend to fight its battles over personalities.

There can be no doubt that Harold Wilson was grateful to his anonymous informer. Lady Falkender has explained that she was a left-winger and thus supported the party's two principal left-wingers, Bevan and Wilson. Left-winger Harold Wilson never was—just left of centre would be more accurate—and few would apply that description today to her.

According to Lady Falkender, Harold Wilson did not know until after she became his secretary, in October 1956, that she had written the unsigned notes to him. He once told me that on his way to Westminster one morning from his home in Hampstead Garden Suburb he saw her standing at a bus stop, recognised her as a Transport House employee and gave her a lift. She then confessed to being the authoress of the letters. Whatever the true version, there could not have been a better basis on which they could start work together.

Thus the girl with a political brain that ministers twice her age would have envied, had her future hitched to a star, a star which through the sudden deaths of Aneurin Bevan (in July 1960) and Hugh Gaitskell (in January 1963) was to become the brightest in the Socialist heavens a decade before anyone could have hoped.

Throughout the bad times—the Bank Rate Leak Tribunal of 1957, which led to the first really damaging blow to Wilson's reputation, the challenge to Hugh Gaitskell for the leadership in 1960, which Wilson afterwards admitted was a mistake—and the good, she was by his side, and there too when, on St Valentine's Day, 1963, he massacred George Brown in the final ballot for the leadership of the party.

She ran his private office until he became Prime Minister in October 1964, and then went with him to Downing Street. She was still only thirty-two and a power in the land, a fact that was to be increasingly demonstrated over the next twelve years.

She often claimed privately that she had 'made' Harold Wilson; that without her he would never have been Prime Minister. Like so much else that was said, it was a lavish exaggeration. He had been the youngest Cabinet Minister of the century while she was still in a gym-slip. But she certainly

M

concentrated his ambition, marked out his target and curbed his natural tendency to go rambling off down the byways of a political argument or situation.

Her relationship with Harold Wilson thrived on extravagant charges and counter-charges. But if she had a point, then it is the greatest irony of our time that, in the end, he was able to say — not only to her but to me and others — that if it had not been for her he would not have stopped being Prime Minister.

The truth of that claim, in turn, has to be measured against the fact that in February 1974 he told a small group of us that he did not intend to stay in office beyond a further two years if Labour won the election of that month, and that he would resign from the party leadership immediately if it lost it.

What is undoubtedly the case, however, is that she was a substantial part of the burden which made him too tired, mentally and physically, to contemplate changing his mind and carrying on. For year after year while I was with him, and with increasing bitterness and anger on both sides, the strain grew, though never to breaking point. At the House of Commons her voice raised in wrath could be heard well down the corridor which leads to the office of the Leader of the Opposition, and was heard. In Downing Street, the rooms were more sound-proof, but not completely.

Visits abroad were often preceded on the night before by a fierce and unnecessary row, hardly the ideal preparation for an international conference. On occasions, when he returned to London a message would be waiting at the airport demanding in imperative terms that he should telephone her to cope with some new crisis in affairs which would be forgotten after a day or two. A successful speech by him could lead to another scene. To others it looked as if any triumph which lifted him above the commonplace had to be impaired and diminished in order to bring him back down again.

Though through her influence she wielded great power, in the end it was wielded so often for trivial ends. She became a force to be placated and appeased rather than to be satisfied. Her demands concentrated more and more on the private and social periphery of the Prime Minister's life. In my first two or three years — in fact, up to the return to Downing Street in

1974—almost every major Prime Ministerial or leader's decision had to await Marcia's comments. Time and effort were constantly wasted by the need to humour her. Speeches were still incomplete as the time for delivery approached because her reaction to the drafts had not been received. When her copy of the draft was returned it often consisted of no more than scrawled comments of 'Rubbish' or 'Nonsense' which grew more indecipherable as they went on. The time eventually came when Harold Wilson deliberately arranged that the drafts would be delivered to her too late for her comments to be received. Finally she ceased to comment at all. It was an area of influence which she lost or surrendered.

What she never lost was her power to claim priority over the other issues with which the Prime Minister had to deal. If she got warning of an unfavourable newspaper article that was to be published about her or her affairs, then she would telephone with a demand that Lord Goodman be instructed to speak to the proprietor. If she, or her sister or her children were unwell – and she was often unwell – then the Prime Minister's doctor had to be sent for. If she needed a car, then she would order the Prime Minister's driver to take her wherever she wanted to go. She was imperious, impulsive and unpredictable.

The left-winger of 1956 was, in 1976, at the age of forty-four a peeress of the realm, the tenant of a splendid mews house in the West End of London and the owner of a detached house in the Buckinghamshire countryside within half a mile of the Wilsons' house and within a few miles of Chequers, the country home of Prime Ministers. She had two cars and three servants and her sons attended fee-paying schools. Lord Stone was her doctor, Lord Goodman her legal adviser, Lord Weidenfeld her escort. She craved respect and respectability and she confused social status with them. When she came into Downing Street in the morning, usually around 11.30 a.m., she came in the Prime Minister's car, driven by his chauffeur; when she left, usually around 2.30 p.m., she travelled in the same car again. When she went shopping on a Friday morning, she used her own car, but it was driven by the Prime Minister's driver.

The unfortunate driver, Bill Housden, caught between the jaws of the nutcracker, would come under fire if she needed the car and the Prime Minister was using it; the Prime Minister, however, was more unconcerned. He did not mind using one of the other cars.

Her treatment of junior members of the staff went from one extreme to the other. If one of them was ill or had domestic trouble she would go to great lengths to help them – or to get the power of Government to help them. When the trouble was over she was just as likely to round upon them and make their lives a misery.

The roll-call of girls and women who were reduced to tears by her sarcasm is a long one: Mary, Fay, Jennie, Clare, Susan, all wept in front of me. Others, especially Christine and Mavis, stood their ground, never cried and never gave way. Bill Housden who had been Harold Wilson's driver, off and on, for more than twenty-five years, could be 'a lovely man' one moment and a target for attack the next. She welcomed me at first, and then, in 1970, on the flimsiest of bases, demanded that Harold Wilson should dismiss me.

There she did not succeed. She went beyond the limit Harold Wilson would tolerate and after that failure I was safe from anything she said or did. But few others were.

The sudden changes of mood were an alarming element of her character. Praise or denigration were equally likely to be lavished upon a colleague without apparent cause. She could move from a captivating charm to virulent denunciation within seconds, from engaging wit to red-faced rage. She welcomed newcomers to the Harold Wilson entourage with grace and generosity – indeed, any newcomer had to have her express approval – but if that newcomer began to enjoy the regard of Harold Wilson then she would turn upon them.

When that happened the Prime Minister would suffer a lengthy harangue about their defects: which usually included the two cardinal sins of disloyalty and 'leaking'. No story about her ever appeared in the newspapers or in *Private Eye* without someone near to Harold Wilson confidently – often with scant justification – being accused of being the source of it.

Her attempt to get me fired in 1970 followed a decision by Harold Wilson that I should write his mammoth book on the 1964–70 Labour Government from recollections dictated by him on tape. Such was her outburst on that occasion that the plan was hastily abandoned. She was appeased; I was retained.

After 1974, Bernard Donoughue became the target. Though she did not secure his departure from No. 10, the vehemence of her constant attacks upon him left their scars. Harold Wilson always prefaced his description to me of the latest charges against Bernard Donoughue by saying that Marcia was 'obsessive' about him, but always there was left the residue of suspicion that there might be something in what she said. But I was better placed than anyone to discover the sources of leaks and I never traced one back to him.

During 1975 and 1976 one could watch with a weary sadness Harold Wilson's apprehension, the frequent glances over his shoulder, that he might be seen by her talking to Bernard Donoughue and me, knowing that if he was it might be the cause of some new eruption.

Lady Falkender has left no lasting impact on public affairs; whatever the distractions she caused, Harold Wilson never neglected any vital work for her. Nor has she left any lasting impact on our public institutions, though through her influence the House of Lords is rather more heavily populated than it might otherwise have been. Her legacy is in the field of the might-have-been; what might Harold Wilson have been but for her unrelenting presence? Would he have been a great Prime Minister? Or would he never have been Prime Minister but for her? Or would he have been a worse Prime Minister? Would he have been any different?

History will decide, but the role of Harold Wilson will never be understood or properly evaluated unless the role of Lady Falkender in his political life is fully comprehended. By adding to the cares of office, did she shorten his time in office, as he was to claim? Or was that all part of the make-believe which formed such a large element of their relationship?

How was she able to compel able men, brilliant men, to defer to her? It was certainly not the protection and patronage of the Prime Minister alone. She did it in Opposition, too, when it appeared probable he might not be Prime Minister again.

An appreciation of Lady Falkender has to start from the fact that she possessed a remarkable personality which, at its peak, was overpowering. If she had been Boadicea, she might not have lost. For a time, when I first worked with her, my admiration for her sheer brain-power was considerable, almost unquestioning. Had she gone into the House of Commons she would have forced her way into the Cabinet at an age when most single women were still hoping to get married. That, eventually, no Cabinet beyond one in size would have been big enough to hold her, is irrelevant. Her great years were her thirties, when she was very impressive indeed. But like so many young men who over the years have illuminated the political heavens, she was a shooting star burning brightly but briefly, the brilliance of a lifetime fading in the fall.

I already knew Marcia Williams when I went to Downing Street in 1969, as did most political journalists; I knew, too, that she was the most important person around the Prime Minister. Then she was thirty-six rising thirty-seven, a tall blonde with a soft, half-frightened expression and blue eyes which slid rapidly from side to side whenever she felt threatened, which she often did. She was feminine, but it was her political brain which left the lasting memory.

She would dominate all about her in a social gathering, but publicly did not domineer. It is a fact about her that, unless she knows a person extremely well, she will rarely be other than friendly and charming face to face.

It is the telephone that she can transform into an instrument of torture. It is her great medium of communication, the means by which she can transmit withering scorn and discourtesy, a talent epitomised in a call she received during the February 1974 election campaign. Lord Balogh, who believed, rightly, that we were trying to avoid holding an election strategy meeting in his presence, telephoned to Harold Wilson's house in Lord North Street from Transport House and demanded he should be invited to join our discussions.

'Thomas,' asked Marcia sweetly, 'how old are you?' A pause. 'You're sixty-eight? Then why are you behaving like a child?' She then hung up. In ten seconds she had dismissed the possessor of one of the most outstanding financial brains of our time.

In the period up to the 1970 General Election I enlisted in the ranks of Marcia's admirers. Though she had no journalistic training, she could transform a pedestrian political speech by the Prime Minister into a highly effective one with a few simple but vivid thoughts, plus a general restructuring of its order. It was the gift of a first-class sub-editor. When she began by saying, 'Forgive me, fellers, for being a poor, ignorant woman, but I do not understand what this paragraph means', she was invariably right in believing it did not mean anything and she was pronouncing the death sentence on that passage.

She was then politically indispensable to the Prime Minister.

If some of her ideas were gimmicky, if others — eagerly adopted — were never followed through, nevertheless it was abundantly clear in my early days at Downing Street that the Prime Minister depended more on her advice than any other's. She was already a legend among the No. 10 staff, who would almost blanch at the mention of her name; ('Marcia's coming to see you', was always a good way of ensuring the sudden collapse of a private secretary in his chair), but it all seemed a bit exaggerated.

From the beginning she was extremely sensitive about any press inquiries about her — and news of them would send her into a panic — but with good reason. It is a tiresome fact that women holding down senior posts are still treated by Fleet Street as sex objects if they are young or good-looking, and Marcia was still both. As much for her feminity as her power she was more closely scrutinised than any of her Conservative predecessors had been. On the other hand, for the average newspaper reader she was certainly more interesting than a man.

Michael Halls, the Prime Minister's principal private secretary who died suddenly in April 1970, was her main contact with the civil service machine. He told me that she had taken objection to the middle-class Conservative attitudes of the Garden Room girls — the secretary-typists at No. 10 — and that in consequence he had had to replace a number of them. He did it, he confessed, by making their lives a misery until they sought a transfer to another department in Whitehall. It was an unpleasant story.

In the pre-1970 General Election days, though there were long periods when she did not come into the office, she was outspoken about Government policy. She was in favour of the trade union 'reform' measures contained in 'In Place of Strife', the advent of which — despite their subsequent abandonment — did as much as any other policy to lose that General Election; she opposed (rightly) the Government's policy of general support for the American intervention in Vietnam and opposed (wrongly) the Government's support for the Federal Nigerian Government against Ojukwu's Biafran rebels. She had a great interest in, and knowledge of, the reforms of the civil service proposed by the Fulton Committee; she was consulted, and sometimes deferred to, on ministerial changes, especially during the 1969 autumn reshuffle.

The legends about her — her violent changes of mood, her flashes, and more, of temper — all seemed to me then to have been embellished in the repeated telling.

It was at the 1969 Labour Party conference at Brighton nine months after I had joined the staff, that I had the first small glimpse of her destructive power at work. We were in a routine discussion about the speech the Prime Minister was to make to the conference and the air was thickening with smoke — Tony Benn — a long-time favourite of hers — and Harold Wilson were smoking pipes, three or four others of us were smoking cigars. Suddenly Marcia began to rage against the smoke which was, she said, upsetting her throat. Everything was wrong, the speech in general and the Prime Minister in particular. She was tired, she said; she was ill; she did not have to put up with it; she was going home, and home she went, back to London.

The work in hand was abandoned for the rest of the night. It was only a minor incident, but it was to be repeated more violently on future occasions. It was part of a pattern: the sudden creation of a crisis, an emotional scene, a tirade, just before the Prime Minister faced a major speech or international conference. Followed by bronchitis or influenza or a sore throat which prevented her from coming to work for some days.

By such scenes it was certainly demonstrated that she was more important than anyone else. If ever she asked the anxious question, 'Mirror, mirror on the wall...' there could be no doubt about the answer. On that occasion at Brighton I dissuaded the Prime Minister from leaving the conference to visit her sick-bed. His departure would have become known almost immediately; the party and the country would have been puzzled, to say the least, if they were given the true reason for his return to London, and if no reason was given then rumours of a sudden party or national crisis would have been rife.

Whenever one of these volcanic scenes took place, the Prime

Minister would be furious with her. When she subsequently fell
ill, then his compassion would take over. But, in truth, in those
early days and months I admired the ease with which she got
her own way. She was decisive, pungent, completely in command. The other side of her personality – the face that darkened,
the ungovernable temper, the unending diatribe – I had barely
seen; anyway, no one was perfect, and I have a bad temper
myself.

Not only did she have a unique talent for disturbing the
calm, she also had a gift for restoring it, which is a greater
quality.

One evening in the early months of 1970, she and I, Gerald
Kaufman, then the Prime Minister's political press officer and
phrase-maker, later M.P. for Ardwick and Minister of State
for Industry, and John Schofield Allen, seconded from Transport House, were with the Prime Minister in his study, holding
one of many discussions about General Election timing. Allen
was there to dispense the drinks, which he would always do
lavishly.

The telephone rang. It was an M.P. being difficult. Marcia
was gentle with him, persuasive and winning. When the call
ended, I said: 'You're such a good diplomat, we should make
you ambassador to Washington.' 'You can't,' she replied. 'I am
not sycophantic enough.' 'That's all right,' I answered,
'Gerald will teach you.'

Gerald, who was slowly sinking into a large armchair, flicked
his empty whisky glass in my direction, a gesture similar in
intent to the upward-thrusting V-signal. Unfortunately, Allen,
assiduously carrying out his duty, had just seen the empty glass
held in the hand jutting at right angles from the depths of the
armchair and filled it.

I was covered in whisky and angry. Gerald was full of
remorse and apprehensive about what might happen next, the
Prime Minister was embarrassed and John Allen was giggling,
his invariable response to most situations. Within seconds
Marcia had efficiently removed the Prime Minister from the
room, Gerald from the building, Allen from the whisky and
had begun removing the whisky from my coat. I still left No. 10
smelling like a distillery, but she had coped, with inspiration
almost.

The final decision on when to hold the 1970 General Election was taken on Monday, April 13, Budget eve, in the Prime Minister's study.

The Parliament elected in 1966 could last, in theory, to the first week of April 1971 but the introduction of decimalisation – due in February 1971 – was held to be so unpopular that the real choice lay between mid-summer and autumn 1970. The Chancellor of the Exchequer, Roy Jenkins, had told the Prime Minister that there were no economic developments likely which could inhibit the timing of the decision.

It was a purely political judgment that had to be made by the Prime Minister. In favour of waiting until the autumn was the fact that the wounds inflicted upon Labour voters between 1967 and 1969 – devaluation, the wage freeze, tax increases, the battles with the unions, Vietnam and Nigeria/Biafra – would have a little longer to heal.

Against the autumn was, mainly, the fact that everyone was expecting the election to be then. The Conservatives were banking on an October poll and were planning to spend over £1 million on political advertising during the summer months. A June election would put a stop to that.

Peter Shore, one-time head of the Research Department at Transport House, former parliamentary private secretary to the Prime Minister and in the Cabinet then as Minister without Portfolio, had been brought into the discussions about a date. He has a first-class analytical mind. He and Gerald were in favour of June; so, more reluctantly, was I. Marcia said she favoured June, provided Labour was not going to lose; otherwise she preferred to go on until the 'bitter end'. After the defeat on June 18, the Prime Minister was to commend Marcia for being the only 'bitter ender'. But she had backed both horses in the race, in which situation it is easy to be right provided everyone forgets that you were also wrong.

One strand of her thinking that made me more uneasy was revealed when she said one evening, 'Remember, fellers, that our loyalty is to Harold Wilson. No one else. Never forget that.' She always saw him as an American-style President above party rather than as a Prime Minister. That was why we had the Presidential style campaigning. From the outset, the election was fought as Harold Wilson v. the Conservatives. The role of the Labour Party was played down. The famous 'walkabouts', which were Marcia's invention, the remoteness from Transport House – Downing Street was his headquarters – all demonstrated the gamble that it was the Labour Party which was unpopular, but that Harold Wilson could drag them back into government on his coat-tails. It was a massive miscalculation.

An outsider, Will Camp, chief of publicity at the British Steel Corporation, was brought in to replace Gerald Kaufman, who had been adopted as candidate for the Ardwick constituency of Manchester. Camp was a Labour supporter, but he was not familiar to the rest of the team. As a civil servant, I could not openly be with the Prime Minister on a political trail. Instead, I stayed at Downing Street, tried my hand for the first time in writing the odd speech and radio broadcast and, with a loyal journalist friend composed about thirty articles for the press, which we issued under Harold Wilson's signature. (At previous elections he had written the important ones himself.) Camp was wrongly praised in the press for inventing the walkabouts and commended for his speech-writing, which he did not undertake. He was probably the only person to emerge from the campaign looking slightly taller. He went back to British Steel and left shortly afterwards following a disagreement over the Corporation's future policy.

During the campaign I saw Marcia each day, and for most of it. The temper began to emerge. Our campaign room was the office of Mrs Wilson's personal secretary, Peggy Field, sister of Marcia, a lovely girl and popular with everyone. One of the typists from the Political Office stood trembling outside the room one evening and asked me to pick up a file which was beneath Marcia's armchair and give it to Marcia. She had tried herself to look, she said, but Marcia declared it was not there. The girl began to cry.

I went into the room and bent to look beneath the chair. Marcia asked what I was doing and I told her. She flew into an immediate rage: face a dark red, eyes glittering, shouting at the top of her voice. I shouted back at her and said I had no intention of letting her bully me. I walked out. A few minutes later Peggy came to me and said that Marcia was under great strain, did not want to row with me and could not stop crying. Would I please go back and apologise? I apologised and the tears stopped.

Everyone was under strain at that time. Tension and the useless dissipation of energy was no help. Had I known how much time and emotional energy was to be consumed in the years to come, with greater storms over issues just as trivial, I might have quit there and then and gone back to political journalism. But I did not and, of course, the more storms there were the more easily they slid off one's back. I quickly realised how Harold Wilson put up with the scenes: he had become accustomed to paying no attention to them.

There was one lesson to be learned from that disastrous General Election campaign and it was learned. Never again should the Labour Party leader try to win a General Election divorced from the efforts and opinions of Transport House. The 1945 defeat of Winston Churchill demonstrated that the British people dislike voting for a President. It was the emphasis on the whole team which was to secure Labour's victories in the General Elections of 1974.

(Curiously, Edward Heath did not learn that lesson. Having won in 1970 more on policy than personality, he fought a one-issue campaign in February 1974 and adopted the walkabout which symbolised the cult of the personality. One can sometimes take a tactical tip from a defeated opponent, but one should not adopt his strategy.)

As soon as the first result came through on the night of Polling Day, June 18, we knew it was all up. Marcia telephoned from Liverpool where she had gone with Harold and Mary Wilson to be at the count in his constituency of Huyton, and ordered the staff to begin work on packing the boxes with files for removal the next day. The Liverpool party returned soon after 7 a.m., the misery of those early hours captured by a splendid *Sun* photograph of a weary Harold Wilson in the back of his car and his head upon his wife's shoulder. It said all that there was to say.

'Well, Joe,' he said as he entered No. 10, 'you were always the one who had doubts.' That was true, though my doubts related more to the actual date chosen. The trade figures, which in those days were, in the public mind, the index of the Government's virility and competence, were due on the 15th and it seemed to me an unnecessary hazard to publish them three days before the vote rather than four days after, if we decided the vote should be on the 11th. We never discussed the decision about Polling Day again.

As I was about to start breakfast, the Prime Minister sent for me. The speed of his physical and emotional recovery from a setback was always surprising. On this occasion it was phenomenal. He told me that on the journey back from Liverpool he had mapped out the chapters of a book he intended to write about the achievements of his first two Governments, those of 1964 and 1966.

The money from the book would help maintain a substantial office staff necessary to the Leader of the Opposition (the contribution from Transport House was only £6,000 a year, which would do little more than pay for two shorthand-typists. We had six or seven of them, as well as Marcia and me). The volume would also serve as a handbook of the successes of the Government which party workers could use during the next General Election campaign. The belief that Harold Wilson never looked farther ahead than the next week-end was not generally true in my experience.

We now had to start thinking of that next campaign, he said (which in the gloom of that morning was five years away) and it would begin with the interviews that he would give later in the day to the B.B.C. and I.T.N., when his rejection by the voters had been confirmed by the votes counted on Friday morning. I urged that our strongest card would be that we had left the Conservatives with a healthy economy, growing stronger month by month, but that we had been defeated by the wounds which the measures to achieve that strength had inflicted. He agreed and he set it out in all the broadcasts and interviews he gave that day. He persisted in that line until the economy did begin to flounder under the Conservative Government and it was the reference point for all his subsequent attacks.

When I went back to the breakfast room, someone else had eaten my breakfast and the tea was all gone. Marcia was in the middle of a bad-tempered denunciation of Joe Kagan, a long-time friend of Harold Wilson's, manufacturer of the Gannex raincoat, and a financial supporter. Kagan, a Lithuanian Jew, had survived the horrors of a Nazi concentration camp. A verbal attack for not providing a pantechnicon to remove all the office equipment was not likely to irritate him too much.

Marcia busied herself with renting a home for Harold and Mary Wilson in Vincent Square (at 80 guineas a week) and supervising the removal from No. 10. Outside a large crowd had gathered to boo any Labour personality and to cheer Edward Heath when he arrived. The bundling out of the old regime is a barbaric ritual, like a public hanging. The only moment that lightened a dark day was the news that two Ministry of Works porters (both coloured), upset by the election result, had refused to move the Conservatives out of their offices at the House of Commons. The trouble was, we needed the offices. On the following Monday we heard that the men had been sacked.

Over that week-end Harold Wilson was busily organising an Opposition. Bob Mellish who, despite his public grumbles, was always a pillar of strength, had agreed to be Chief Whip. Marcia wanted Harold Wilson to resign the leadership but he refused to consider it, except for one moment when Barbara Castle announced that she intended to stand against Roy Jenkins for the deputy leadership of the party.

Harold Wilson knew that if she did so the party would split immediately along the right-left lines of old and begged her not to. But Barbara was adamant. She had to do what was right, she said; everyone was free to do what they liked. Wilson agreed; if she opposed Jenkins, he said, he would do what was right for him and resign rather than lead a rabble. He added brutally, almost as if it were an afterthought: 'If you do stand, you won't get fourteen votes.' Barbara left saying she would stand, but she never did. When she had gone from the room, the leader's defences fell away and he visibly sagged. For a time he was utterly dejected, depressed and defeated. At that moment he might have resigned. But by the next morning he was back to planning a role for the Opposition and the writing of his book.

Then we had another scene, though of a different kind.

On the Friday afternoon, a week after ejection from Government, Marcia arrived in the Leader of the Opposition's office, sat down and quietly began to weep. Calmly, however, and with some dignity, she announced that she was resigning her post. She had, she said, sacrificed all hope of happiness in her personal life by devoted work for Harold Wilson and the

Labour Party. She had done more than enough. She was under-paid (£30 a week, she said) and over-worked. She had a family to consider and they must come first. She had come into the office only to tell us of the decision and to say goodbye. She continued to weep quietly. I was much moved.

She rose. 'I am now going to the country,' she said, 'to start a new life.' Then she left.

I was stunned. I asked Harold Wilson: 'What are we going to do?' 'Oh, pay no attention to all that,' he said cheerfully. 'I've seen it a hundred times before. She'll be in on Monday as though nothing's happened.' He was absolutely right. On Monday she came in and as far as I know her resignation was never referred to again. The distinguishing of fantasy from reality was not always easy.

Though she was not resigning, Marcia was determined, she said, to act only as Wilson's private secretary. Someone else would have to run the office and be its general manager. She asked if I would do it. I agreed (I had joined Harold Wilson on the strict understanding that my service would be for two years only, but I still had six months of that to serve and I needed to fill in my time).

The work of the office clearly needed organising and the duties of the shorthand-typists allocated. There was an enormous volume of mail to be answered. I looked forward to the task.

When I arrived the next morning to begin my duties I found that in the girls' workroom a lengthy notice, signed by Marcia, had been pasted up on the door, stipulating the hours each girl would come in and leave, when they would take their lunch, and forbidding them to make tea or coffee in the room. I quit there and then, or at least I would have done if I had had the chance. But my appointment was never mentioned again. For the first time, but not the last, I felt I had wandered into the pages of *Alice*. 'Off with his head' or 'promote him' meant the same thing, because orders once issued were forgotten or never carried out.

Ideas on every conceivable subject were fired off like rockets into the night, blazed spectacularly for a moment, and were then neglected as a new rocket lighted the political skies before its spent stick fell into a dusty corner of the mind.

In those early days of Opposition we never actually did

anything, except react to events. And since the House of Commons was not sitting much during the summer and early autumn, and since Edward Heath had decided not to do anything in his first hundred days, there was little to which Harold Wilson could react.

We meandered through that July and Wilson signed a contract to write his book and I signed a contract to assist him by doing the actual writing. I was learning fast now that things never happened in any way remotely resembling what was planned, particularly where Marcia was involved. What went wrong with my participation in the book was, literally, a piece of cake.

One of the typists who disliked Marcia as much as Marcia disliked her had decided to leave the office. On her last day she bought a cake and made some tea (strictly forbidden) for a small party to which I was invited. Marcia was not. The girl also wanted to say her farewells to Harold Wilson, but was reluctant to ask Marcia to arrange it. I told her that formality was unnecessary and that I would take her down to his office when I knew he was free, which I did. Marcia was out of the office at the time.

It was a commonplace episode, barely worth recording in a typist's diary. But when Marcia heard about it, all hell broke loose. She stormed into Harold Wilson's office and denounced me for being sly, crooked, devious, a cheat, and a conspirator, as well as being disloyal – the thrust to the heart. Tennessee Williams would have portrayed it better. One charge against me I never forgot: she accused me of 'treating the girls as equals' and I pleaded guilty to it.

Finally, she shouted: 'If you think you are going to write that book, you are mistaken. It is not going to be in your style.' And nor was it. Although I had already begun work upon the first chapter, Harold Wilson later told me he had decided against continuing to dictate into a tape machine because it would make the book too long. He had decided to write it himself. He wrote nearly half a million words, more than half by hand, in five months. It took me several months to correct and amend it; for him the physical and mental toll was such that he did not recover fully from the effort for more than a year.

Between the resumption of Parliament after the 1970 party

conference season and Christmas that year Marcia came into the office at the Commons almost every day. But in December that year a strike by the electrician's union made working conditions difficult, and so she stayed at home. After a few days the electricians returned to work, but Marcia did not. Apart from occasional spells she never came into the office again on a regular basis until after the General Election of 1974. She never liked hearing Harold Wilson's speeches and rarely attended the House of Commons. Nor did she often go to Transport House. Sometimes four or five months would go by without my seeing her. All work was done at home. If Harold Wilson wanted to see her, then he had to make the journey.

I believe this absence from the political scene for so long began the damage to her political judgment. She was a stranger to a large part of the Parliamentary Labour Party and they were strangers to her. Staying away dissipated her main asset.

Still, life in the office became tolerable again. It was not a question of out of sight out of mind, because she continued to control the office by telephone from her home, but one can always pull a face on the telephone.

She wielded the instrument like a slave driver his whip. Once launched upon a harangue, there was no stopping her, except by replacing the receiver. Harold Wilson frequently hung up on her. So, too, did Terry Lancaster, Political Editor of the *Daily Mirror*, one of the very few people with whom she would sue for peace; so did her brother, Tony Field, the first of three office managers appointed in less than three years of Opposition; so did Albert Murray, the third of those managers (the second of them, a first-class organiser and former Transport House official, Ken Peay, left after four months when he gave Harold Wilson the choice of choosing between him and Marcia because he could not stand her tantrums any longer).

So frequently did people hang up on her — or she on them — that a formula for making peace gradually developed. It was, quite simply, the responsibility of the person who slammed the telephone down to initiate the next call.

Marcia would use the telephone at almost any hour of the day or night. On one occasion when the Prime Minister phoned her when she was asleep, she waited for an hour and then

N

phoned him back and woke him 'to see how he liked it'.

On the telephone she could be withering, scornful and biting without enduring the physical presence of the person under attack; for the same reason she could be just as acid by letter. Every private secretary at No. 10 knew what it was like to receive a typewritten note – typewritten by her secretary – berating them for some fancied discourtesy or failure to perform their duty properly. But a personal meeting was different.

One private secretary who shocked his colleagues, and himself, by hanging up on her during a particularly unpleasant call, would nevertheless go into her office to see her, slump into her armchair and disrespectfully drape his legs over the side without reprisal. If she was especially difficult with the civil servants on occasion, Bernard Donoughue and I would be consulted or asked to intervene: we were their nominees to bell the cat.

Others outside the office suffered too from this telephonic torture. One day in 1974, soon after the Soviet Government had granted exit visas to the dissident Kirov ballet husband and wife team, the Panovs, I was lunching privately with the Israeli ambassador, Gideon Rafael, at his London home. Rafael is a man of great dignity who, though elderly, fought as a volunteer private soldier on the Golan Heights during the Arab-Israeli war of 1973.

Just before we sat down to eat, the telephone rang. Rafael's side of the conversation was familiar:

'Yes ... yes ... of course ... no ... no ... no ... of course I would like you to meet them ... yes ... no ... of course not ... not trying to exclude you ... please ... they're here tomorrow ... 5.30 ... please come ... '

and so on. 'That,' said Rafael to me when the call ended, 'was Lady Falkender.' 'I know,' I said.

The explanation of that episode is that Lady Falkender had asked the Prime Minister, as had many others, to press the Soviet Government to issue the exit visas for the Panovs. When it did so, he awarded her the credit. Rafael's stuttering responses were in no way reflecting an ambassador frightened by the political secretary of the Prime Minister to whose nation he was accredited; rather, they reflected the unrelenting quality of her telephone conversations. Once on the slipway no interruption could impede or deflect them. Only replacing the receiver had any effect at all. At least, I suppose it had an effect.

The principal exception to her 'no-confrontation' rule was Harold Wilson, Prime Minister or no. He was, of course, her source of power. But there was more to it than that: the way she treated him, how she spoke to him, what she said to him was a public demonstration of that power. If the Prime Minister is to be shrewishly denounced in front of civil service witnesses, those witnesses would be extraordinarily obtuse not to take heed. It did not, however, command their respect, only caution and a determination not to give cause, just or not, for a further tirade.

Party conferences were another time of trial for everyone. For Harold Wilson, for any Labour leader, the conference speech is the most important one of the year. However much the N.E.C. may posture, however much the Tribune or other groups may bluster during the year, it is the party in conference that the leader must keep at his side. The delegates to it were always the fount of Harold Wilson's strength. He must have known more of them than any man alive.

Sometimes Marcia came to the conferences, sometimes she did not. Always she was expected, but when she might arrive, when she might decide to depart was as uncertain as the Blackpool weather.

When she came in 1972, Harold Wilson, in order to placate her for some now forgotten injury, worked almost exclusively with her on his speech (though the first draft had been prepared in London). I was at that time almost permanently in her disfavour; Harold Wilson and I only discussed his speech when she was absent. The final production of the typescript, the checking of it – a tired typist may omit a whole paragraph or even a page – was left to Marcia. She went over it with Harold Wilson, as a last precaution, after breakfast before he left for the conference centre at Blackpool's Winter Gardens. I went down with him.

It has become the custom at Labour conferences for the leader to make his main speech of the week on the Tuesday morning immediately after the announcement of the results of the elections to the National Executive Committee, which is a bad moment because it means that the delegates are still discussing the voting as he begins his speech.

Harold Wilson would use much of the time taken by the announcements to go through and underscore those parts of the speech to which he wanted to give the greatest emphasis. The 1972 speech was important. In it, he intended to commit the Labour Party to the nationalisation of all urban building land, to fulfil the promise of the Liberal Party sixty years earlier to restore to the people the land that the Almighty had given to the people and which the speculators had got their hands on.

As he went through his typescript that morning on the platform, Harold Wilson realised that it contained one major omission: there was no reference in it to the public ownership of land. It had all been left on the cutting room floor, as it were. The checking and the re-checking had failed to notice that the main point of the speech was absent.

Mrs Shirley Williams, who was sitting next to him on the platform, came hurrying off to tell me what had occurred. Fortunately, Bill Housden was standing nearby and he drove me back to the headquarters hotel, the Imperial, as fast as he could go through the morning traffic. It took about seven minutes. At the moment of our leaving the Winter Gardens Harold Wilson had just risen to his feet.

The floor of the typists' room at the hotel was literally covered by hundreds of discarded pages of earlier speech drafts. There was no time for a systematic search. I grabbed one handful of paper while Bill Housden looked at another. I dropped it and snatched at a second; then a third, and third time was lucky. Within five minutes of sinking to our knees to find the missing pages we were on our way back to the conference hall. While Bill drove, I put the pages in order. We re-entered the hall exactly twenty minutes after leaving it. As I reached the platform the delegates began a lengthy hand-clapping for a just-completed passage in the speech. I handed the land proposals to Shirley Williams and she placed them in front of Harold Wilson. I then went to the front of the platform and gave him the thumbs-up sign.

At the back of the hall I asked Terry Lancaster, 'How's he doing?' 'All right,' said Terry, 'but he's a bit slow.' Slow he might have been, but if he had gone much faster he might have finished his shortest-ever conference speech before I got back. There were no words of reproach afterwards. But whether as a consequence or not, Marcia never took charge of a conference speech again.

The fear she engendered among the staff was often a cause of matters going wrong. For more than three years in Opposition the daily post was a source of irritation and inefficiency. Marcia believed in answering every letter, even those from compulsive correspondents, such as all politicians receive, and even those from mental hospitals which are not infrequent. She also said she must see every letter that came in. The girls who opened the post took that instruction literally.

If, therefore, a letter arrived addressed to Mr Wilson asking for a press or television interview it was automatically sent out on the twice-daily run to her home in Wyndham Mews, despite the fact that the girls knew it was for me to deal with. From then on, the absurd took over again. Instead of returning the letter with 'Joe' written on it, Marcia would first dictate on tape a formal acknowledgment: 'Mr Wilson has asked me to thank you for your letter. His Press Secretary, Mr Joe Haines, will be replying to you in due course ... '

That tape, when completed by the addition of a number of other letters would then be collected by Bill Housden and returned for transcription to the staff in the office at the House of Commons. As no priority was ever apparently accorded, the typing of a tape might take several days before it was completed. Then all the letters from it would be duly returned to Wyndham Mews for signature and despatch. And then a note to me would be dictated, saying: 'Mr Haines (or Joe), I have acknowledged. This is for you to deal with ... ' Back it would come to the office on tape, be transcribed, go back to Wyndham Mews for initialling and eventually land on my desk. At times, this process took up to ten days, by when the point of the interview might be lost or the visiting journalist returned to the U.S.A. or from wherever he came. If he wrote us off as being too lazy or uncaring to answer, he was wrong.

I was beginning to see what Lord Wigg had in mind when

he buttonholed me in New Palace Yard, Westminster, on the morrow of Polling Day in the 1970 General Election and said: 'Until Harold gets rid of Marcia the Labour Party will never be in office again.' Wigg and Marcia were renowned for their dislike of each other. But when the crunch came, it was Wigg who left Downing Street, where he had done a first-class job in tightening security which had grown lax in the Conservative years.

If she alienated colleagues, she was also able to inspire devotion from a few. I remember Gerald Kaufman, after he became an M.P., leaving our office one day deeply troubled and upset by something she had said to him. 'She is wicked,' he said. 'I will never, never speak to her again until she apologises.' The next day he appeared in the office – and kissed her.

John Allen was a permanent target who never bore any sign of scars. On one occasion when he was judged to be at fault – for allegedly disclosing her ex-directory telephone number to Lord Balogh – he was barred from entering the office – where he worked! – during her displeasure, which lasted about three weeks.

He haunted the corridors of the House of Commons until he was sure that Marcia was not there. Then he would come into the office. She had, however, a habit of suddenly appearing in an empty space, as though summoned by a genie's lamp, and Allen inevitably would be trapped. 'Out!' she would say, 'out!' for all the world like a Victorian parent expelling a fallen daughter from the household. And out he would go at all speed consistent with not dropping his cigar or spilling his drink. And always laughing.

He retained some affection for her, as did Lord Balogh, who was used to being treated in peremptory fashion. On one occasion, when he was disturbing Harold Wilson's concentration by noisily crushing ice with his teeth, he felt the headmistress's wrath. 'Thomas,' she said severely, 'leave the room!'

Jane Cousins, a strikingly pretty research assistant, whose arrival in the office had the same impact on morale as did General Buller's at Ladysmith, was a constant target for attack, especially after her photograph appeared in *The People* showing her barefooted at the Labour Party's special conference in 1971 on the Common Market. She was accused – inevitably – of leaking, the gravest crime in the charge sheet, whenever she was reported to have had a drink with a journalist. These stories were usually repeated to me. When I defended Jane, Marcia told me I was 'always blinded by a pretty face'. Jane was too independent to put up with it and left.

One of the worst incidents concerning the staff led to the dismissal of Susan Lewis, a young girl who had first worked as Marcia's assistant when in her 'teens. Marcia had decided not to attend the 1970 Labour Party conference at Blackpool (we never knew until she arrived whether she was going to attend a conference or not. In 1975 we hired a furnished flat for her, at a cost of £100, on the South Shore at Blackpool because the hotel accommodation was inadequate for her. But she never came and the flat stood empty for the week).

The first draft of the leader's conference speech having been prepared in London, Susan was instructed to bring Marcia's copy of it up to us in Blackpool in order that we might incorporate her amendments into the text of the next draft. These amendments to speeches were not always clear.

Susan was sent on the overnight train on the Friday evening, arriving early on Saturday morning. By then, a second version of the speech was ready and Susan returned to London and Marcia with it. She was then dispatched back to Blackpool on the Saturday evening train, with further amendments, arriving Sunday morning. She then returned to London with the further amended draft and then was sent up to Blackpool once more by the overnight sleeper. Marcia telephoned Harold Wilson with instructions that Susan was to be sent straight back to London again. Susan, whose mother was a Transport House employee and in Blackpool for the conference, as were many of her friends, cried 'enough' and said she was staying in Blackpool for the night. She was sacked instantly after a distressing interview, which I witnessed, with Harold Wilson.

In Opposition, almost every week had its melodrama. If Jane Cousins was not under attack, then I was. If not me, then it was Marcia's brother, Tony, though these were often family quarrels and no concern of mine. But their personal disputes were a factor in the eventual removal of Tony, who found when he returned from his honeymoon in June 1973 that Ken Peay was doing his job and there was no place for him. By October, Peay had gone, too.

Ken was a great loss. He was a man with a disciplined and orderly mind. He understood what the central weakness of the office was and he faced Harold Wilson with the logic of his thinking: unless Marcia went, he said, he would go. He went.

He was succeeded at my suggestion by Albert Murray, a quick-witted Cockney, Fleet Street print-room worker, and a former junior Minister until the 1970 election defeat, when he lost his seat at Gravesend. The only worry was that he might be too closely associated with me and therefore at a disadvantage. But Marcia proclaimed, 'I like Albert', at which Harold Wilson sighed his relief and announced that Albert was Marcia's choice. She and Albert existed for more than a month without a sharp word.

Looking back now on those days, it is disturbing how much time was spent by everyone – including Harold Wilson – in discussing, forestalling, circumventing or opposing Marcia. There were matters which were really too petty for us to take account of, yet take account of them we had to. Her obsessions created counter-obsessions.

Had we been the office of a small private business, these bad working relationships would have mattered only to ourselves. But we were not ordinary or insignificant. We were the machine, however imperfect, which was supposed to sustain the Leader of the Opposition – the alternative Prime Minister – in his constitutional and political duties. It was our task to prepare his speeches and statements, to conduct the necessary research, to advise and discuss both tactics and strategy.

I and others who were involved knew that we were not adequately performing our tasks. The best jockey and trainer in the world will not win the Derby with a horse that has three sound legs and a wooden one. The choice was always whether to go or to stay. Jane Cousins and Ken Peay left. I stayed. The balance was always a fine one. As I had more influence with Harold Wilson than anyone else except Marcia – influence in the sense that he would always listen to whatever I had to say, however much he disliked what I was saying – it seemed to me right that I should not leave. Also I liked the man.

But the strain, at times, was felt by everyone, including

Harold Wilson. Because she refused to come into the office except for meetings with Transport House officials about his speaking engagements, he had to go to her house at Wyndham Mews. Attempts to telephone her were usually frustrated by a servant who would state in broken English that 'Mrs Williams ees not here'. These meetings at Wyndham Mews often degenerated into quarrels that would go on past midnight.

Harold Wilson's most successful period in Opposition, when even *The Times* said he had recovered his old form, came after Marcia had gone too far and had been offensive to Mary Wilson. Harold Wilson was more angry than I have ever seen him and he banned Marcia from coming into the office (a gesture whose impact was somewhat lessened by the fact that she rarely came in anyway) and had virtually no communication with her for six weeks. But passions faded, reconciliation followed and disorder was restored.

One of her abiding obsessions was about the Royal Family. Having accepted the C.B.E. in the 1970 Dissolution Honours List, she refused to go to Buckingham Palace to receive it on the grounds that the Queen 'is a Tory'. Eventually, the C.B.E. was sent to her by the Palace authorities and she then complained that it came 'in a brown paper parcel'.

According to Harold Wilson she was convinced that the Queen did not invite her to Palace functions because she was aware that Marcia was of Royal blood (through a wrong-side-of-the-blanket relationship between a Royal Personage—George IV or Edward VII, I was never sure which—and one of her forebears). Such an attitude by the Queen, if true, would, I imagine, exclude a great many of her subjects from consideration: Charles II and William IV had more than two dozen bastard children between them.

There was an extraordinary incident at a dinner given on April 16, 1975, by the Prime Minister to mark the departure from his office of his principal private secretary, Robert Armstrong, who had held the post since his appointment by Edward Heath in July 1970. Armstrong was the principal link between No. 10 and Buckingham Palace and thus worked closely with the Queen's private secretary, Sir Martin Charteris. Lady Falkender had been placed next to Sir Martin, and the other dinner guests—there were a couple of dozen of us—were abuzz afterwards with her reported greeting to Sir Martin: 'I suppose you realise I loathe all you stand for?'

Incidents like that are usually fortified by the wine and in the retelling, but whatever the actual words used, the Prime Minister felt it necessary later in the evening to excuse his secretary's behaviour and to tell Sir Martin that she did not mean what she had apparently said.

The Queen and Marcia eventually met on the night she came to dinner after the announcement of the Prime Minister's retirement and to mark his years of service. The dinner was notable in three respects: the Queen's speech, which was witty and brief, and totally unlike the stilted clichés her advisers think it right for her to utter in public; Michael Foot's dinner jacket, which no one present had ever seen before, its middle-class conformity relieved only by a National Union of Mineworkers pin in its lapel; and Marcia's curtsey when the Queen moved along the line of guests. It was superbly executed outdoing all others, an example either of natural grace or hours of practice.

Any appreciation of Marcia written, say, at the end of February 1974, could not have been wholly bad. If she had more enemies than friends, that is not an unusual situation in politics. On the credit side, I had seen in the early days a clear, incisive and sometimes inspired political mind; a determined, ruthless, magnetic personality which, masochistically, some people enjoyed. Publicly and privately she had demonstrated total loyalty to Harold Wilson, though the private side was overladen by violent language and scenes and lurid threats of what would happen if she did not get her way. The loyalty however was primarily to him, and not to the Labour Party.

Politics was his life and she shared that life.

Harold Wilson and I were once discussing the impact of non-political events upon the political scene – to which commentators have not given enough attention – and he recalled how he had been worried in 1953 that the ascent of Everest by Hillary and Tensing, announced on the eve of the Queen's Coronation, would enhance the popularity of Churchill's Government. I said that in those days I was too young to think in those terms. He replied: 'I have been thinking like that since the day I was born.' Marcia thought like that, too, and was the only other person I ever met who did so.

Marcia could be extremely persuasive with those whom it would be risky to bully. I never saw her, for example, other than completely at ease—appealing, feminine, but exceedingly intelligent—in Dick Crossman's company. Dick was a bully who hated being bullied, but he enjoyed flattery, especially by an intellect which had received the endorsement of university success, as hers had. Crossman paid a lot of attention to Marcia's arguments because she paid a lot of attention to winning his agreement. With many people he was too clever by half, but with her he was never half clever enough.

Though always liable to outrageous behaviour, neurotic (her word to describe herself) suspicion and appalling rudeness she still seemed to me at the beginning of 1974 to offer a marginal advantage to Harold Wilson, especially because the excesses were seldom translated into bad decisions on policy matters. My view then, however, as I have said, was that her long absence from the House of Commons had impaired her usefulness. Westminster is a place to *be* in; when things are happening, the old hand can smell it in the air; it activates the politician's sixth sense. (This necessity for Westminster involvement is one reason why so many academic writers on politics know so much about the theory of their craft but understand so little of its practice.)

But if by 1974 she was a wasting asset, there was no doubt that she had contributed much to Harold Wilson's success. If she had retired in 1970 when she said she was going to, then the historical verdict on her role as the party leader's and Prime Minister's closest adviser and confidante would have found much to her credit. But during the two years of Harold Wilson's last administrations the entries on the debit side multiplied.

When the snap General Election was announced by Edward Heath on February 8, 1974, with polling day twenty days later, the first decision taken by Harold Wilson and Marcia courted disaster. Once again, Transport House was to be ignored and the appeal to the electorate was to be concentrated on the polling power of the leader, which had become more dubious. We were to fight the campaign from the Leader of the Opposition's Office at Westminster, separate from the party's headquarters a few hundred yards away in Transport House.

It would have been an appalling blow to party morale,

apart from being inefficient. Ron Hayward, the party's General Secretary, was horrified at the proposal and urged me to press Harold Wilson not to do it but to move into Transport House where he had been allocated a set of offices some months before. I did so, and so did others. After a day's hesitation when no one was sure what would happen the decision was reversed and we moved into Smith Square. The Westminster office was left to a small team of voluntary workers, headed by George Wallace, former M.P. for Norwich North and subsequently made a life peer, who dealt with the flood of correspondence.

In the event, the Wilson team during that campaign worked better and more happily than at any time during my membership of it, certainly more happily than it was ever to do again. More important, it worked in harmony with the staff at Transport House, who welcomed us back into the fold ungrudgingly and without recrimination.

Our team consisted of the three permanent members of the Wilson staff – Marcia, Albert Murray and me – and Bernard Donoughue, then senior lecturer in Politics at the London School of Economics, former secretary of the highly-suspect Campaign for Democratic Socialism – the engine room of Labour's right-wing during the 1960s – and a hard man. Bernard Donoughue had been overseeing the preparation of private opinion polls for Harold Wilson for some months but I had never met him before the election was announced because of Harold Wilson's erroneous belief that I hated all academics.

In fact, Bernard Donoughue and I got on from the start, became firm friends and sustained each other in what were first difficult weeks and then difficult months ahead. He was an academic figure sprung from the working class. His boyhood home had been in a Northamptonshire village near to where the Field family (Marcia, her parents and brother and sister) had lived.

In the hysterical atmosphere of a one-issue election – typified by the *Observer* which had the inscription 'The Miners' Election' over every election story and feature on the first Sunday, though it dropped it subsequently – in which most of the press and the B.B.C. were on the side of the Government, it was essential to have a clear and unswerving view of how the battle was going to be fought.

In a situation like this, Harold Wilson was at his best, and at his best he was better than anyone else. He never deviated from the strategy he laid down on the first Sunday of the campaign: to fight Heath to a standstill on the trade union issue – this to be done principally by Jim Callaghan, who had the unions' trust and was also the most effective television speaker – and to win the election on the other issues on which the voters were disaffected by turning that disaffection into votes for Labour.

That meant that Harold Wilson would concentrate his speeches and statements on food prices in particular and inflation in general; on pensions, where Labour had by far the most appealing policy; on unemployment, on which the Tories were always suspect; and on the Common Market pledge to hold a referendum, the popularity of which among the public had consistently been under-estimated by the press and the Conservatives.

The strategy was undoubtedly right. The manner in which we sought to implement it during the first few days of the campaign was abysmal.

Harold Wilson had a nasty bout of 'flu in the week the General Election was announced. When he spoke at Middlesbrough on February 9 he sounded jaded and he looked exhausted and journalists who saw him said he knew he could not win and the knowledge was showing.

The legend is now firm that we never thought we would win, but it is not true. From the very beginning our small group and a large part of the Transport House staff, including Ron Hayward, thought we would win – though we feared what would happen both to the country and to the party if we did lose. (One immediate result would have been the resignation from the leadership of Harold Wilson, who had told us he would stand down on the afternoon following polling day.)

Unwell though he still was, Harold Wilson decided he would dictate all his own speeches and statements to the daily press conferences at Transport House. There was no reason why he should do this unless he feared any speech-writing by me would create tensions within the office. But the first speech took three hours to dictate, subject as it was to constant interruptions. It was lifeless.

It then fell to a small group of us, augmented by Lord

Balogh, to discuss it. Tommy Balogh was popular with everyone, but he could be a trial. When we worked on a Wilson
speech he was rarely on the same page, let alone the same
paragraph, as the rest of us. He brought back memories of
reading classes at school. His financial and economic judg-
ments were always treated with great respect and consideration
by Harold Wilson but he tended to get irritated very quickly
by Tommy's political advice.

By the time the first speech was ready for delivery it had
taken more than five hours to prepare. So late was it that no
copies were available for the press covering the meeting. The
troop of reporters with him were understandably annoyed and
hostile and their annoyance inevitably was reflected in their
coverage.

For our part, we were dispirited. The day was too short for
five hours of it to be taken up with one speech. In any case, I
was always firmly convinced that committees could not write
speeches, or even rewrite them. Facts they can insert, but
phrases they cannot.

A speech drafted by one man, however badly, will sound and
read better than the contributions, however good, of half-a-
dozen people which have been spatchcocked together. I
travelled with Harold Wilson for the first few days of the
campaign and watched the speeches fall from tired lips onto a
leaden audience. With the after-effects of the 'flu still hanging
about, with mandatory television interviews, campaign committees, rushed travel, essential reading, there was no hope of
giving the campaign a lift unless we radically altered our
methods.

While he was out of the office one day we all agreed that
his system of working was endangering his strategy. He had
asked us to provide him with themes for his speeches, but he
had already laid them down himself. We decided to go much
farther: propose to him that I should draft the speeches which
he could then amend and improve, and save several hours of
his time each day. With some relief he agreed. I then wrote a
speech on food prices for delivery on Friday, February 15 at
Manchester, which brought him the best press coverage he had
received in the campaign during that first week.

Albert Murray then accompanied him on his nightly

speaking engagements while Marcia, Bernard Donoughue and
I decided on the structure of the next night's speech; I would
then write it and Marcia would take the speech to the Wilsons'
home at Lord North Street and leave it on his bed for him to
read before he slept, well after midnight. However tired he was
from one night's speech, there was never any escape from the
next night's.

For all of us, Marcia included, it meant a fifteen-hour day,
but a renewed, in the event temporary, comradeship had been
forged between us which made it not only a bearable period
but an enjoyable one.

Albert Murray and I knew there would be a reaction when
it was all over. Marcia, as she freely admitted, was kept going
by the tranquillisers which she kept in a locket she wore, but
victory was more important to us than any imaginable aftermath.

In the last ten days the campaign was perceptibly moving
our way. The private opinion polls we received each day
showed that while the Tories still held a comfortable lead when
the voters were asked for which party they would vote, that lead
was not held in the marginal constituencies where we had the
advantage; most important, the order of priority awarded by
the voters to the issues in the campaign had changed dramatically. At the beginning, the Conservatives' chosen issue, 'Who
governs Britain?', was the dominant one, reflecting the overwhelming press and television treatment of it.

But while Heath stubbornly clung to that question, Labour
had shifted the voters' attention to the issues we were fighting
upon.

The influence which an election campaign has upon the final
result is greatly over-rated; most people have decided how they
intend to vote before it gets under way. They like to appear to
be gravely weighing the merits of the contenders, but elections
are usually won in the three years before polling day, not the
three weeks.

The February 1974 campaign, however, was different. The
electors appeared to be heavily on the side of the Government
in the battle against the miners. That was a temporary movement, quickly abated, but the underlying trend was not good
for us. Heath then announced that having called the election

on the principle of 'Who governs Britain?' he was handing over the Government to the Pay Board. (He did not put it quite like that: he merely announced that the Government would accept the findings of the Pay Board's inquiry into the miners' claim. But everyone knew the inquiry's settlement would cost more than the Government had been prepared to concede to the miners, thus making the election unnecessary.)

The Pay Board in the middle of the campaign then unexpectedly gave us the bonus for which we had been looking to make our efforts take off. In a non-attributable briefing to the press one of its members disclosed that an apparent mistake had been made in the calculation of miners' wages compared with other industries and that the miners were not so high up in the 'league table' of industrial incomes as had been thought. It looked as if the Government had made an elementary mistake.

That was how the B.B.C. news presented it that night; their concentration on the miners' dispute had at last been to our advantage. And that was how most newspapers presented it the next day.

I gave the news of the Pay Board's briefing to Harold Wilson just before he left his home to speak at Hampstead and Ilford. He was then seen on television that night denouncing the Government without any response from Ministers. It was the turning point of the campaign, when our belief that we would win became solid conviction. Suddenly for the voters it seemed that the election, the blank television screens after 10.30 p.m., the three-day week, the darkened streets, the constitutional crisis, every misery that tainted an unusually sunny February, was the fault not of the miners' intransigence but the Government's incompetence.

The whole episode was a lesson to those who run election campaigns. With our tiny organisation—only Marcia and I were in the office when the news broke—we were able to react immediately. Harold Wilson spoke off-the-cuff at his first meeting and we had an updated script ready for his second.

The Tory machine, which by all accounts was over-staffed, over-confident and bureaucratic, failed to get in touch with Mr Heath who only heard of the Pay Board's press briefing some five hours or more after the press had told me. I discovered later that his staff at No. 10, who did want to alert him, could not get in touch with him because the Garden Room girl, who was the only civil servant with him, was travelling between one speech centre and the next. At the crucial moment of the campaign, Downing Street was unable to reach the Prime Minister.

(During the October General Election we paid heed to the lesson. Whenever the Prime Minister was speaking in more than one town an office in each town was manned. Contact was never lost.)

Our only fear now was that we would not have sufficient time to swing enough voters for a clear victory. Everything was going our way, despite the public opinion polls which were being published almost daily. The price of food – linked with the Common Market – had become the main issue. Jobs, housing, inflation – all had come to the forefront of the electorate's mind. Harold Wilson, the effects of the 'flu having disappeared, was living on the adrenalin which battle produces. There was a feeling of optimism right through the camp. We even took an odd hour or two off to eat a meal which did not consist of ham sandwiches, an apple, and tea in plastic cups.

It was at one of these meals at the St Ermin's Hotel that I felt my relationship with Marcia had been so restored that I could risk joking at her expense. We were idly discussing parallels between present day politicians and the figures of the past. I suggested that she might be most closely compared with the daughter of Pope Alexander VI.

She did not recognise the allusion, but to say the least she was suspicious. Bernard Donoughue, seeing her uncertainty about the value of the compliment, unhelpfully explained who that Pope's daughter had been (Lucretia Borgia). The eyes flashed and I saw nothing had changed, though I suppose that even as a joke it was offensive.

We were all to spend Polling Day in Liverpool before going on to Harold Wilson's Merseyside constituency of Huyton, where he was assured of a substantial personal victory. Unless something totally unexpected happened, we were sure it would be a national victory, too.

The unexpected then happened, or nearly so.

A reporter from the *Guardian*, Gareth Parry, called to see me at Transport House a few days before the poll to ask about a story his paper had received to the effect that Harold Wilson had been involved in land speculation in the Wigan area. I told him there could not be any truth in the story at all; he accepted the denial and left.

I immediately reported our conversation to Harold Wilson. He reacted sharply. There were clearly dangers in a Labour leader being accused of being concerned in land deals when the party was so committed to ending speculation of that kind. He telephoned the then editor of the *Guardian* (Alastair Hetherington) to repeat my denial to Parry. Hetherington had known Harold Wilson more closely than almost any other newspaper editor and accepted the refutation without question. The *Guardian* did not use the story.

The next evening a Transport House official told me that a *Daily Mail* reporter was asking to see Marcia (who was, in fact, at home). The *Daily Mail*'s interest in Marcia, whatever it was, was unlikely to further Labour's chances of electoral success. I went to see the reporter.

He insisted on speaking to Marcia, saying it was a personal matter. My first thought (unjustified) was that the paper might be intending to run an article about her two sons, whose existence was not then generally known. I refused to let him see her until he divulged what his inquiry was about. He told me it was about land deals in the Wigan area involving, he said, Marcia Williams and Harold Wilson. I told him what I had told the *Guardian*'s reporter: that any story involving Mr Wilson in land deals must be false.

He then told me that the *Daily Mail* had documents concerning the deal. I said they must be fakes. I told him that Mrs Williams was not available (which was true) and he left. That was the beginning of the affair of the land deals, the slag heaps at Ince-in-Makerfield, the so-called 'Wigan Alps'. Its ripples were not to abate during the twenty-five months of Harold Wilson's premiership which followed.

It first diverted our attention in those last vital days before the vote; it later irremediably damaged our relationships with the press; it occupied the time and energies of those people around Harold Wilson who ought to have been his companions and advisers in the early weeks back at Downing Street. It was wholly destructive, and to my mind Marcia was never the same person again.

She and her family suffered from a hounding by Fleet Street for which, looking back, it ought to be ashamed. For our part, we lost our tempers at the very time when we ought to have kept cool. We believed at first and subsequently that the motive of the inquiries by the *Daily Mail* was political at some point, either on their part or on the part of their informant. The events of the spring and summer of 1974, with the constant emphasis on the personal conduct of Labour personalities was squalid: the episode of the forged Harold Wilson signature, which was an integral part of the land deals story; the forged Geneva bank account purporting to belong to Edward Short, deputy leader of the party and Lord President of the Council; the running story of the corrupt architect John Poulson with the sometimes far-fetched association of him with prominent Labour names; the investigations into the private lives of a number of leading Labour figures because someone had made a scabrous allegation against them. Perhaps it was all part of the transatlantic shockwaves from Watergate, but it did press and politics no good. It certainly did not help the Prime Minister's office.

From the outset I was given a categorical assurance by Harold Wilson that nothing improper or illegal had occurred over the Wigan (more precisely, Ince-in-Makerfield) land deals. I had known, of course, for a long time about the involvement of Tony Field in the possession of land near Wigan. He had frequently discussed its prospects with me and made no secret about it. Though he was a friend of Harold Wilson's, no one ever regarded him as a passionate and committed supporter of the Labour Party.

Until the story broke, I was not aware that his two sisters were also his partners in the site, though I would not have been particularly incensed had I known. Tony Field had bought a slag heap in the 1960s, intending to market it, I believe, as hard-core for motorways. His purchase long preceded the Labour Party's decision to take all urban building land into public ownership, and the scandalous rise in land values during the early 1970s.

Nevertheless, I would have been naïve not to recognise that

o*

had that story appeared on the eve of poll or on polling day itself it might have cost Labour just that handful of votes which would be enough to lose it a few marginal constituencies in Lancashire and possibly elsewhere.

The last few days of the February campaign were therefore concerned more with keeping Marcia out of the hands of the press than anything else. Fortunately few journalists knew at that time where she lived.

Once Polling Day came we knew we were safe from a last-minute scare. The anti-Labour newspapers had all written off our chances anyway. The only unresolved question, apparently, about the election, whose actual result had been firmly decided by the published opinion polls, was the size of the Conservative majority.

But all the reports coming to us throughout the day were of heavy polling in strong Labour areas, particularly in the Midlands. In calling the election the Conservatives never realised that a three-day week meant that in at least half the country the workers—in the main, Labour voters—would not be at work; that they would have plenty of time to go along to the polling station and to vote. They did so.

There were four sips of nectar that night. We had returned to our hotel in Liverpool as the polling booths were closing, crossing a foyer in which a group of bored journalists were standing, the men who had been with us throughout, disconsolate at being assigned to a certain loser and wishing they were back in London where the action was going to be that night. None of them said a word to us.

Independent Television had carried out a number of interviews with electors coming out of the polling stations during the day, hoping by that method to discover not how they *would* vote but how they *had* voted. The first returns after the polls closed were showing that a Labour victory was probable.

There was a knock at the door of our hotel suite and Albert Murray answered it. It was one of the reporters from down below. He had just seen the I.T.N. programme. 'It's looking good for you,' he said. 'Does Mr Wilson want to say anything?'

The next enjoyable moment came a little later, after the first few results had been announced. The local manager of British Rail came up to our suite, offering to lay on a special coach, with press conference facilities, to take us back in triumph the following morning. He was politely thanked, but we had decided to fly back.

The third, the one with the most meaning, came at almost the same time. A number of Liverpool Special Branch detectives suddenly appeared outside Harold Wilson's suite. They had decided that the next Prime Minister was in there and they would be taking no chances with his safety.

Finally, Huyton and Harold Wilson's own count. There could now be no question that whatever the final figures nationally, Edward Heath had lost his majority. Michael Charlton, the B.B.C.'s Election Night reporter at Huyton, dashed towards Harold Wilson seeking an interview. 'Prime Minister ... ' he began. We had worked for nearly four years to hear him say that.

The people who had never believed we were in with a chance were now undergoing the kind of mass conversion which a Chinese Christian general is said to have imposed on his troops when he baptised them with a hosepipe.

In the event, we were disappointed at not getting a majority of the seats in the House of Commons and Harold Wilson did not become Prime Minister until the following Monday evening, when Edward Heath conceded that there was no way he could stay in office. Together with his team – Marcia, Bernard, Albert, me – Harold Wilson entered Downing Street just before 9 p.m. on March 4, 1974. We had two more years before the mast.

9

1974–1976

Old and young, we are all on our last cruise.

ROBERT LOUIS STEVENSON

The exhilaration of those early days back in Downing Street were never to be equalled, not even by the further election victory of October, which was less than expected and which on a personal level had soured before the polls closed. Within minutes of re-entering No. 10 as Prime Minister, Harold Wilson asked that the T.U.C. and the C.B.I. should be brought to meet him and his new Ministers. The miners' pay claim was swiftly settled on the basis of the Pay Board's report, which must have added to the pain of Edward Heath; the three-day week was ended in triumphant publicity; the street lights were again switched on, and television for insomniacs restarted. The Civil Service, as was its custom, had provided alternative copies of a Queen's Speech and the Cabinet adopted the bolder one. Marcia said that Harold would be captured by the civil servants as he had been before, and Harold said he would not. Things were definitely going to be different this time, and as an earnest of the change it was decided that we would all lunch together each day. Wonder of wonders, the arrival of the new regime at Downing Street was going to be signified by the hiring of a cook/social-secretary and an assistant.

Mary and Harold Wilson had already decided that they did not want to live 'over the shop' again. Our luncheons, therefore, would be held not in the second-floor flat at No. 10 but in the small and elegant dining room which is a kind of annexe to the State Dining Room. The Prime Minister would sit at the head of the table with Marcia on his left, the guest of the day – the occasions were to be used for discussions with people like Ron Hayward and other senior staff from Transport House – on his right and Bernard Donoughue, Albert Murray and I would complete the table.

The first few lunches were highly successful. They gave us an opportunity to get through a considerable amount of useful work. It was the only time that anything approaching the mythical kitchen cabinet – strictly, a dining room cabinet – had ever operated. But Albert Murray and I, with some experience in this field, had noticed the testy edge creeping back into Marcia's voice. She was looking for a fight. Faults were being found, slights were being imagined and the ominous description of 'civil servants' was being increasingly applied to Bernard Donoughue and me, in the tones an evangelist might use about a street walker whose prospects were more of hell-fire than salvation.

It was not long before the pot boiled over. One day Marcia tried to get the Prime Minister – and he *was* the Prime Minister, after all – to rise to her baiting. She was unsuccessful. The next day, the niggling was resumed. The Prime Minister was refusing to respond and the rest of us were feeling uncomfortable; suddenly, she threw down her napkin, red-faced and angry, and stormed out, lunch largely uneaten. She never ate informally with us again.

Her departure from the table, after weeks of close if deceptive co-operation, was a pity but it was not disastrous, and it certainly was not unexpected by the Marciologists in our ranks. What was a tragedy was that the Prime Minister suddenly stopped coming, too. He told us that he wanted to lunch at the House of Commons, to meet the new members, eat with the Chief Whip, invite this Minister and that to his table there. They would all have been praiseworthy reasons for not eating with his staff each day, if they had been the genuine reasons. But when the House of Commons was not sitting he would eat alone in Downing Street, joining us occasionally for coffee and saying that he liked his food cooked more simply. Of course, that problem could have been met by instructions to the cook.

But the squeeze was on again. If he could not eat with her – and he could not, because she would not attend the table – then he could not eat with us, if only because lunch followed by a scene is no aid to the digestion. So the practice of appeasement was resumed, the first of many such episodes in the two years that were to follow.

Later in 1974 the lunches were stopped altogether, on the orders of the Prime Minister. After he and Marcia had left we had asked all the private secretaries at No. 10 to join us. We shared and discussed each other's problems to our enormous mutual advantage and to the advantage of No. 10's work. The transition, for us, from suspected political advisers to office colleagues was speedy and complete. But there was then continued criticism by Marcia to the Prime Minister—which he adopted and repeated to us—about the 'scandal' of civil servants eating in the splendour of the small State dining room. (That only happened, of course, when the room was not being used for an official lunch.) When the cook/social-secretary had to leave later in the year, no replacement for her was allowed and her deputy, another superb cook, was asked to leave, too.

So useful had the lunches been, however, in our civil service capacity that we later hired a cook for two days a week at our own expense; we sat at an ordinary kitchen table in an unheated and tiny pantry above the roof of the Press Secretary's office. There could be no justification for banning that arrangement, though I hope future Prime Ministers will allow their civil servants to come in from out of the cold.

But overshadowing, even overwhelming, everything else in the early days of the 1974 Government was the so-called land deals affair. On March 18, two weeks to the day after Labour became the Government again, the day on which the Conservative Opposition had threatened to bring down the Government by defeating them in the vote at the end of the Queen's Speech debate—a threat they hastily withdrew when they discovered it was not the Queen's intention to send for Mr Heath if the Government lost—the *Daily Mail* published, on an inside page, a lengthy article headlined, 'The case of Ronald Milhench and his £950,000 land deals'. Milhench, a Wolverhampton insurance broker, had been negotiating with Tony Field for the sale of the land at Ince-in-Makerfield. The details of the Field family's involvement was set out in great detail. The article was the outcome of the inquiries which the newspaper had been making since the latter part of February.

Surprisingly, there was little reaction to the article from the rest of Fleet Street. The *Daily Mail*'s stable companion, the London *Evening News*, made a routine inquiry but showed little enthusiasm about the story; the *Birmingham Mail*, presumably because Milhench was in their circulation area, also telephoned my office, but no other newspaper pursued it.

The invariable reaction to unfavourable or unpleasant newspaper stories concerning Marcia was to invoke the aid and advice of Lord Goodman, who was not only the Prime Minister's solicitor and trusted adviser on wider issues but was also the chairman of the Newspaper Publishers' Association, one of the major appointments among what appeared at times to be several hundred that he held. Lord Goodman was proud of the fact that he had never asked an editor or a proprietor not to use a story; he would do no more than make them aware of all the considerations that were involved. He had been called in just before Polling Day to reason in this way with Mr Vere Harmsworth, the proprietor of the *Daily Mail*, pointing out the damage a last-minute election stunt story might do to democracy. The *Daily Mail*, after all, had something of a past record in that regard.

Though the *Mail*'s story had no reference to the alleged involvement of Harold Wilson – which had been the basis of the first inquiries by the *Guardian* and the *Daily Mail* – Lord Goodman was to be constantly consulted from then on. But without the expected follow-up from the rest of Fleet Street, the article seemed no more that a 'one-off' one; if so it could be forgotten.

But there was a circulation war going on among the Fleet Street 'populars' at the time, and the *Daily Express*, whose major Scottish offshoot had just closed down, was losing it. On April 3 it published a different story about dealings in land, concerning one of Tony Field's business associates. The *Mail*, getting advance warning of what the *Express* was up to, countered that same night with a more sensational and readable article than their rival's: they disclosed that someone had forged Harold Wilson's signature on a letter to Milhench – a story which had, of course, been known to them for several weeks.

This time Fleet Street did not, or could not, ignore the story any longer. The next two weeks were hellish. In the national press alone between April 3 and April 11 over 6,000 column inches were devoted to the written and pictorial coverage of the story. Writs alleging libel were issued by the Prime Minister and Marcia against several newspapers. Her house at Wyndham Mews was besieged by reporters and photographers, a few of whom were so rude and importunate that they blackened the name of every journalist. For days, anyone entering or leaving the house was photographed or questioned. I watched from inside while three or four reporters tossed a coin to see which of them would be the next to knock on the door. On one occasion, children were encouraged to do so, too. Despite requests, the police made no attempt to stop the harassment or the obstruction of the path to and from the house. Inside, the curtains remained drawn because reporters had tried to peer into the living room. Bernard Donoughue, Albert Murray and I went out there on several occasions, at the Prime Minister's request, to advise and console Marcia. We were all intensely angry at the sight of the continuing siege.

Harold Wilson's relationships with the press were never worse than at that time, and neither were mine. Looking back from the calm of more than two years later, I wish we had all reacted with less obvious feeling. But each of us had been working a ninety-hour week for more than two months; the anti-Labour press during and after the election campaign had been more virulent than at any time since 1945; the behaviour of some of the journalists outside Marcia's house was dis- reputable – the worst in my experience, and I had been a journalist myself for more than twenty years – and at a time of acute national crisis we had been distracted by a personal matter which had no connection with that crisis. We saw behind the pursuit of the land deals affair the larger ambition of discrediting the Labour Government.

Were a similar situation ever to arise again, I hope I would still go to the aid of the person on the receiving end, though more dispassionately. Perhaps before it happens we might in Britain get an effective code or law on privacy. Though my handling of the press throughout that period was in the manner desired by the Prime Minister – except on the occasion when I

walked out of an off-the-record meeting with lobby correspondents when one of their number, half drunk, went too far
in his insinuations against Marcia – I never dissented from, or
disagreed with, his wishes. Most of us at No. 10 shared, or even
exceeded, his passion. However, everyone's work – from the
Prime Minister downwards – suffered in consequence. Solici-
tors were consulted; they in turn brought Queen's Counsel in
with their advice; and the police began their inquiries to find
out who the forger might be. Marcia said she would not see the
police unless they gave a guarantee that the contents of the
meeting did not leak. They did not press the point about her
and they never asked to see me. It was clear that they already
had a good idea who the forger was.

Despite the widespread anger, we could not lose sight of our
principal duty, which was to protect the Prime Minister and
to isolate him and his administration from a row which did not
involve any of them. Questions in the House of Commons were
inevitable from Conservative M.P.s. But the Prime Minister
could not be interrogated about events which had taken place
when he was out of office, as many of them had, and we urged
him to confine any other statements to robust answers to
questions which were relevant.

But he insisted on going farther and he drafted a statement
on the affair which he intended to make in the House of
Commons. In one of the rare joint minutes we ever submitted
to him, Bernard Donoughue and I wrote: 'To issue the statement in its present form, whether in the House or in any other
way, invites disaster. You would inevitably involve yourself in
the transactions which ... were not your concern.'

A somewhat modified version of the original statement was,
however, made. A sentence in it which specifically referred to
'reclamation' of the land at Wigan rather than 'speculation'
in it – a sentence which we had urged in particular should be
struck out – brought ribald laughter down upon his head. The
House had taken the statement badly, the Labour benches
were dismayed, the press's hostility had been further aroused
and the coverage of the story continued.

For Marcia, the worst moments were yet to come. One
Friday afternoon we heard that the editor of the *Daily Express*
was intending to print a story about her private life outside

politics, a life which was not the concern of the Government, the Labour Party or Fleet Street. We spent a frantic few hours with Lord Goodman's help trying to trace the newspaper's proprietor, Sir Max Aitken, who was airborne in the Bahamas area, in the hope that he might instruct his editor to drop the story. In the event, the editor did so, just before his edition time, without any word from Sir Max. By the end of that evening, however, Marcia looked to me as if she was in a state of shock, neither hearing nor seeing us, slumped silent in a chair.

Finally, after Milhench had been arrested and charged with the forgery of Harold Wilson's signature (he was later sentenced to imprisonment) the newspaper interest in the story petered out.

Before it was all over, Marcia had issued a statement exclusively to the *Daily Mirror* in which she explained that she had become involved in the Wigan venture because she hoped that the income from it could be invested in a pension for her when she eventually retired, her job as secretary to the Prime Minister being non-pensionable. When I saw the first draft of this statement I thought it was so self-pitying that it could only do her harm. So I slipped it into my pocket and took it away from Wyndham Mews in the hope that she would forget about it. She did not and asked for it back. I returned it with a substantial number of amendments designed to strengthen and improve its impact. Most of them – I think all but one – were accepted. The statement eventually issued was favourably received. The *Guardian*'s leader-writer declared that Mrs Williams was the only person to emerge with dignity from the whole affair but that the Prime Minister would be well-advised to get rid of his Press Secretary, Joe Haines. I was never more hurt by anything written about me. Marcia telephoned to express her sympathy. I said I did not think much of the (then) editor of the *Guardian* but I did not intend to issue a statement from 10 Downing Street saying he should be sacked.

Marcia did not come into the office at No. 10 for some weeks, nor did the Prime Minister visit her. Isolation at Wyndham Mews brought a renewal of the old conflicts. Bernard Donoughue, Albert Murray and I had resumed our normal work and stopped our visits to her. Before long, all the old antagonisms had been revived; it was as though we had never helped her. It was at that point that the Prime Minister decided to write another chapter in the saga, a chapter which was to provoke more controversy, rightly excite Fleet Street and worsen even more the strains and atmosphere within the office.

Shortly after his return from the Scilly Isles where he had spent Easter, the Prime Minister told me that he was preparing a new list of life peers to strengthen the ageing and thinning ranks of Labour supporters in the House of Lords. Marcia was to be among them. Everyone in the office was chilled by the prospect – me especially, for only a few weeks before I had been categorically instructed to deny a story which included a forecast of her elevation to the Upper House.

The denial was right at the time, but who was going to believe that? The primary point of the story – in the *News of the World* – had, in any case, been that Marcia was going to join the Government as a Minister of State, which at the time was legally impossible without legislation – the number of vacancies at that level is limited by law – and politically more so. What is more, I had had a total assurance from the Prime Minister that in no circumstances would he ever make her a member of his Government. If ever he had gone back on that undertaking I would have had no option but to resign. But there had been no reservations about either part of the story when he told me to deny it. I was further told not to give briefings of the press if the journalist concerned was present (which was not often). All this I did. I thus felt strongly that the Prime Minister had an obligation – a loyalty – towards his Press Secretary not to make even partly true a story which I had been asked so vehemently to deny.

He was not, however, to be moved by argument, which meant that he was committed to going ahead with the honour. The civil service were unhappy as well as Bernard Donoughue, Albert Murray and me. The civil servants concerned were, quite properly, anxious to protect the Prime Minister from further criticism. So were we, though we were thinking more widely and more politically. In order to restore Marcia's reputation by demonstrating his faith in her and the propriety of her actions, the standing of the Government itself might suffer, which was not a fair exchange. We were all sunk in gloom at what we knew would be the reaction both in the press and the party.

So strongly did we feel about it that in the early afternoon of May 23, 1974 – only a few hours before I was due to give the information, under embargo, to political correspondents – we decided that I should lead a small deputation of four to the Prime Minister urging him, even at that late stage, not to go ahead with her ennoblement. Though the list of peerages had already received formal approval from the Queen, we were convinced that Buckingham Palace would not resist a last-minute amendment to the list.

Three of us – the only civil servant concerned had rightly decided to wait outside the study – repeated the arguments I had stated before, but with greater emphasis: that the announcement would harm his reputation and dismay the party at a time when we were not discouraging, for tactical reasons, the idea that there would be a mid-summer General Election. It would restore the passions and the publicity of April which we thought had been stilled (though not for the first time I was struck by the thought that she actually enjoyed the limelight) and, 'What is more,' I said, 'I do not see how any longer I can protect her.' The Prime Minister, ceaselessly walking up and down as usual, spun round and demanded to know what I meant by that. I told him: we had always sought to protect her from publicity by arguing that she was only an employee, a private person with a right not to be microscopically examined by the press and public. What he was now proposing to do was to make her a Member of Parliament, a legislator and a legitimate figure of public interest. Though legislators are also entitled to a private life, its protective scope would inevitably be more narrowly drawn. We could certainly not complain any longer at press comments on her power and influence.

The Prime Minister answered that she would be, in fact, surrendering her influence to the three of us in return for the peerage. It was probable that she would leave his service altogether and take a post as an executive with a publishing firm. There was nothing we could do in the face of that, except silently welcome the news. But of course it never happened. We had been disarmed and the battle was lost.

The public reaction was as bad as we feared it would be, but Marcia was in her element. She felt, I am sure, that she had triumphed over Fleet Street. There was, of course, the expected abuse and the expected M.P.s said what was expected of them, but a large number of ordinary party members were dismayed, if the reaction within my own constituency party was typical. The nauseating flattery which seems inseparable from the creation of a title was there, too. But for Marcia what seemed to matter most of all was that she had gained a new respect, the status which was always so important to her. Whether or not the Prime Minister told her of our deputation to him I do not know, but relationships between us became more and more distant.

The only light relief for me came when she chose her title, Falkender. The news was passed to me when I was at Chequers for a Prime Ministerial meeting with Brian Faulkner, the Chief Executive of the Northern Ireland Assembly, which was then on its last legs, and Gerry Fitt, his deputy. Due to a mishearing on the telephone, I thought she had chosen the name 'Faulkner', which would have been strange at any time but inexplicable during the strike by the Ulster Workers Council which was currently trying, and succeeding, to bring Mr Faulkner down.

But apart from the name, nothing else changed. One still did not know from day to day who was principally in her disfavour; there seldom seemed a discernible reason why she switched from one target to another; but irrational though the attack might have been, she never fought on two fronts at once.

Albert Murray was in deep distress one evening when we left Downing Street together. The criticisms of him had been accompanied by a failure to pay his salary into the bank. He was not cushioned by an ample account and he needed the money. He did not, however, want to bother the Prime Minister and involve him in a further dispute over Marcia, who was responsible for ensuring that the Political Office salaries were paid. Albert was a loyal worker and colleague. I was so incensed on his behalf that late that night I telephoned the Prime Minister and told him that Albert's salary was several weeks overdue. The Prime Minister was aghast and he dealt with the matter the first thing next morning.

Later the attacks switched back to me (they were always

relayed secondhand: there was rarely the satisfaction of being able to face one's accuser) and there were rumours of a move afoot to 'clip his wings'.

Peter Davis, a publicity expert who had once run a Fleet Street news agency and who, with another public relations man, Dennis Lyons, had worked hard for Transport House during and in between general election campaigns, was among the uncritical admirers of Marcia's abilities. He was a frequent visitor to her office, both before and after he received a peerage (becoming Lord Lovell-Davis) in the same list as Marcia received hers. Dennis Lyons, who was not a frequent visitor, received his peerage six months later.

The rumours current in No. 10 went as far as prophesying that Lord Lovell-Davis would be replacing me as Press Secretary, but there was never any truth in them. I do not believe he had any ambitions along those lines; in any case, he had been seriously ill earlier in the year and I doubt if he would have wanted to risk a recurrence. For his part, the Prime Minister vehemently repudiated to me a suggestion in the *Daily Mail* Diary that my position was to be 'eroded' by Lord Lovell-Davis. But he and Dennis Lyons were allocated a room in No. 10 from which they could work in the run-up to and during the election on October 10, the date which had been decided some months before. (The office they were given, incidentally, was that which had been used by the cook/social-secretary; it was the simplicity and the symmetry of killing two birds with one stone, rather than the economy, which made it so attractive.)

It was clear therefore that it was in the political arena of the General Election that the wing-clipping was to take place.

The formal announcement of the election date was to be made on September 18 and the Prime Minister convened an election strategy meeting to take place in his study at Downing Street a few days before that day. Those invited included Bernard Donoughue, Albert Murray, Marcia, Lord Lovell-Davis, Dennis Lyons and me, plus one or two other people from outside upon whom we could rely.

Bernard Donoughue and I waited outside the study for some time for the Prime Minister to appear – it is never unlocked when he is absent – and we waited for a long time. Then we heard that a separate meeting, more private, was being held in the drawing room of the largely unused second-floor flat. What had happened in the February election to Lord Balogh was now happening to us. We returned to our offices. It is difficult to convey just how wearing this eternal pettiness could be, or how demoralising the constant appeasement of an obsession was. The news that we had abandoned our vigil outside the study was rapidly conveyed to the Prime Minister and we were summoned immediately to the flat.

If that was a strategy meeting, we had no strategy. The talk was desultory, the planning confused. One of our outside friends who had joined us attempted to get something settled and said: 'Joe will write the speeches, of course?' There was an unmistakable silence. Lady Falkender looked at the Prime Minister; the Prime Minister looked at a spot two feet above the head of no one in particular. Eventually he said, 'Under Marcia's direction ... the speeches.' That was all. Seeing that among her talents the writing of speeches – or the direction of them, whatever that meant – was not included, the evasion merely confirmed what we had already heard was the case: that Lord Lovell-Davis and Dennis Lyons had been or were to be recruited as the speech writers. What was far less certain was whether they knew about it. Their talents lay elsewhere but the proper use of them, and mine, was to be sacrificed to a different objective. In the event, the outcome of this episode, like so many others, was farcical.

When the election date was announced an uncomfortable Prime Minister told me that the Lovell-Davis–Lyons combination would be 'having a shot' at composing a draft for his first speech, which he wanted me to look at. After labouring for some hours on a warm September afternoon a draft was produced and shown to me. Delivered as it was, the Prime Minister would have concluded his address within ten minutes – but he rarely spoke for less than forty at an election meeting. I told Peter and Dennis it would not do, neither did it lend itself to rewriting. I advised them to put it to the Prime Minister for his verdict. So far as I was concerned, I added, it had been a hard year and if I was not needed during the General Election campaign I thought I would take a short holiday.

It was becoming clear to both men that they were pawns in

a struggle which had nothing to do with them. Peter asked the question outright: did I think they were being used by Marcia against me? I said I thought that was possible. They both made it plain that they were not prepared to be so used. Peter said he was not a speech-writer and could not begin to learn to write in the Harold Wilson style in the time available. Dennis Lyons pointed out that he was a businessman and could not afford to neglect that business in order to prepare speeches, particularly if they were to help the Transport House effort as well. Bernard Donoughue told them that I *had* decided to go home, which caused them further considerable concern.

Later the Prime Minister sent for me to ask what the speech was like. 'No good,' I said. 'You do them,' he said, and that was the end of it. Once again, time and emotion had been spent to no purpose. But the resolution of this situation helped to end another which was concurrent.

Lady Falkender, who controlled the Political Office accounts, was insisting that during the three weeks of the campaign I should sleep each night at 10 Downing Street, in the Prime Minister's unwanted flat, or at an hotel controlled by a friend of the party. There was not enough money in the kitty, she said, to meet the cost of a bed-and-breakfast stay at the nearby St Ermin's Hotel, where I had lived during the February campaign. The likely cost was about £175. Knowing the financial help that was available, and from whom, I also knew that £175 was a drop in the bucket. Nevertheless, I offered to meet any cost above £150 from my own pocket. I did not want to be the recipient of private aid by staying at the other hotel which had been suggested.

The trouble with staying at No. 10 was the series of minor, but time-wasting, problems it would bring in its train. Shopping for and preparing breakfast. Washing up. Delivering dirty washing to the laundry and collecting it when clean. Everything that living alone entails. It just did not seem to me sensible to add all that to a fifteen- or sixteen-hour day. But Lady Falkender insisted. The Prime Minister, uncomfortable again, was involved – all this to ensure, as she put it 'that Joe Haines is not going to have breakfast in bed at our expense'. For my part, I did not welcome the thought of breaking off writing every speech and every radio and television broadcast for the Prime Minister in order to scribble instructions about the starching of my shirts, or in order to get to the grocery department of the Army and Navy Stores to buy the following morning's breakfast before they closed.

Finally, I said that rather than stay in No. 10 – where, incidentally, sleep is often impossible because of the penetrating quality of the chimes of the clock on Horse Guards' Parade – I would go home each night. As always when faced with an ultimatum, there was a cave-in. There was a sudden, unexpected donation to office funds from a wealthy supporter; the cost of my hotel bill could be met, without a contribution from me being necessary.

These distractions though irrelevant always assumed a disproportionate importance, like a toothache on honeymoon. Because of them, the contrast between the February and the September–October campaigns was already dismal. The happiness and comradeship of eight months earlier had been dissipated six months earlier. There was to be no reconciliation.

We were at the centre of power of a great national party – the party which all of us believed was the only one capable of solving the economic, social, and industrial crises the country was facing. We were employed to sustain and buttress the leader of that party – the leader who, day by day and in speech after speech, was forever proclaiming that only Labour could unite the people; and yet we could not even afford the luxury of unity in an office team of half-a-dozen. We were fighting a General Election on which the hopes of millions might rest and we were doing it in the midst of a personal vendetta. As a result of the General Election, hundreds of millions of pounds might be transferred across the exchanges of the world, yet hours of valuable time had been wasted on whether or not to spend £175 for a hotel room for the Prime Minister's speechwriter.

Again and again, it might be asked: 'Why did you put up with it?' Bernard Donoughue and I never ceased posing the question to ourselves. Always the balance of the argument tilted towards the proposition that things might get worse if we ceased to put up with it. That may have been conceit, but there were many times we might have quit if we had thought our going would not matter.

It was not to be an elevating election campaign nationally, either. On the political side it began with sharp practice on economic statistics coming from both major parties and the tone of the campaign rarely rose above the level of misrepresentation and electoral bribery, like reduced mortgage interest charges and the abolition of household rates.

Worse, we were on continuous watch for the warnings of an election scandal story – of which we had been hearing for several months – to bear their fruit. The most frequently mentioned subject of these stories was the Prime Minister's income tax returns, given added weight by his discovery that some of his tax papers were missing from his home in Lord North Street.

The Prime Minister moved decisively to cut out one possible source of embarrassment, when Lord Brayley, a personal friend of his and the junior Minister of Defence for the Army, became involved in a dispute with a company of which he had been chairman. The Secretary of State for Trade, Peter Shore, told the Prime Minister that he thought it right to order a Board of Trade inquiry into the affair and Lord Brayley's induced resignation was announced within hours. Lord Brayley was bewildered and shattered by the suddenness of it all, but there was no alternative to his going if he was not to become an election issue.

But the rumours persisted, not least in Fleet Street, that there were other stories, unnamed horrors, which were going to be released upon the electorate in time to sway its vote. Here again, the desire to exclude us from the Prime Minister's inner council led us into dangerous territory. We were aware that there was one matter which was being discussed only between Lord Lovell-Davis, Lady Falkender and the Prime Minister. For once our information network – almost a choir of Deep Throats which we had built up on both the official and the political side – was unable to help us.

One afternoon a well-known journalist came to see me with information about a 'scare' story which, he said, another newspaper was pursuing. I reported his news to the Prime Minister, who told me that it accorded with information that Lord Lovell-Davis had received – it was that matter which they had been discussing privately. Only after the election did

I learn that a colleague of the journalist who came to see me had been informed by Lord Lovell-Davis that another newspaper was planning a last-minute 'exposure' story. It was not confirmation which I had received, only repetition.

Our relations with the press had dramatically worsened again after a speech by the Prime Minister at Portsmouth on September 20 in which he said that 'cohorts of distinguished journalists' (the phrase should be read sarcastically) had been combing obscure parts of the country with a mandate to find anything – 'true or fabricated' – for use against the Labour Party. Certainly he knew that money had been offered to people who had worked with Tony Field in return for information about his business activities, but he was not intending to publish it at that stage.

What tipped the scales was an article in the *Daily Express* that morning in which Chapman Pincher, whose hostility to the Prime Minister was of long-standing, had written about the claim by the widow of Michael Halls, the Prime Minister's principal private secretary until his death in April 1970, for compensation for the loss of her husband. Mrs Halls maintained that his death had been caused by the strain of his work at Downing Street, especially in relation to Mrs Williams, as Lady Falkender then was. She was seeking the sum of £50,000 in her action against the Civil Service Department.

The terms of her claim had become widely known in Fleet Street. One Conservative M.P. had passed on copies of the writ to journalists and one of them had reached me. Lady Falkender was upset by the Pincher article; the Prime Minister reacted by drafting the Portsmouth speech himself. When I saw it I urged him, and so did others, to delete the passage which was to become notorious. At first he agreed. But then, a few minutes before he left for Portsmouth, he picked up the typescript again and said, 'Joe, you have cut too much out.' He reinstated the 'cohorts' paragraph which was to provide fuel for the Parliamentary questions of Conservative M.P.s for the next eighteen months.

Once again, over-reaction had led to recklessness. The main opponent in the election campaign was not the press, but the Conservative Party. The policy of the party and its leader was not to protect the reputation of Lady Falkender but the future

P

of Britain. Mrs Halls and her claim were important to her, of course; but news of it – old news at that – ought not to have deflected the Prime Minister's attention, at the very outset of the campaign, towards an attack on the press.

For the press, or part of it, Labour's attitude towards the newspapers remained part of the news, though it is doubtful if the public were much interested. But the fear of a last-minute stunt occupied too much time in our thinking and private discussions. Even on the last Monday before Polling Day the Prime Minister became involved in a pointless squabble with two *Daily Mail* reporters at his morning press conference.

I had a temperature that morning and was shivering; the natural depression that caused was added to by the press conference. After it was over, I left Transport House for Downing Street and went to bed. A couple of hours later I was awakened by Bernard Donoughue asking me loudly whether I was asleep. He told me that Sir Joseph Stone, the Prime Minister's doctor, was on his way to see me, adding: 'They are worried about who is going to write the speeches.' Then Sir Joseph walked in and prescribed a day's rest, which was impossible.

The Prime Minister had asked for a speech to be delivered at Chatham the following evening (he had by now a standard speech; the new matter would be about 600 words for distribution to the press and television networks), a script for a radio broadcast (about 1,200 words) and another (about 800 words) for his final television appearance. Though I hardly felt inspired, I laboured throughout the evening, comforted by the knowledge that those scripts would be the last. The Prime Minister returned from his Monday evening speech-making soon after 11 p.m. and we gathered for a meeting in my room. He did not like either the radio or the TV scripts and the speech for Chatham was on the wrong subject – his instructions to me had been mistaken or misunderstood. He was right about the scripts: they were flat and unsuitable.

The Prime Minister decided that the best way to proceed would be for him to dictate the TV broadcast himself and a succession of shorthand-typists rapidly produced copies of it for us all. Lady Falkender was brief and cutting: 'Having read that,' she said, 'Joe's looks good.' It was nearly 1 a.m. by then and we abandoned work for the night. I went to see the Prime

Minister at Lord North Street the next morning, more or less recovered, and we decided the line both broadcasts would take. The rest of the morning sticks in the memory.

I began to write in a tiny office at Transport House at 10.45 a.m. As I completed each page of the speech, and the television script, and the radio broadcast I handed it to a girl for retyping. At 12.55 p.m., two hours and ten minutes later, as I was on the last sentence of something like 2,500 words, the Prime Minister put his head round the door.

'Are you going to be much longer?' he asked. 'We are waiting to get on!'

It was with a feeling of relief that the personal tensions, not the electoral ones, were nearly over that we flew by private plane to Speke airport, Liverpool, for the Polling Day count at Huyton. There was a rainstorm throughout most of the flight, but the atmosphere inside the aircraft was little better. On the brink of a fourth General Election victory it was as if we were sunk in the aftermath of defeat.

Albert Murray took on the role of target that day. Shabbily, he was excluded from the team due to accompany the Prime Minister to the count. Even as he edged towards a fourth term, the Prime Minister refused to defend his office manager from such pettiness. Albert's ticket was given instead to Terry Boston (former M.P. for Faversham, defeated in 1970; created a life peer in the Resignation Honours List), who had been a help, but not outstandingly so, during two election campaigns. Bernard Donoughue and I decided we would not go, either. I said to Bernard, in the Prime Minister's suite at the Adelphi Hotel, Liverpool, as we waited for the first results to come in: 'From now on it's all downhill.'

The problem of what to do about Albert at the count was avoided by the Prime Minister asking the three of us, at the last moment, to 'keep an eye' on the results while he answered the Returning Officer's call to be present at the declaration of his own result. We were glad to sit there and cheer the news that young Margaret Jackson had won Lincoln back for Labour by defeating Dick Taverne.

Another attempt to humiliate Albert Murray by sending him back to London by train while the rest of us flew in the HS 127 was thwarted when Bernard Donoughue and I said we would travel with him; however microscopic the issue, if two or three people ever stood together the pressure would be relaxed. But the flight back was hardly that of a Prime Minister on the morrow of a famous victory. The nearest expression of thanks for the efforts which had been put in came when Lady Falkender said to Bernard Donoughue that 'civil servants' had involved themselves in matters in which they ought not to be involved. Presumably, like winning elections.

At least after the February result a generous gesture towards the staff had been made: the Prime Minister bought up the last remaining stocks of a commemorative medal that had been struck to mark the campaign: two silver and thirty bronze. (They were never distributed, because Lady Falkender objected, but the thought was kindly.) This time, there was nothing. Donoughue, Murray and Haines were as popular as if they had spent the three previous weeks working in Conservative Central Office.

The worst part about it always was that one seldom knew what it was one was supposed to have done; what offence had been given; what slight, however unintentional, that might be overcome with an apology. One only knew, usually at second or third hand, that *something* had caused an upset. It was when that upset was transmitted to the Prime Minister and then to a temporary coldness towards his staff that work suffered.

Immediately after the election we heard, through one of our most reliable informants, that the No. 10 Policy Unit was to be moved out of Downing Street and into the Cabinet Office. The attacks on Albert and me could be shrugged off because when it came to the point of serious conflict the Prime Minister would dig in his heels – he said to Lady Falkender at the beginning of the election campaign: 'Why is it you are always right and everyone else wrong?' – but an attack upon the Unit was serious politically.

I have explained elsewhere in this book how important the Policy Unit had become to the Prime Minister. It was an essential source of alternative advice to that of the official machine; very frequently, because of the high quality and dedication of its staff, the Prime Minister proclaimed the superiority of that advice. In six months it had produced more fresh thinking, laced with an understanding of the Government's political commitments and obligations, than any other part of the Government, certainly more than the Central Policy Review Staff – Edward Heath's 'think tank' – which had been absorbed into the Civil Service. Its departure from No. 10 would be a real loss. We had no doubt at all that its removal into the Cabinet Office would be the result of a personal animosity. Our information had come from the best possible source outside the Prime Minister.

The distance between 10 Downing Street and the Cabinet Office is the thickness of a door and Bernard Donoughue's Unit was sited only a few yards away from that door. But in terms of influence, that door is the gateway to oblivion. Many a Minister, in both Conservative and Labour Governments, has been told that by agreeing to operate from the Cabinet Office he would have access to Downing Street itself; that though he (or in one case, she) would be without a department there, the Prime Minister, the source of political power, was only a few yards away. It is not true. The Cabinet Office for a Minister, or a Prime Ministerial adviser, is what a Mongolian power station is to a Kremlin politician. That door is always kept locked; access to Downing Street means much more than applying for the key. To have put the Unit there would have been to destroy it. It would have become part of the Cabinet Office, an addition to its strength as it increasingly rivalled the Treasury in the Whitehall power struggle. Like the C.P.R.S., its independence would have gone.

Bernard Donoughue and I discussed the implications of the move at great length. We decided to oppose it, to the point of resignation by both of us if it had to come to that.

Once again, of course, the weirdest aspect of it all was that nothing was said officially to either of us about what was being contemplated. Though we received regular reports of developments we still depended upon others for our information. There was little that we could do except wait.

There was, however, one opportunity for a demonstration. A victory party had been arranged for those who had helped in the election campaign, for Transport House and Parliamentary party staff as well as the staff of the Prime Minister's Political Office. Bernard Donoughue and I arrived together for the party, greeted the Prime Minister and Mrs Wilson and then promptly left together, watched by Lady Falkender. The next day, we heard that the plans to transfer the Unit from No. 10 had been abandoned. Bernard Donoughue was invited to lunch with the Prime Minister and Lady Falkender and was given champagne in her room as an aperitif. After lunch he went to the study with both of them and more champagne was served. Lady Falkender then left the room and the Prime Minister told Bernard Donoughue that he wanted him to take over a new and bigger responsibility, occupying the prestige office next to the Cabinet Room—the office which belonged to Lady Falkender. He was to take charge of the Political Office, with more power. The Prime Minister mentioned—as he was later to tell me—that the Cabinet Office had been trying to take over the Policy Unit but that he would not allow it to happen.

Bernard Donoughue had been taken by surprise. He asked for time to think over the offer. In the event, he could have had all the time he wanted. It was never mentioned again.

The memory of one incident blurs into another, like the gunfights of a thousand televised Westerns. Only the 'High Noons' are remembered: the refusal by Lady Falkender to be positively vetted by the security forces, which was a total and inescapable obligation on everyone else who worked in Downing Street; the complaints against Bernard Donoughue which led to his being excluded from the Prime Minister's journeys abroad, even though the essential briefing for the trip had been prepared by his policy unit; her appointment to the committee to inquire into the British film industry and her threat to resign after she had been criticised by the *Evening Standard*'s cinema critic; her insistence that the Prime Minister should send a letter of introduction on behalf of her brother to the Prime Minister of Saudi Arabia, to coincide with a visit Tony Field was making to the Middle East (the then Foreign and Commonwealth Secretary was asked to deliver the letter while he was in Saudi Arabia). Each of these events produced minor crises and there were scores of others.

The private secretaries at No. 10 were more bothered by all this than I ever was. The private secretary who had to assist in getting a visa for a Filipino servant was embarrassed. His colleague who arranged the Prime Minister's official engagements was often in hot water. The practice of leading Israeli Ministers approaching the Prime Minister through her rather than through the official channels was a source of irritation to the Foreign and Commonwealth Secretary. Her interest in foreign affairs grew and was not only confined to the Middle East.

In late 1975 she arranged a private meeting between the retiring Spanish ambassador to Britain, Señor Fraga, and the Prime Minister. Señor Fraga had acquired a reputation as a liberal in the Spanish context and therefore an acknowledged meeting was probably acceptable to party opinion here.

But not long before that meeting, I had been at a private lunch at the Israeli ambassador's house given to mark Fraga's return to a Spain where Franco was slowly dying. A mild criticism of Franco by Harold Lever, another guest, sent Fraga into a rage: beating the table he declared, 'I am part of the Franco regime; I am proud to be part of the Franco regime.' He did not seem to me to be all that liberal-minded. Given the state of Labour Party feeling about Spain, a secret meeting with Fraga was injudicious. It ought not to have been arranged in the way it was.

The desire to be associated with show business folk, which was always part of her character, also grew. It was not unknown for her to alter the table placings at an official No. 10 dinner to ensure that she sat next to a star of stage or screen. No one minded. But one incident which was resented – on the night of May 15, 1975 – occurred when the Prime Minister of Fiji was the guest of honour at a No. 10 dinner. He was not, of course, ranked among the major statesmen of the world, but Harold Wilson had a gift for making his guests feel that for that night at least no one counted for more. After a short and graceful speech by the Prime Minister, and just before the Fijian Prime Minister rose to his feet, Lady Falkender rose to hers. She left for 'another engagement'.

To walk out in that way offended many guests. They were outraged three-quarters of an hour later when she returned with Frank Sinatra and Barbara Marx, who later became Mrs Sinatra. The American singer was immediately introduced to the Prime Minister, who then took him round the room to meet most of the other guests, leaving a lonely Fijian Prime Minister in the shadow of a show business star. Incidents like that did not make for good public relations or good Common-wealth relations.

But the rules never applied to Lady Falkender, even at dinner. It was the practice at No. 10 for all couples, which included staff members and their wives, to be split up so that one of each would sit at a leg of the U-shaped table. Lady Falkender, however, would ensure that her escort sat next to her. The escorts varied: Sir George (later Lord) Weidenfeld most frequently filled the role, but others included Iltydd Harrington, the colourful deputy leader of the Greater London Council, Gerald Kaufman, and John Cordle, Conservative M.P. for Bournemouth East, who was regarded by other guests as a somewhat eccentric choice for a Labour Prime Minister's secretary.

Early in 1975 it became increasingly clear that the Prime Minister was determined to go ahead with his often-expressed ambition to give up office. The physical and mental strains of thirty years at the top were beginning to show. In March, Lady Falkender asked us if we knew that he intended to resign 'within a few months', which was earlier than we had expected. She asked what we were going to do about it. For my part, I had made up my mind that if he wanted to go I would never argue against it.

The incredible stamina which had always allowed him to do the work of two men was beginning to flag. He no longer had the time or the inclination to play golf. Where once he could depart for Chequers on a Friday evening looking grey and tired and return on the Monday morning looking tanned and youthful, he now often looked tired still on Monday. Apart from anything else, his week-end workload had greatly in-creased and there were occasions when his red dispatch boxes contained up to 500 submissions. Once upon a time he would acquire a tan if he only put his head out of the window to see if it was raining. Now he rarely had a bronzed look.

For his health's sake it seemed to me right that he should retire. Though most of the time he was still fit and strong, working at the pace he had done had demonstrated that the strength was no longer inexhaustible. I doubt if Lady Falkender could have realised just how tired he was getting. There were frequent reports of lengthy quarrels between them at the week-ends at Chequers – she used to go there from her home nearby to enjoy the swimming pool with her children – spanning both Saturday and Sunday.

Overseas visits were always the cause of added strain. For forty minutes one evening in the Paris Embassy official business had to wait while the Prime Minister sought to smooth over another 'crisis' concerning Lady Falkender back home. When we arrived at Heathrow late one night from one international conference, there was a message saying that Lady Falkender was on the way to the airport. He had to wait while an embarrassed official staff drifted slowly away to their homes. In the end, to avoid arousing the curiosity of the waiting press, the Prime Minister got into his car and drove away – around the airport perimeter until the reporters had dispersed and then back to the V.I.P. lounge. It was bizarre.

Throughout the winter of 1975–6 she fought and argued with him over his decision to resign. She demanded that he should not go to the Scilly Isles that New Year because there was 'so little time left'. New Year's Day is the Wilson wedding anniversary and he ignored her. But though she opposed the decision, the arrangements for a writing and television career for the future ex-Prime Minister went ahead. Even as early as January a dinner party was arranged at David Frost's house to include some of the people who would be involved in the eventual television series about British Prime Ministers which was being planned.

For most of us, the sadness we felt about the impending resignation was leavened by the thought that a strain was to be lifted from our lives.

A final luncheon party given by the Prime Minister to his closest advisers, political and civil service, in a way symbolised what the previous years had been about. We were due to meet at 1 p.m. for lunch at 1.15 p.m. Lady Falkender did not arrive until 1.35 p.m. If it had been anyone else, even a Minister, lunch would have started. Until the end, she was proving that no one mattered so much as she did.

It was all so unnecessary. Few people associated with Harold Wilson had ever sought to dispute her pre-eminence, hard to understand though many of them found it. We were prepared to concede the fact. It was for the Prime Minister to define the limits of her influence and if we felt those limits were too far-flung, in matters of State they were definite. Her flights of temper were uncomfortable and embarrassing, though we were uncomfortable and embarrassed for him.

Her especial fire was held for those she suspected of becoming too close to Harold Wilson. The attacks upon them were her way of asking the 'Mirror, mirror on the wall' question. Respect and importance were what she wanted. Recognition that she was out of the ordinary. Well, she *was* out of the ordinary. But like the rest of us, she was in the end only an appendage of the Prime Minister, because he was the Prime Minister. She con-fused power with respectability; influence with admiration.

The Labour Party has been, and is, a lifetime allegiance for me. Its ideals and principles have shaped the whole course of my working and private life. As long as it does not change, then neither will I. The loyalty which any party member has is readily transferred to its leader, even if at times he is uncertain whether or not that leader fully embraces those principles. In my case, loyalty to Harold Wilson as the Labour Party leader was sustained by my affection for him as a man. At the Cabinet meeting at which he announced his resignation, Jim Callaghan, in a spontaneous tribute, said: 'Harold, I believe history will treat you more kindly than your contemporaries.' I believe Jim Callaghan was right. But the judgment of history must be founded upon all the facts, and in the life of Harold Wilson Lady Falkender is a considerable fact.

The loyalty which I and others gave to Harold Wilson naturally covered those for whom he showed concern. But affection cannot be transferred as readily. Long before Harold Wilson resigned I had made it clear to him that I intended to break cleanly away. Even if there was a job for me to do for an ex-Prime Minister – and there was not – I did not want to do it. I had decided that the role which Lady Falkender had played should at least in small measure be disclosed, because I believed her influence had been too great; it is right that in politics no one should count too much. For too long, Lady Falkender counted for too much. If the verdict of history's jury is that among British Prime Ministers Harold Wilson did not count for too much then I hope it adds a rider about what might have been.

Index